IMAGES
of America

MIDDLESEX FELLS

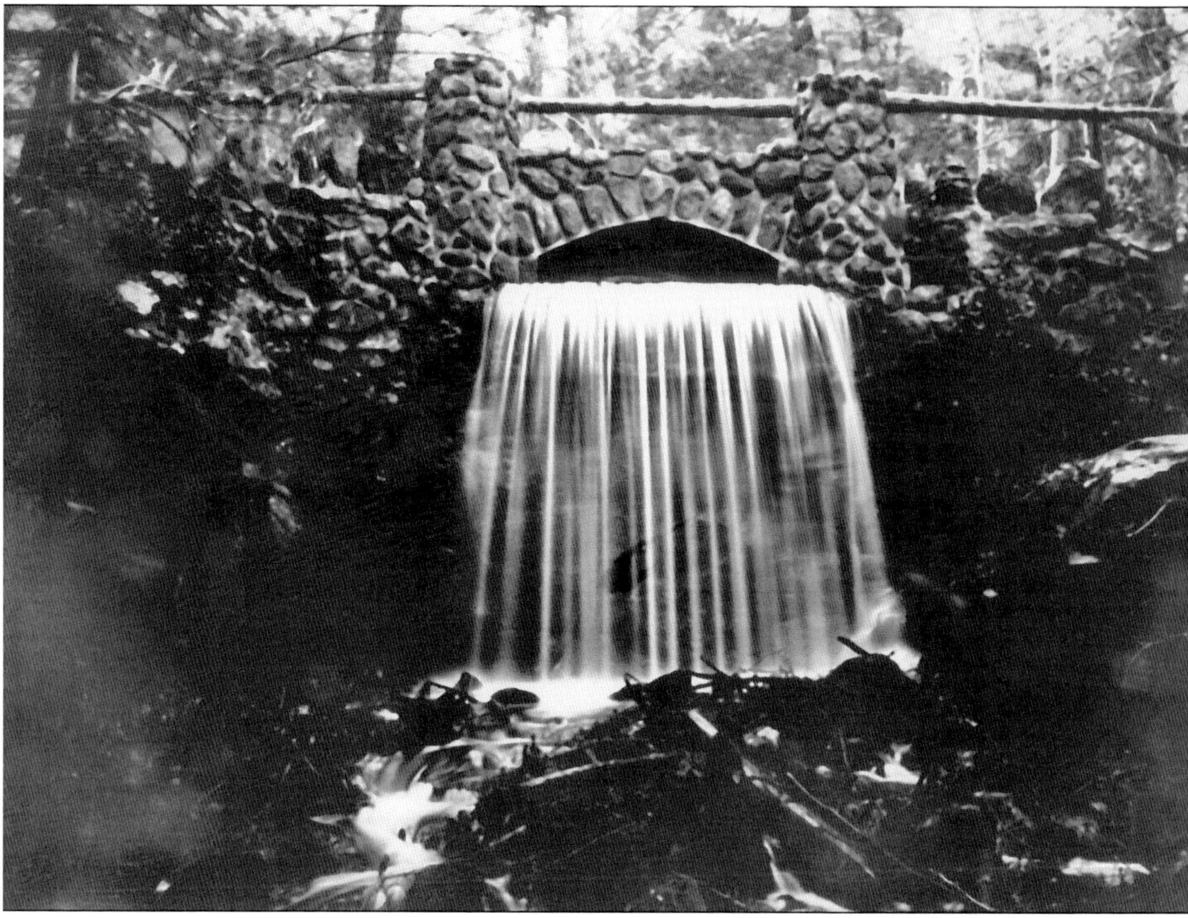

In 1862, William Foster wrote, "A few days ago the Bunker Hill paper published an article of the rare beauty of a water-fall at Wyoming or Spot Pond—sometimes dry, when the miller chooses to shut down the gate. This Fall among the high forest trees and over the craggy rocks is really worthy of notice. It is not mine but the brook which is the only issue from Lake Wyoming runs through my forest of very lofty trees, nearly a hundred feet high." Douglas Heath photographed this waterfall in May 2013, using 19th-century glass-plate methods. (Authors' collection.)

On the Cover: Oliver Tryon of the Metropolitan Water and Sewerage Board took this photograph on June 23, 1912, of young people, perhaps on a Sunday outing from Boston, enjoying a day at Spot Pond. From 1910 to 1946, electric streetcars gave people in the Boston area access to the Fells. Trolleys stopped at Porter Cove on Spot Pond and at the Sheepfold. People enjoyed getting off at Porter Cove for a drink at the well (far left of image) before strolling to Pickerel Rock at Spot Pond's south end. Forest Street, on the right side of the photograph, was later widened and paved and renamed Route 28. In 1959, Interstate 93 was built parallel to Route 28, and part of Porter Cove was filled. (Courtesy of Massachusetts State Archives.)

IMAGES
of America

MIDDLESEX FELLS

Alison C. Simcox and Douglas L. Heath

ARCADIA
PUBLISHING

ISBN 978-1-4671-2270-2

Published by Arcadia Publishing
Charleston, South Carolina

Printed in the United States of America

Library of Congress Control Number: 2014942217

For all general information, please contact Arcadia Publishing:
Telephone 843-853-2070
Fax 843-853-0044
E-mail sales@arcadiapublishing.com
For customer service and orders:
Toll-Free 1-888-313-2665

Visit us on the Internet at www.arcadiapublishing.com

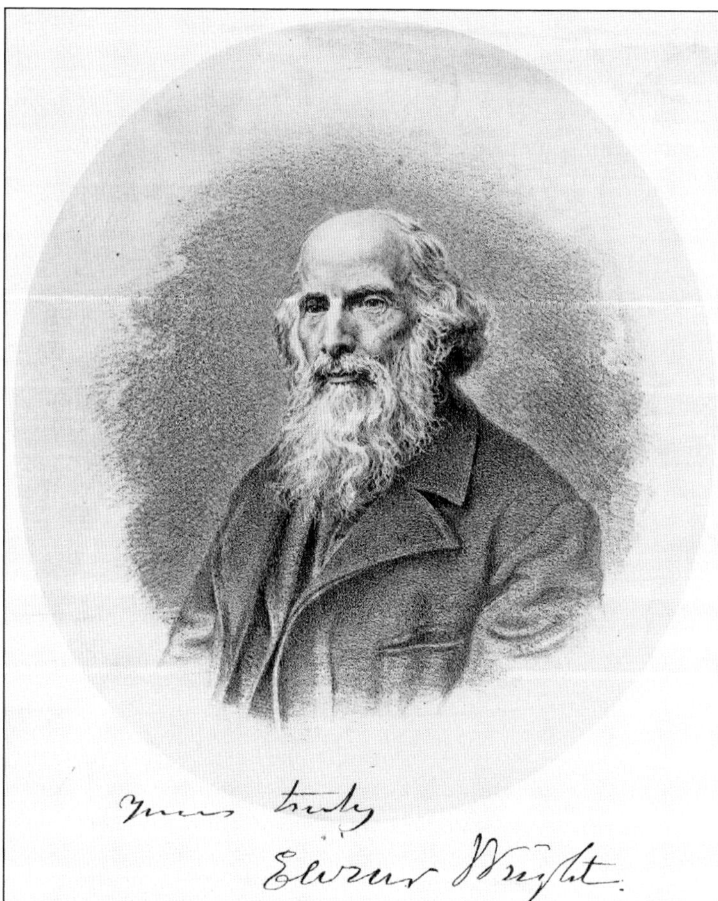

Elizur Wright (1804–1885), sometimes called the "Father of the Middlesex Fells," wrote the following in the *Melrose Journal* in March 1883: "The people must move and act spontaneously, if anything is done. It is everybody's axe; and if nobody grinds it, it will be dull for generations to come. The wood-choppers are sure to grind theirs while a tree is left. Here is work for the press, the pulpit, the platform, for everyone who likes to breathe pure air, drink pure water, and see green things." (Courtesy of Mike Ryan.)

Contents

Acknowledgments		6
Introduction		7
1.	Prehistory to Colonial Settlement	11
2.	Haywardville and Virginia Wood	19
3.	Waterworks	35
4.	Creation of the Fells	55
5.	Gypsy Moth Wars	83
6.	Stone Zoo	91
7.	Early Years of the Reservation	101
8.	Modern Age	117
Bibliography		127

ACKNOWLEDGMENTS

We are indebted to many people for helping make this book possible. First, we thank Mike Ryan, former executive director of Friends of the Middlesex Fells. Mike enthusiastically shared his knowledge about the reservation's formation in the 19th century. He kindly agreed to review drafts and gave excellent suggestions that resulted in a better book. Sean M. Fisher, archivist for the Massachusetts Department of Conservation and Recreation (DCR), deserves equal thanks. Sean offered his time and expertise and gave us great access to records and photographs in the DCR Archives. Other images from state collections were generously provided by Judy Greene, Mike Nelson, and Tom Walsh of the DCR and by staff at the Massachusetts State Archives.

Lester H. Stephenson Jr. and his son Donald generously contributed their 1940s photographs of the last trolleys to run through the Fells with Lester's father at the controls. Kyna Hamill and Allison Andrews of the Medford Historical Society and Museum gave us access to their wonderful collection. Becky Fullerton, archivist for the Appalachian Mountain Club (AMC), shed light on the AMC's important role in helping to make the Fells a reality. The following groups also lent us materials from their collections: Stoneham, Melrose, and Medford Public Libraries; Stoneham Historical Society (SHS); New England Historical Genealogical Society (NEHES); Middlesex Registry of Deeds; Frederick Law Olmsted National Historic Site (ONHS); Winchester Archival Center; Cleveland Colby Colgate Archives; American Antiquarian Society; Historic New England; Robert S. Peabody Museum of Archaeology (PMA); and Wakefield Department of Public Works.

We also thank Meg Thompson, professor emerita of geosciences at Wellesley College; Ryan Hayward of the Preservation Collaborative; Mary Marchant (SHS); Michelle Clark (ONHS); Bonnie Sousa (PMA); Tom McCarthy, great-grandson of George Davenport; Ellen Knight, archivist at the Winchester Archival Center; Oskar and Bill Rogg, descendants of William Bailey Lang; Joseph P. Kopera of the Massachusetts Geological Survey; and Sally Rege Carroll. We also thank Ian and Alec, our wonderful sons. Special thanks go to our acquisitions editor at Arcadia Publishing, Caitrin Cunningham, who was supportive throughout. We dedicate this book to Doug's brother, Peter Heath.

INTRODUCTION

Middlesex Fells Reservation, a rugged, forested park just north of Boston, is the legacy of a remarkable 19th-century preservation movement. Beginning about 150 years ago, a small group of people—notably Elizur Wright, Wilson Flagg, George Davenport, Sylvester Baxter, and, later, Charles Eliot—worked tirelessly to set aside this area of outstanding geological, scenic, and historical interest to provide a refuge from city life and to preserve the natural landscape. It was a daunting fight against vested interests, with no guarantee of a favorable outcome. Ultimately, the Fells movement led to the creation of the Metropolitan Park System of Greater Boston, the first regional park system in the United States.

Although Interstate 93 passes through the heart of the Fells, many drive this highway regularly with little awareness of this special place. Over 2,500 acres in size (over 3,000 including reservoir areas), the Fells lies within five Massachusetts cities and towns: Malden, Medford, Melrose, Stoneham and Winchester. It includes two north-south valleys of rocky outcrops, woodlands, meadows, streams, ponds, wetlands, archaeological resources, and historic structures. It also includes Virginia Wood, the first gift of land to the world's oldest regional land trust, the Trustees of Reservations.

The story of the Fells (whose name is a Saxon word for wild, rocky hills) appropriately begins with its rocks. The uplands of the Fells are bounded on the south by a dramatic cliff marking the Northern Boundary Fault, which separates the Boston Basin from uplands that extend into New Hampshire. The oldest rock type in the Fells, the Westboro Formation (quartzite), dates back as far as 912 million years. The next oldest rocks are part of the Middlesex Fells Volcanic Complex (undated, but older than Dedham granite). About 609 million years ago, these were intruded by the Dedham granite. From 573 to 226 million years ago, many basalt dikes intruded older rocks. About 380 million years ago, landmasses collided to form a supercontinent called Pangaea. About 194 million years ago, as Pangaea began to break apart and give rise to the Atlantic Ocean, the Medford Dike cut through older rocks. This dike, which has maximum thickness of 460 feet along the west flank of Pine Hill, was the focus of 19th-century quarrying, and stones from these quarries were used to build mansions on Spot Pond's eastern shore and to line paths of Boston Public Garden.

The topography created by this complex geology was further shaped by ice during the Wisconsin glacial period (extending from about 110,000 to 10,000 years ago), which left a landscape of scoured and rounded bedrock covered by glacial till and outwash sediments and dotted with kettle ponds, including Spot Pond. About 10,000 years ago, after the ice receded, Paleo-Indians migrated to New England. Hunting and gathering parties had easy access to the Fells from base camps on the Arlington Plain, about one mile to the southwest, and from the lower Charles River. The Fells, like other upland areas around the Boston Basin, was rich in plant and animal resources, including mastodons and other large game, and stone for manufacturing tools. Sites dating back 9,500 years exist on the Arlington Plain and lower Charles River, along the shores of the Mystic Lakes, and along the length of the Saugus River. One of these, Ossini's Garden in Wakefield, Massachusetts, on a tributary of the Saugus River, is only a few miles from the Fells

There are several sites in the Fells that predate the arrival of Europeans. Evidence from these indicates that this area was occupied from early Paleo-Indian times. Three sites near Spot Pond have been identified as Late Archaic or Woodland period (6,000 to 450 years ago) stone-tool workshops. At the time of European contact, native people in the Fells area were the Massachuset (or the Pawtucket, according to some scholars), and their leader was the sachem Nanepashemet. After he was killed by Mi'kmaq raiders (also called Tarrantines) in 1619, his wife, known only as Squaw Sachem, took over as chief. Under pressure from the growing English colony, Native Americans left the coastal lowlands, where they were concentrated, and moved to upland areas, including the Fells.

In February 1632, John Winthrop, the first governor of the Massachusetts Bay Colony, explored the northern part of the Charlestown territory and wrote in his diary, "They came to a very great pond . . . and the pond had divers small rocks standing up here and there in it, which they thereupon called Spot Pond." Two years later, Spot Pond was included on the first published map of the Massachusetts Bay Colony. In 1639, Squaw Sachem sold her land to the colony, including much of the acreage that now comprises the Fells. By this time, disease and conflict had reduced her people to a fraction of their former size.

The first farm in the Fells was built about 1645 at Bear Hill, the highest point in the Fells (317 feet). In 1707, a sawmill was built on Spot Pond Brook, which flowed out of Spot Pond, and other farms appeared near Bear Hill and north and west of Spot Pond. In 1658, Charlestown territory, previously common land, was divided amongst taxpayers. Colonial settlers sought agricultural land and avoided the swampy and rocky areas of the Fells. Towns emerged at its periphery, including Medford, Malden, Stoneham, and Woburn. Medford became a center for shipbuilding and brickmaking; Malden became an agricultural community with links to Boston markets; and Stoneham became a shoe town. But the upland areas of the Fells remained sparsely populated and, except for one cart road (Fulton Road) built in 1641 to connect Charlestown with its northern territories, access was limited to footpaths. Despite difficult access, colonial industries, especially shipbuilding, brickmaking, and cobbling industries, consumed much of the forest for wood resources.

Meanwhile, Spot Pond Brook became a focus of industrial activity. From the early 1600s, its rushing waters powered mills, first producing lumber, and later, snuff, and spices. William Barrett operated a mill for dying cloth from 1814 to the 1840s. In 1846, Elisha Converse (of tennis shoe fame) and Benjamin Poland bought the land and resold it to Elisha's brother James. In 1858, James Converse sold the property to Nathaniel Hayward, an inventor of vulcanization of rubber. Hayward then bought some of Hurd's land, making him owner of all but one mill property along Spot Pond Brook, and the area became known as Haywardville. But the village's golden days had already passed when the Spot Pond Water Company began regulating flow in 1869 between Spot Pond and Spot Pond Brook, decreasing flow in the brook. Today, all that remains of Haywardville are millponds, waterfalls, waterwheel bases, and stone foundations.

While mills were grinding on Spot Pond Brook, several Boston businessmen saw an opportunity to develop an estate district on Spot Pond's scenic eastern shore. In 1846, William Foster, James Eaton, and William Bailey Lang bought 120 acres from merchant Joseph Hurd and created the Wyoming development. They auctioned off lakeside lots, but kept some for themselves, on which they built Italianate mansions designed by Lang and built with Fells granite. Foster initially owned half the Wyoming acreage, including six house lots. Although he never lived on Spot Pond, his daughter Fanny (who married the brother of "Ice King" Frederic Tudor) lived in one of the mansions. In the 1870s, Lang's nearby estate was converted into the Langwood Hotel. A 1902 fire destroyed most of the hotel, but spared the mansion (razed in the 1980s). Today, the only remaining stone mansion, the Botume House, is used as the Middlesex Fells Visitors Center.

As Boston's population grew, so did demand for drinking water. In 1867, businessmen from Medford, Malden, and Melrose formed the Spot Pond Water Company. Two years later, the towns bought the company's water rights. In 1898, the Metropolitan Water Board hired Olmsted Brothers (successor to Frederick Law Olmsted's firm of Olmsted, Olmsted & Eliot) to develop plans to improve Spot Pond as a reservoir while retaining its natural beauty. The project, completed in 1901, entailed excavating shallow areas and raising the water level by nine feet.

Since colonial times, the Fells has been known for its natural beauty. In 1856, naturalist Wilson Flagg advocated setting aside "the wild region extending from Stoneham to Salem, for the purpose of one or more preserves." In 1869, Elizur Wright published a pamphlet urging the state to designate the Five Mile Wood as Mount Andrew Park. In an 1879 *Boston Herald* article, Sylvester Baxter calls the area Middlesex Fells for the first time—and the name stuck.

In 1880, Wright and Flagg founded the Middlesex Fells Association, which pushed for legislation to enable towns to preserve land. The following year, George Butterfield, owner of the Langwood Hotel (converted from William Bailey Lang's stone mansion), cleared the Ravine Road hemlock groves (now in Virginia Wood). In a lantern-slide lecture, botanist and photographer George Davenport decried the calamity of replacing the hemlocks with "acres of unsightly stumps." This destructive act became a rallying cry to preservationists and helped in the passage of the Public Domain Act in 1882.

In 1890, landscape architect Charles Eliot, alarmed that areas of exceptional natural beauty were vulnerable to development, urged the state to create a board of trustees to preserve land. The next year, the Trustees of Public Reservations was founded. Its first property was a gift of 20 acres beside Spot Pond from Fannie Foster Tudor in memory of her daughter Virginia. Eliot and Baxter then led an effort, supported by the Appalachian Mountain Club (AMC), to create the Metropolitan Park Commission (MPC), which resulted in creation of the Metropolitan Park System of Greater Boston (see chapter 4). Within two years of the commission's founding in 1893, it had established four reservations—Blue Hills, Middlesex Fells, Stony Brook, and Beaver Brook—and soon began to build parkways to connect the reservations with Boston.

During this period, Boston's suburbs were changing as routes for horse-drawn vehicles were converted to trolley lines. Using trolleys and nearby railroads, people could now live outside the city and commute to city jobs. In 1905, the Boston Elevated Railway Company and the Boston & Northern Street Railway proposed to extend trolley service from Somerville to Stoneham. Construction of roadbeds and trestles began and, in 1910, the first trolleys ran through the Fells, with popular stops at "the Sheepfold," former site of a piggery, and Porter Cove. The trolleys ran for almost four decades, but service ended in 1946 when they could no longer compete with automobiles.

During the Great Depression, Pres. Franklin D. Roosevelt established the Works Progress Administration (WPA) and Civilian Conservation Corps (CCC). Men from a nearby CCC camp in Breakheart Reservation traveled to Middlesex Fells on work details, where they sprayed trees for gypsy moths and built trails and fire roads. WPA workers also battled insects, built roads, and worked on larger projects, including constructing Wright's Tower and bridges in Virginia Wood and improving Bellevue Pond.

Today, Middlesex Fells features one of the largest forests existing within a large metropolitan area. Despite widened, busier roads surrounding it and Interstate 93 (built from 1959 to 1961) cutting through its center, the Fells remain a retreat for people seeking greenery, exercise, and solitude. The reservation, however, continues to face challenges, including a proposal to build a large office complex at the former site of the Langwood Hotel on Woodland Road. Friends of the Middlesex Fells and others fear that such a development would transform a historical Fells parkway into a busy traffic artery. Other challenges are ecological. A recent botanical survey showed that the Fells still has many wild areas and habitat types, but many native plants survive in only one or two locations, and nonnative species have tripled since the 1890s, from 110 to 305. The Fells provides breeding, migratory, and wintering habitats for hundreds of wildlife species, but some species are threatened by habitat fragmentation, disturbance from recreational uses, and climate change. These modern threats to the forest are different, but in many ways as challenging, as those faced by 19th-century preservationists.

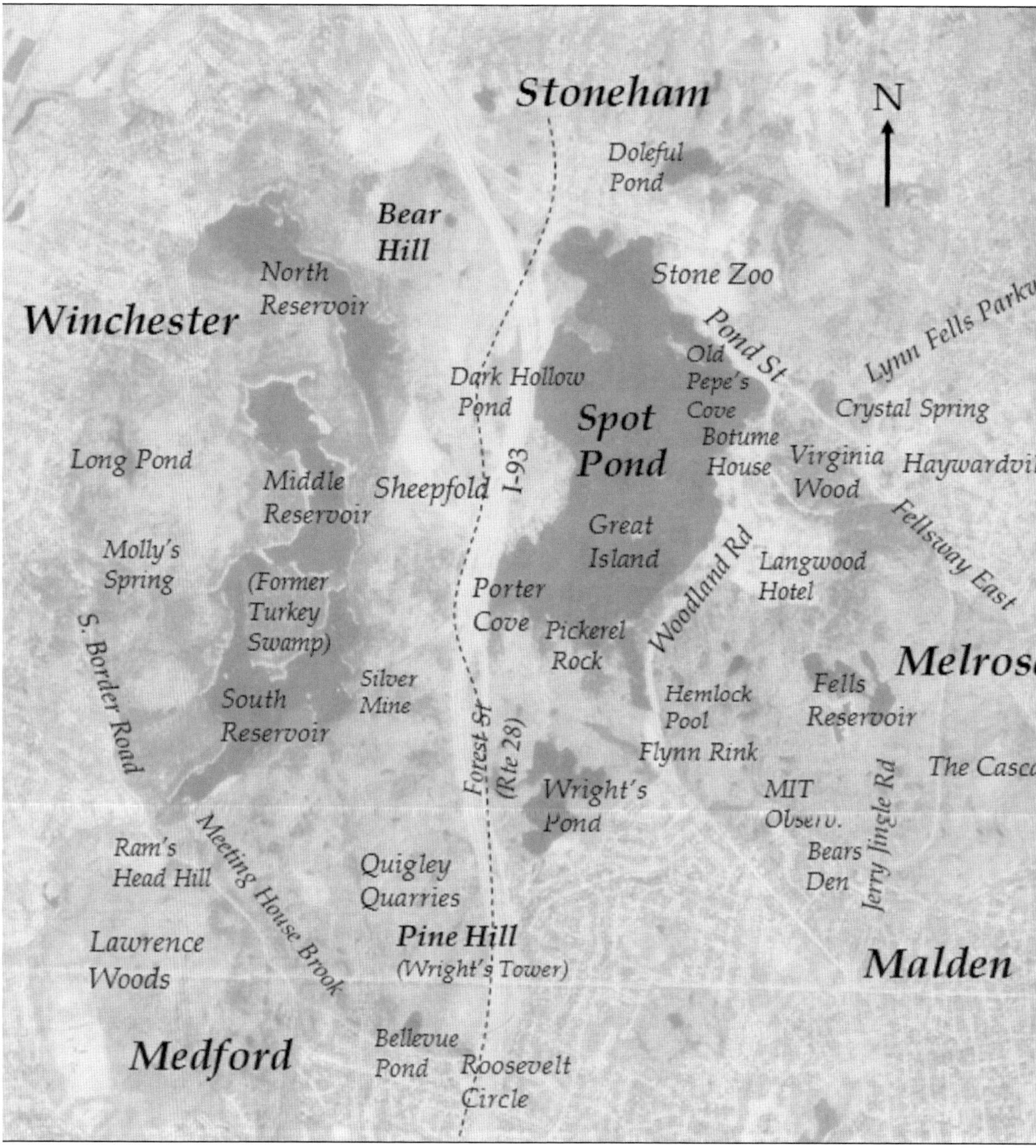

This map of Middlesex Fells Reservation shows the location of features discussed in this book. The dashed line shows the 1910–1946 trolley route. The base map is an aerial photograph taken in 1974. A trail map for the reservation is available online. (Courtesy of Wakefield Department of Public Works.)

One

Prehistory to Colonial Settlement

Middlesex Fells Reservation is part of upland with ancient bedrock that has recorded cataclysmic events, including volcanic eruptions and continental rifting. The most recent event to shape the topography was the Wisconsin glaciation, when thick ice covered most of Canada, the Midwest, and New England. Fourteen thousand years ago, the ice front had receded to a location near the northern border of Massachusetts, leaving a landscape covered with glacial till, pocked with kettle ponds, and littered with boulders. The central feature of the Fells, Spot Pond, formed as a kettle pond, but was enlarged for use as a reservoir in the 19th century (see chapter 3).

In the early 17th century, when Europeans began to settle in Massachusetts, the land was home to thousands of native people from many tribes. In northeastern Massachusetts, including the Fells area, these people were called the Massachuset (identified by some scholars as Pawtucket) and their sachem (leader) was Nanepashemet, whose name translates as "New Moon." In 1619, well before John Winthrop's party arrived in Charlestown, Nanepashemet was killed by the Mi'kmaq from the north (also called Terratines). Nanepashemet's wife, known only as Squaw Sachem, took over his domain.

In 1632, Winthrop and others explored the Fells, then part of Charlestown's northern territory, and came upon a pond with islands and rocks protruding through the ice and named it Spot Pond. Seven years later, Squaw Sachem sold her land to the Massachusetts Bay Colony. By this time, the Massachuset people had been decimated by epidemics and war.

By the end of the colonial period, the Fells area, known variously as Charlestown End, the Rocks, or the Five Mile Woods, remained sparsely populated, except for a cluster of mills along Spot Pond Brook (see chapter 2). Early settlers avoided the rugged topography of the Fells in favor of land that was more accessible and favorable for agriculture. Towns emerged at the borders, including Medford (shipbuilding, brickmaking), Malden (agriculture), Stoneham (shoemaking), and Woburn (agriculture, tanning). The eastern side of Spot Pond, including parts of Stoneham, Melrose, and Malden, was called Lap Parish because of the many shoemakers in the area. The word *lap* refers to a shoemaker's stone held in the lap and used to beat leather. But despite difficult access into the Fells uplands, colonial industries, particularly shipbuilding, brickmaking and shoemaking, cut down much of the forest for its wood.

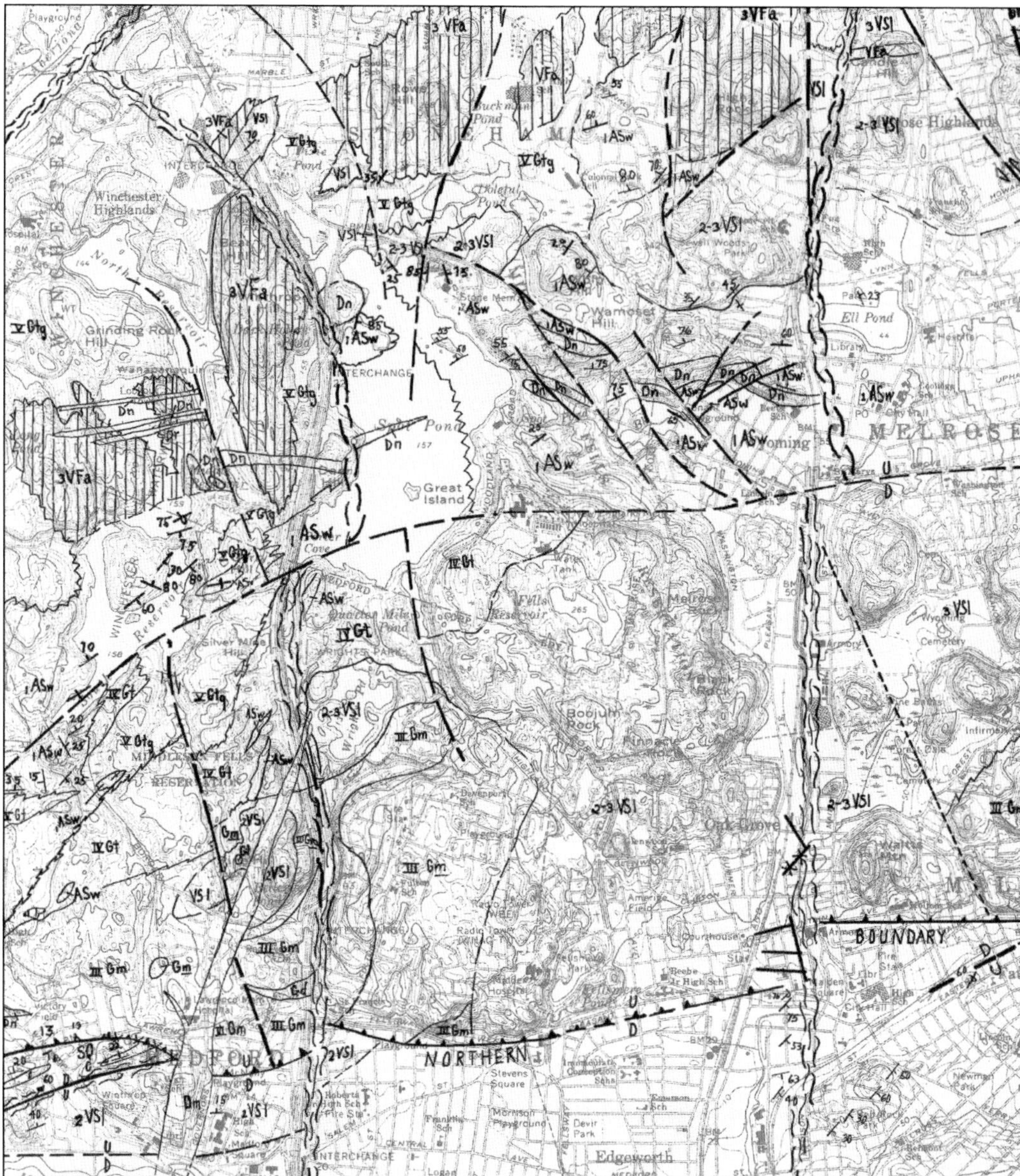

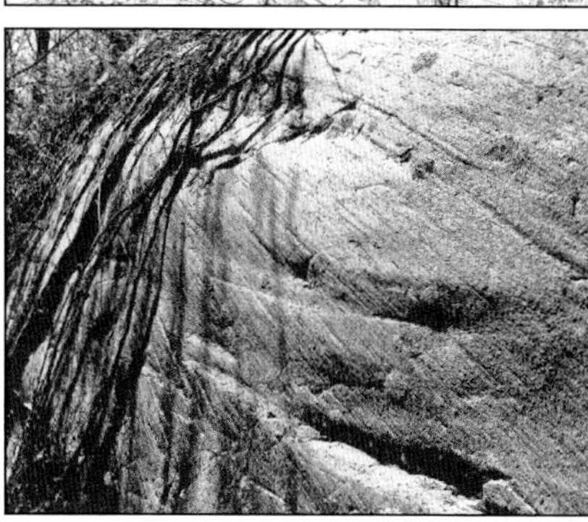

This 1980 geologic map was drawn by Clifford Kaye of the US Geological Survey. From oldest to youngest, rocks include the Westboro Quartzite (ASw, 912 million years [my]), the Middlesex Fells Volcanic Complex (VFa, VSI, undated), Dedham Granite (Gt, Gm, 609 my), Basalt dikes (Dn, 573 to 226 my), and the Medford Dike (Dm, 194 my). At left is an outcrop of a basalt dike located at the entrance to Virginia Wood. The striations and grooves formed as ice moved over its surface during the last glacial period. (Above, courtesy of Massachusetts Geological Survey; left, authors' collection.)

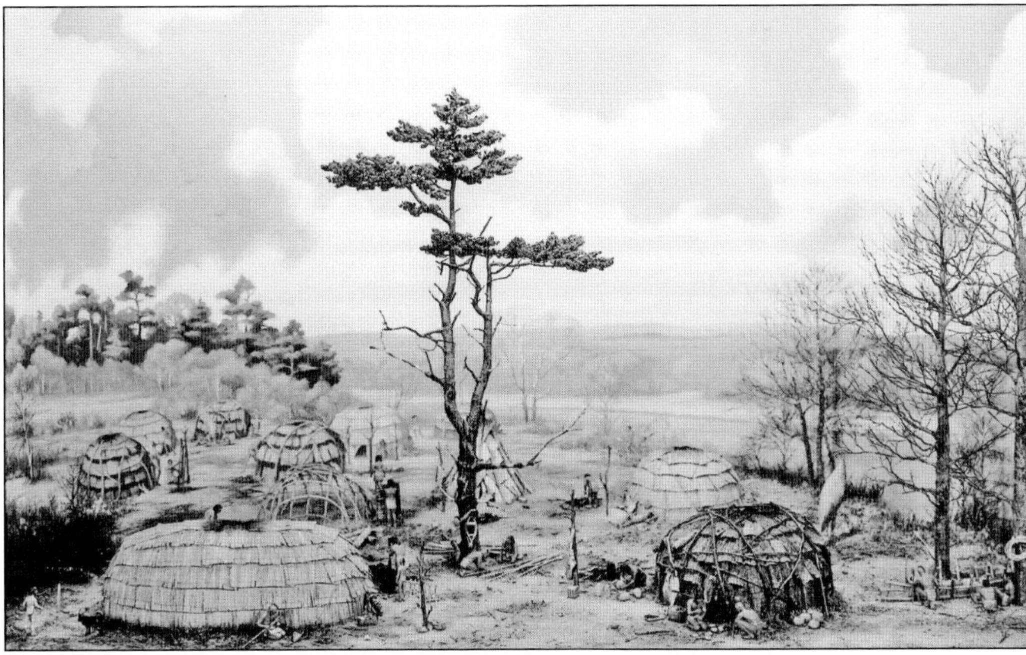

Five centuries ago, the Fells region, particularly near Spot Pond, may have contained one or more Native American settlements or winter camps similar to the one shown in this diorama of a Pawtucket village beside the Merrimack River. Daily life focused on activities such as planting corn and beans, hunting and fishing, preparing food, and making tools. (Courtesy of Robert S. Peabody Museum of Archaeology.)

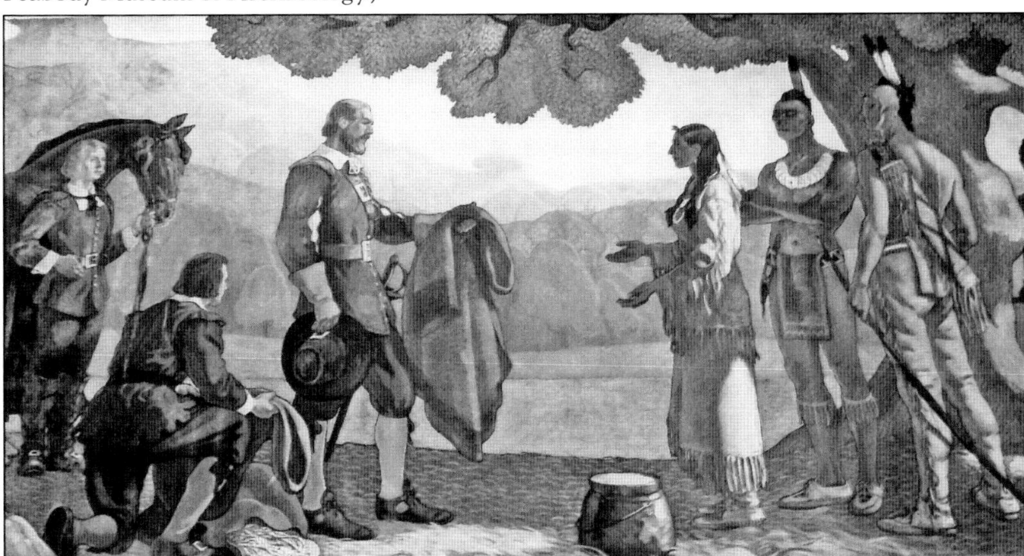

Squaw Sachem was the wife of Nanapashemet, chief sachem of the Massachuset Federation. After Nanapashemet was killed by a neighboring tribe in 1619, she became tribal leader and was called "Queene of Mistick." This 1934 mural by Aiden Ripley in Winchester Public Library depicts Squaw Sachem accepting "21 coats, 19 fathom of wampum, and three bushels of corn" from John Winthrop in exchange for land around Charlestown, including much of Middlesex Fells. (Authors' collection.)

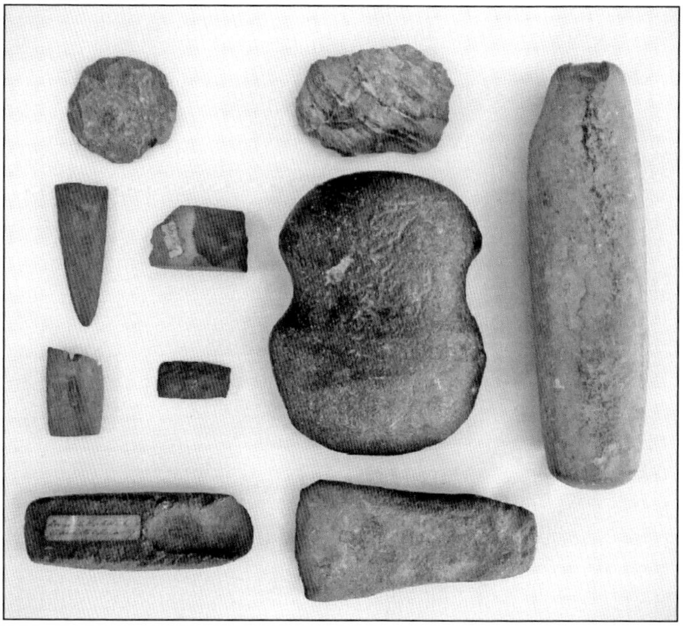

This prehistoric set of tools found in the Middlesex Fells area includes pestles, gouges, and a plummet. A pestle, shown at far right, was used for grinding nuts and grain (and later corn). Gouges were used for working wood to make canoes and other carved objects. The large grooved stone in the center is a plummet, possibly used to anchor a fishing net. (Courtesy of Medford Historical Society and Museum.)

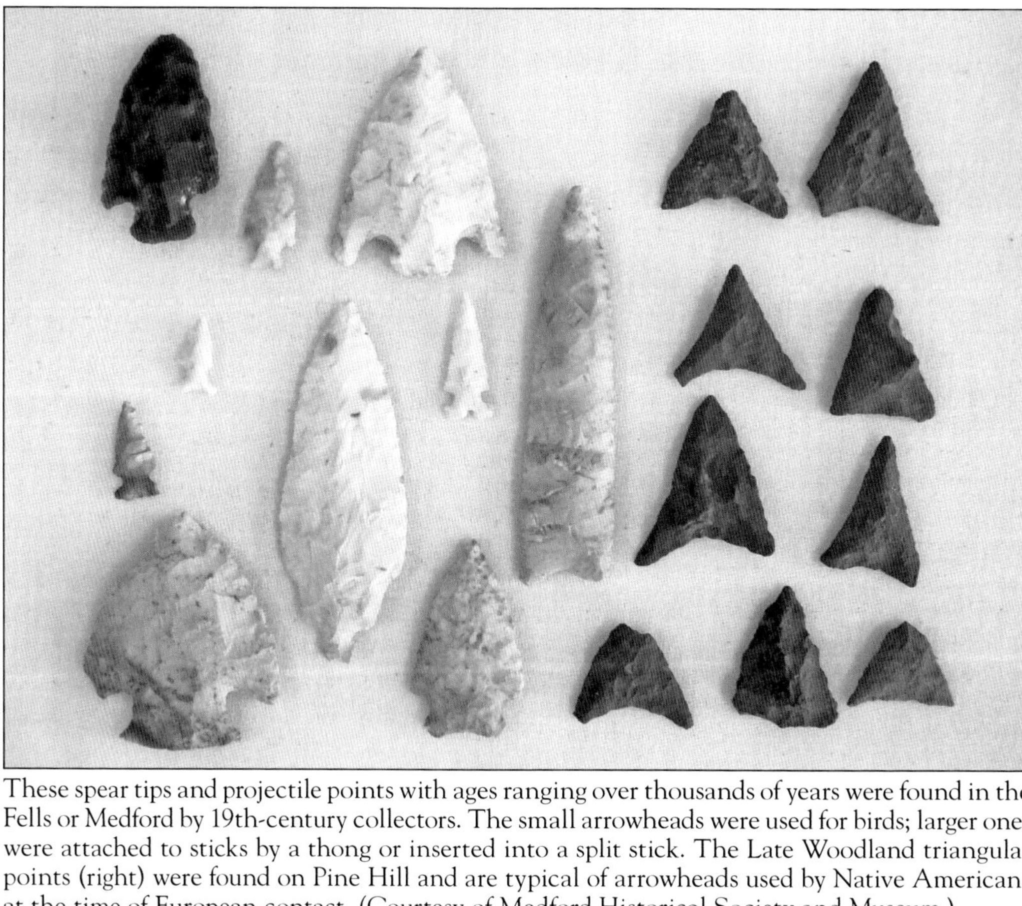

These spear tips and projectile points with ages ranging over thousands of years were found in the Fells or Medford by 19th-century collectors. The small arrowheads were used for birds; larger ones were attached to sticks by a thong or inserted into a split stick. The Late Woodland triangular points (right) were found on Pine Hill and are typical of arrowheads used by Native Americans at the time of European contact. (Courtesy of Medford Historical Society and Museum.)

In February 1632, Gov. John Winthrop (1588–1649) explored the northern part of Charlestown territory. He wrote that he, Increase Nowell, John Eliot, and others "came to a very great pond, having in the midst an island of about one acre, and very thick with trees of pine and beech; and the pond had divers small rocks standing up here and there in it which they therefore called Spot Pond. They went all about it on the ice." (Courtesy of American Antiquarian Society.)

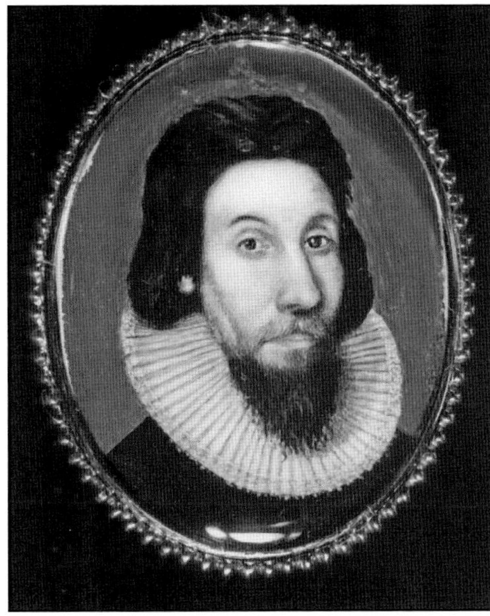

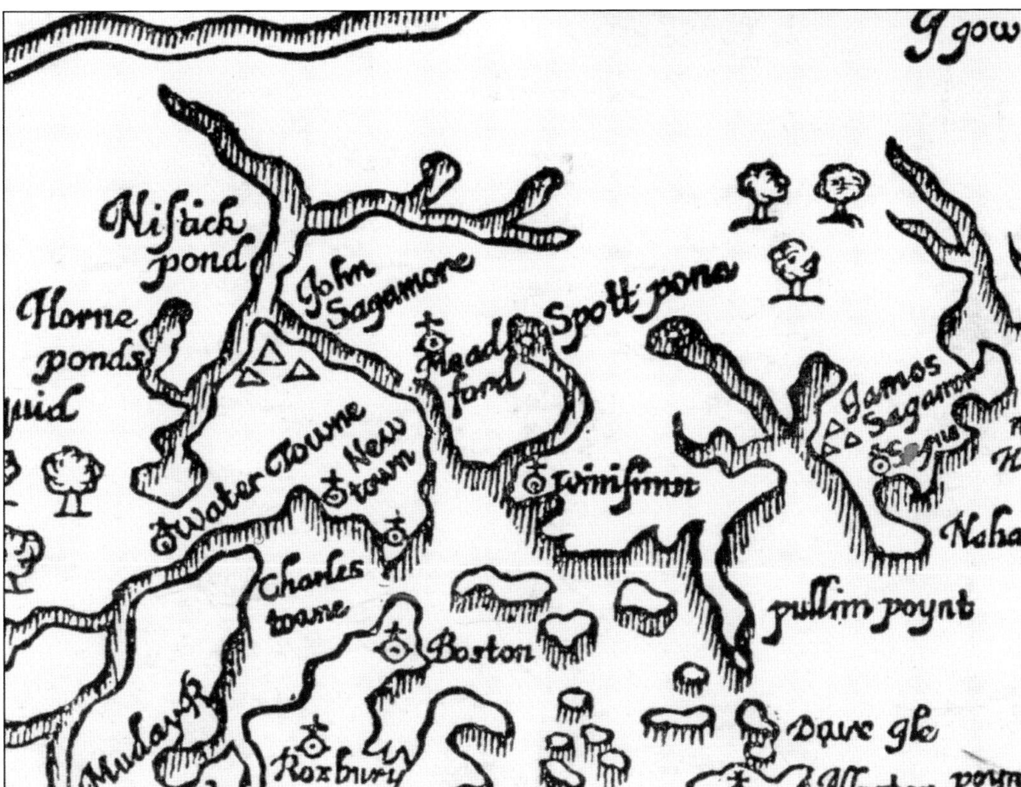

The first map of Spot Pond was included in William Wood's book *New England's Prospect*, published in London in 1634. Wood and his father, John Wood, traveled from London to America in 1629. Governor Winthrop gave the younger Wood permission to trade with Native Americans. This book was one of the first to provide details about Native Americans and life in the Massachusetts Bay Colony. (Courtesy of Boston Public Library.)

THE LEGEND OF "CHEESE ROCK,"

FOR THE FOREST FESTIVAL, JUNE 17, 1882.

In sixteen hundred thirty-one,—
It was a winter day,—
When Winthrop, Nowell, Eliot,
To northward strolled away.

The frozen Mistick flood they crossed,
Ere Cradock's mansion stood;
O'er swamps and rocky hills they pressed,
Through miles of lofty wood.

They crossed a lovely ice-bound lake,
With islands here and there;
"SPOT POND" they called it, from the rocks
That showed their noddles bare.

Then up northwestwardly they climbed
A hill well crowned with trees,
And hungry there, as well might be,
They dined on simple cheese.

For, why, the guv'nor's man in haste,
And careless how they fed,
His basket loaded with the cheese,
And quite forgot the bread.

This fact, so simple and so grand,
To us they handed down;
"CHEESE ROCK" they named that lovely hill,
Those men of high renown.

Some smaller men cut off the trees,
And then they named it "Bare";
And when the bushes wildly grew,
They spelled it "B-e-a-r."

But Nature still asserts her rights
Against all vulgar spells,
And cries aloud, "Restore the pines
To these my favorite Fells.

"Mount Winthrop you may call this spot,
If you'll preserve the trees
That canopied with winter's green
The guv'nor's lunch of cheese!"

Elizur Wright wrote this amusing poem about Governor Winthrop's famous 1632 lunch, which reputedly took place at the top of Bear (or Bare) Hill. The poem was read at one of Wright's Forest Festivals, which were held annually in different parts of the Fells. About 1890, George Davenport captured the view below of two men standing near the summit of Pine Hill. This scene overlooking Spot Pond is similar to what Governor Winthrop and his party saw some 250 years earlier from nearby Bear Hill. (Both, courtesy of the Medford Historical Society and Museum.)

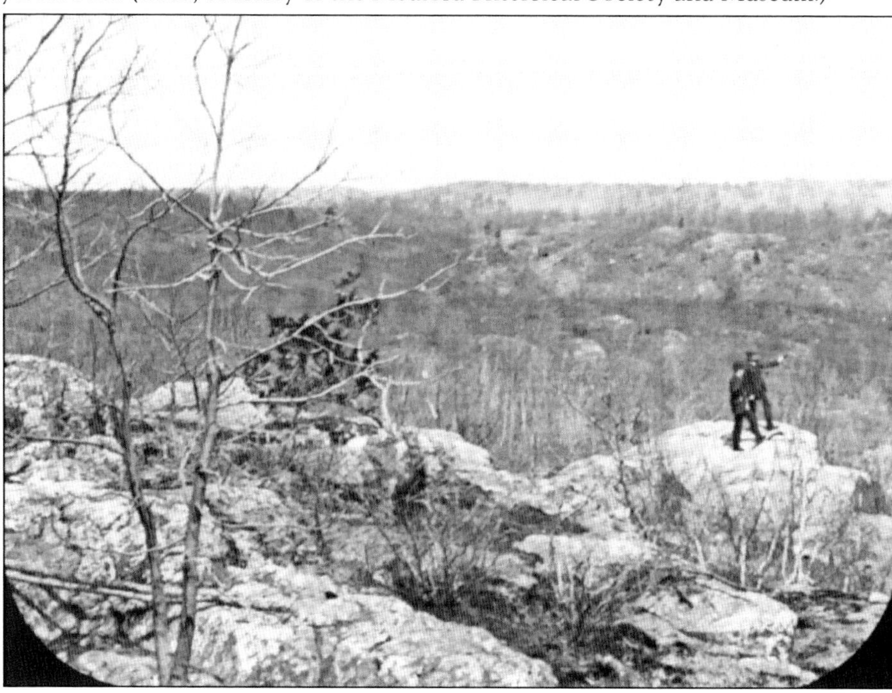

This stone wall near Spot Pond Brook in Virginia Wood is one of the few remaining range lines built in 1658 by Charlestown citizens, and is mentioned in a 1715 deed as the northern boundary of a sawmill property on Spot Pond Brook. Range lines ran parallel in an east-west direction and many served as property boundaries. Colonists called the stones that littered the land "fieldstones" or sometimes "hardheads" or "cobbles." Many of the stone walls in the Fells may have been a source of rocks for lining the shores of Spot Pond when it was rebuilt in 1900. (Authors' collection.)

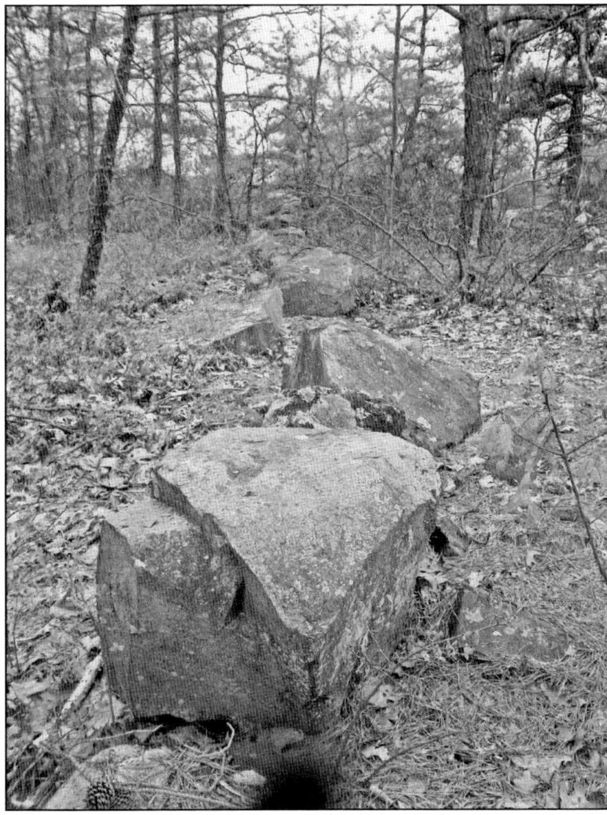

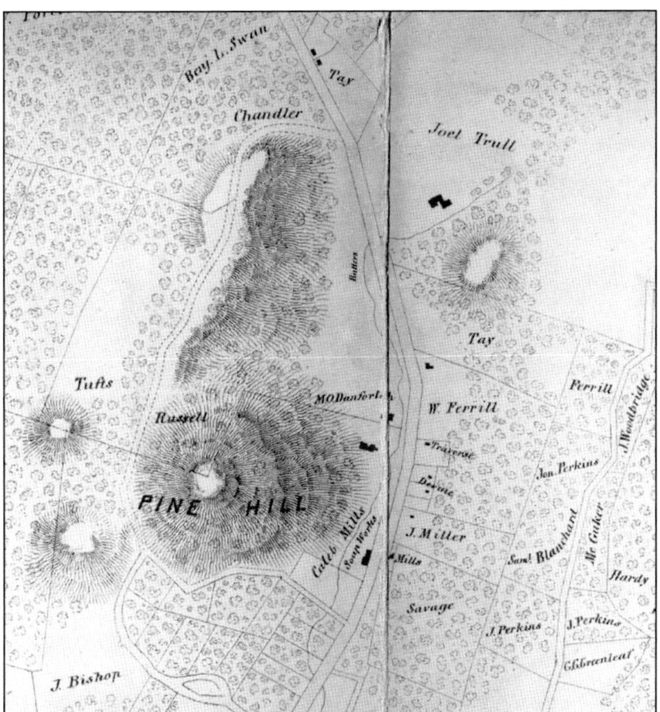

This portion of an 1855 map of Medford by H.F. Walling shows old roads and property owners in the Pine Hill area and along Forest Street. At that time, Elizur Wright's house, east of Pine Hill, was owned by Caleb Mills, who owned the Soap Works. Wright, sometimes called the "Father of the Middlesex Fells," (see chapter 4) moved here from Boston in 1864. (Courtesy of Massachusetts State Archives.)

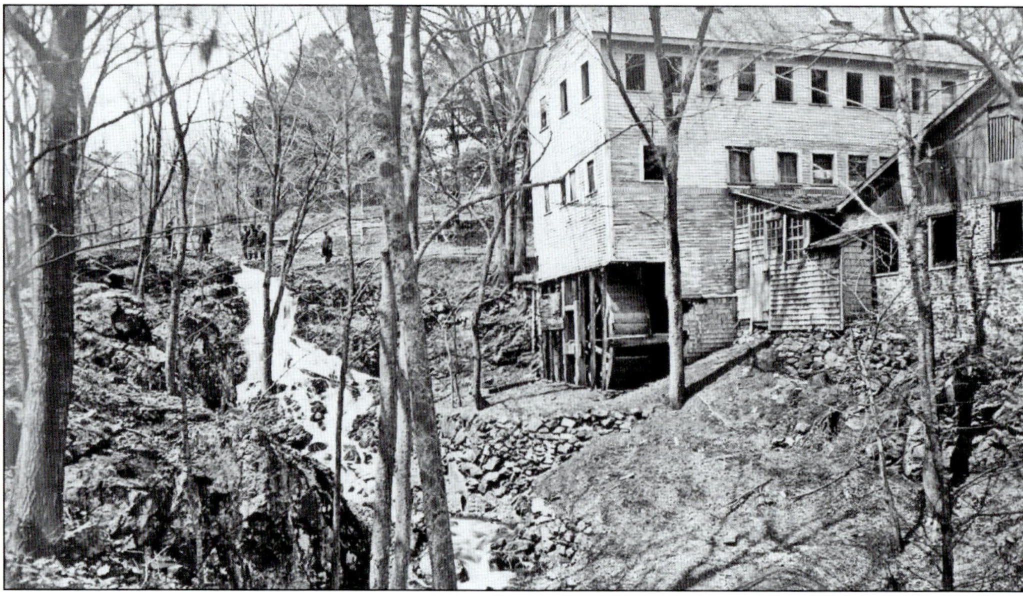

George E. Davenport took this photograph of Joseph Hurd's mill in the 1880s. The mill, located on the north side of Spot Pond Brook and downstream from the milldam and waterfall shown on page 2, dates back to at least 1792 when Ebenezer Bucknam sold the property to John Rand. It was originally used as a sawmill. Later owners used it to manufacture wagon wheels, boxes, and furniture. (Courtesy of the Medford Historical Society and Museum.)

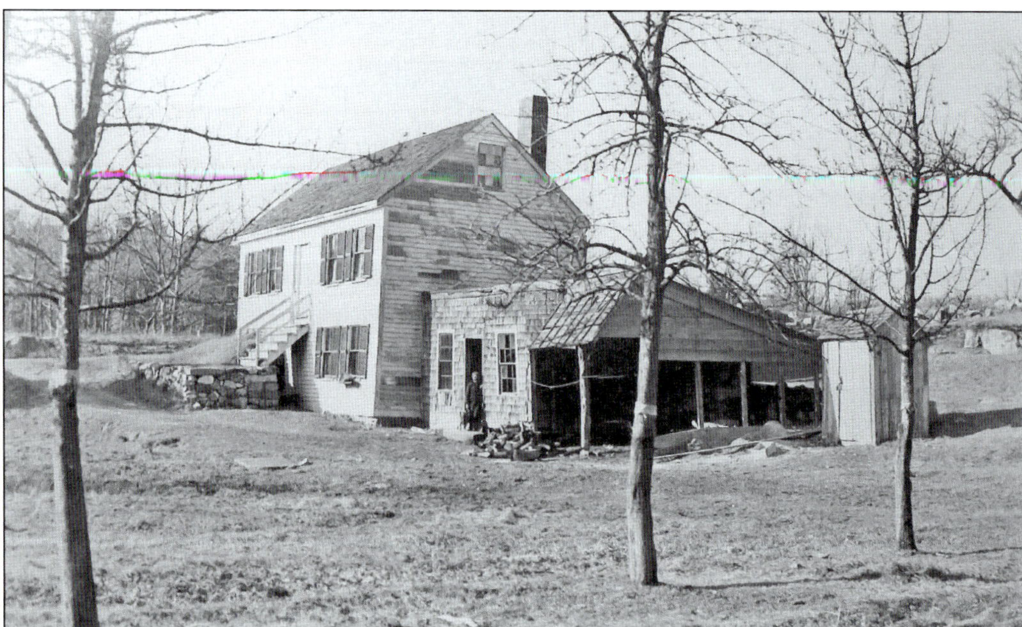

In 1840, Samuel Tay of New Hampshire bought this property on Forest Street south of Spot Pond in Medford (now Route 28) from blacksmith Nathan Wait. In 1876, Tay's son Samuel Jr. married Ida Russell Wright (Elizur Wright's daughter). The 1880 census lists Samuel and Ida (Wright) Tay Jr. and their two children, Dorothy and Winifred, living with Elizur at his house at 288 Forest Street (see page 58). (Courtesy of Massachusetts State Archives.)

Two

HAYWARDVILLE AND VIRGINIA WOOD

From the 18th to mid-19th centuries, Spot Pond Brook, which flowed out of the east side of Spot Pond, provided power to a mill community that no longer exists. Although land ownership is complicated, deeds show that, by the mid-18th century, Timothy Sprague owned much of the land beside Spot Pond Brook, and, by 1790, the Bucknam family owned land along the brook from the upper millpond to the Old Stoneham-Malden Road (see lower map on page 29). At this time, the brook area was sparsely settled by extended families.

Between 1810 and 1813, housewright James Hill Jr. and gunsmith Aaron Hill bought most property along the brook. In 1814, they sold the land to Joseph Hurd, who was successful enough in international trade to be included in a book entitled *The Rich Men of Massachusetts*. Hurd owned a spice mill on Spot Pond Brook (see upper image on page 18).

In 1814, William Barrett bought eight acres in the eastern part of the settlement and ran a silk-dying business. In 1846, Elisha Converse (of tennis shoe fame) and Benjamin Poland bought Barrett's land and resold it to Elisha's brother James. In 1858, James Converse sold the property to Nathaniel Hayward, an inventor of vulcanization of rubber. Hayward then bought some of Hurd's land, making him owner of all but one mill property along Spot Pond Brook, and the area became known as Haywardville.

In 1846, Hurd sold 120 acres along Spot Pond's eastern shore to Boston businessmen William Foster and James Eaton. These two, in partnership with William Bailey Lang, developed the land into an estate district called Wyoming. In 1862, Foster gave Lot 8, which included an Italianate mansion built of local granite, to his daughter Fanny. After her husband Henry Tudor died, Fanny moved to France with her daughter Virginia. In 1886, Virginia died in Paris. In her memory, Fanny donated 20 acres, bounded by Woodland Road, Pond Street, Haywardville, and Ravine Road, to the newly formed Trustees of Public Reservations. The Trustees gave this land, known as Virginia Wood, to the Metropolitan District Commission in 1923 and it became part of Middlesex Fells Reservation.

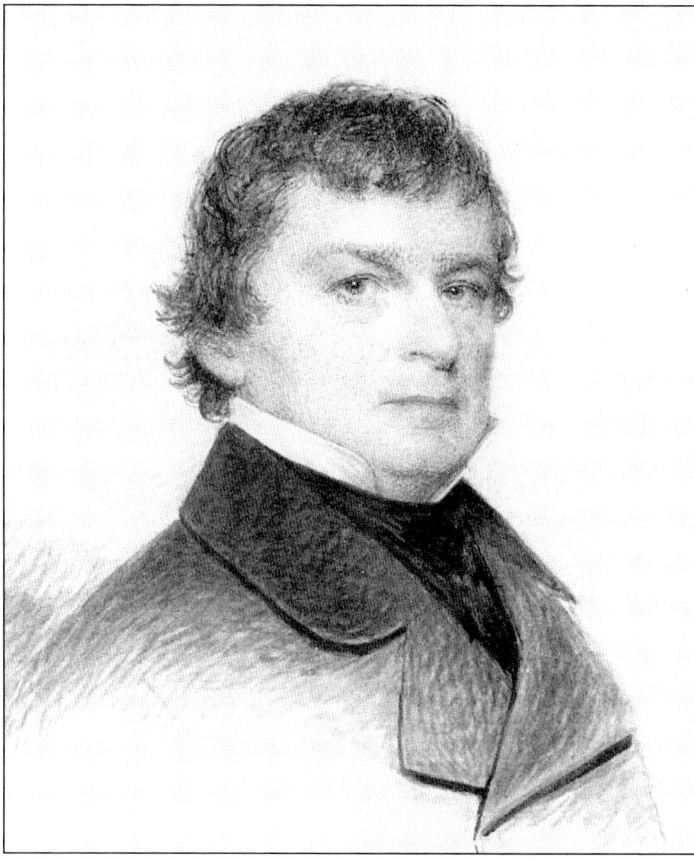

Henry James Tudor (1791–1864), shown here in an 1843 sketch by Boston artist Alvan Clark, was the younger brother of "Ice King" Frederic Tudor. An 1810 graduate of Harvard College, Henry worked as a field agent in his brother's ice business. In 1844, he married Francoise "Fanny" Foster, daughter of William Foster. In 1846, William and two business partners developed the Wyoming estate district on the eastern shore of Spot Pond. (Courtesy of NEHGS.)

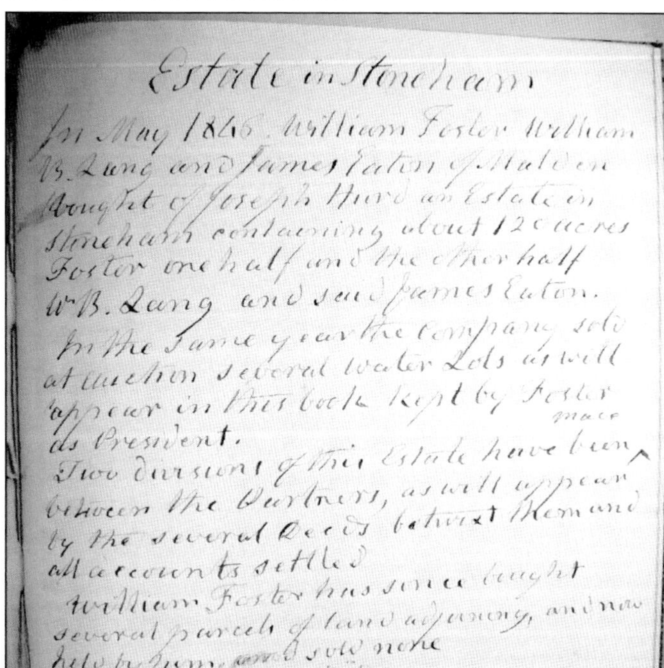

Estate in Stoneham

In May 1846 William Foster William B. Lang and James Eaton of Malden bought of Joseph Hurd an Estate in Stoneham containing about 120 acres Foster one half and the other half Wm B. Lang and said James Eaton.

In the same year the Company sold at auction several water Lots as will appear in this book kept by Foster as President.

Two divisions of this Estate have been made between the Partners, as will appear by the several Deeds betwixt them and all accounts settled

William Foster has since bought several parcels of land adjoining, and now held by him, and sold none

In this 1846 excerpt from an account book, William Foster recorded his purchase (with William Bailey Lang and James Eaton) of 120 acres of land on Spot Pond's eastern shore from Joseph Hurd, owner of Hurd's spice mill. Some of the 13 waterside lots were sold at auction to wealthy Boston businessmen, while others were kept by Foster and his partners, who built Italianate stone mansions designed by Lang, using local Fells granite. Today, the only remaining mansion is used as the Middlesex Fells Visitors Center. (Courtesy of NEHGS.)

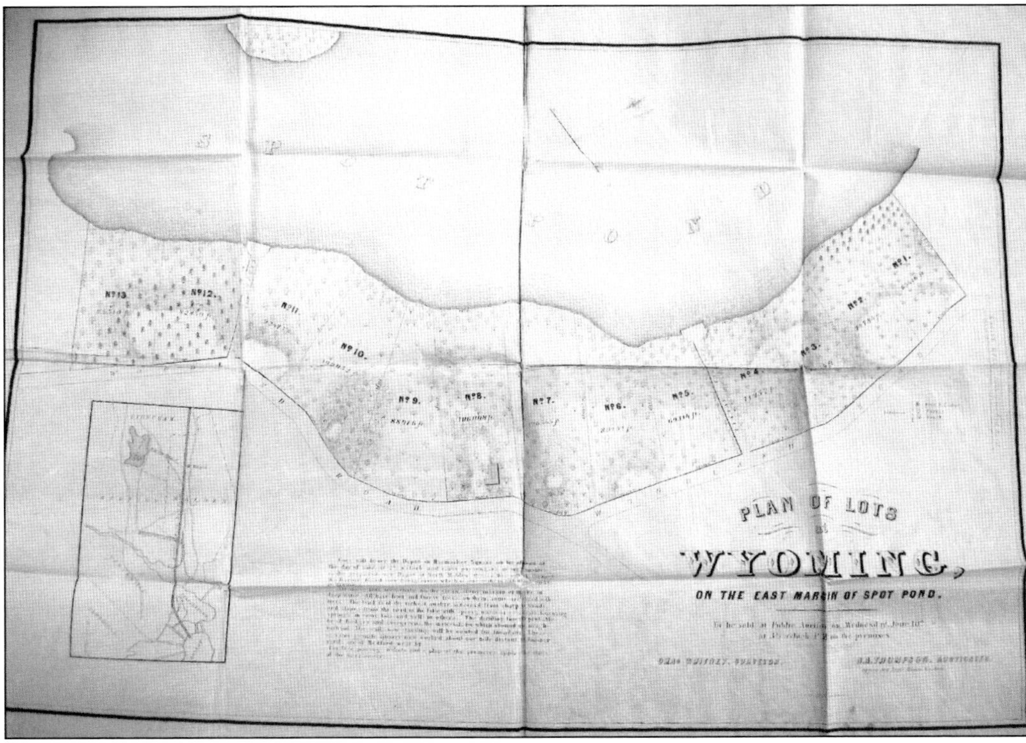

This 1846 plan of lots, surveyed by Charles Whitney of Roxbury, belonged to William Foster. It was used to advertise 10 of 13 Lake Wyoming (Spot Pond) lots, and potential buyers were encouraged to take the train from Boston to Melrose, where an omnibus (horse-drawn coach) would transport them one mile west to Spot Pond. (Courtesy of NEHGS.)

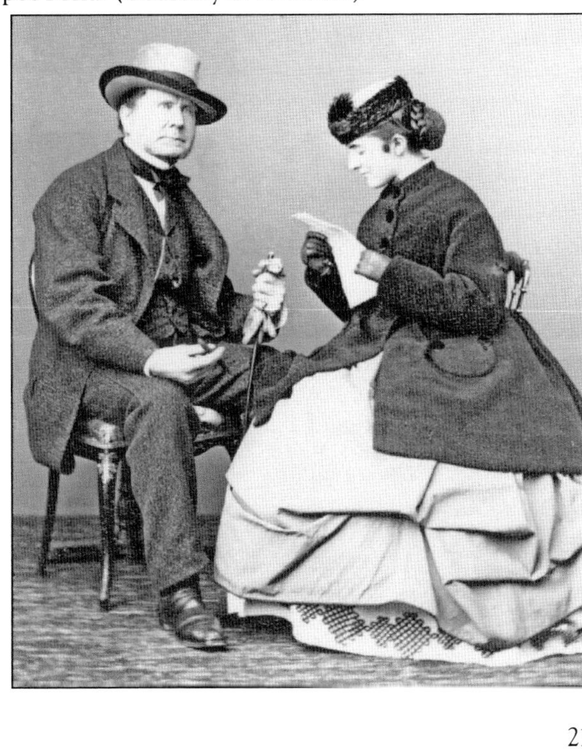

William Bailey Lang (1801–1887) and his daughter Frances sat for this 1865 photograph in Paris, France. Nearly 20 years earlier, Lang, an iron and steel merchant, designed stone mansions for himself, William Foster, and James Eaton beside Spot Pond. These designs were inspired by American landscape architect Andrew Jackson Downing. In 1854, Lang sold his house and moved to Scarsdale, New York, with his wife, Eliza, and their three daughters. (Courtesy of Cleveland Colby Colgate Archives, Colby-Sawyer College.)

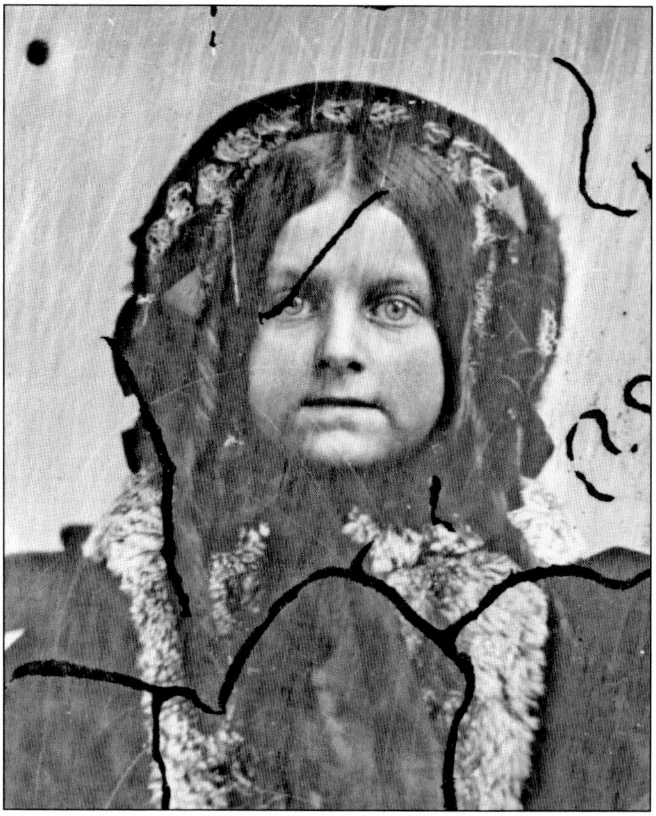

Photographer David E. James took this haunting ambrotype of Virginia Tudor in Boston about 1856. Virginia, the third daughter of Henry James and Fanny (Foster) Tudor and their only child to reach adulthood, was born in Boston in 1850. From 1862 to 1867, the Tudors lived in the Spot Pond mansion shown below. According to family letters, Virginia had a garden and loved to play in the woods. After Henry Tudor died in 1864, Fanny and Virginia moved to France to join Fanny's sister (also named Virginia). The younger Virginia died in Paris in 1886. In memory of her daughter, Fanny gave the newly formed Trustees of Public Reservations their first property—Virginia Wood, a 20-acre parcel beside Spot Pond. (Both, courtesy of NEHGS.)

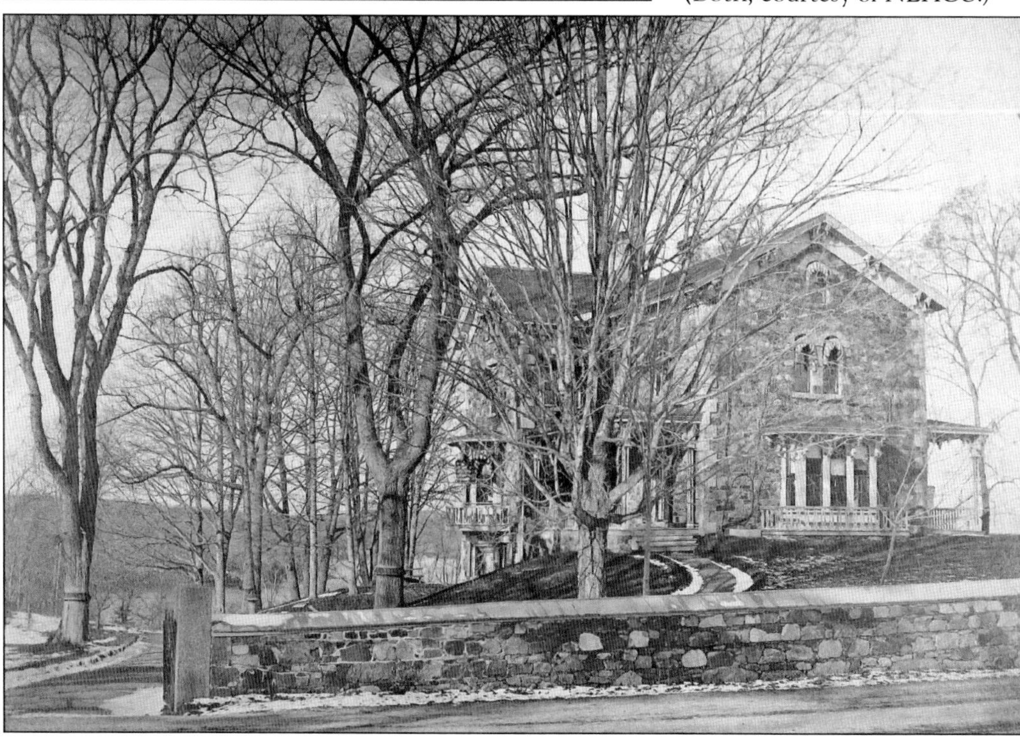

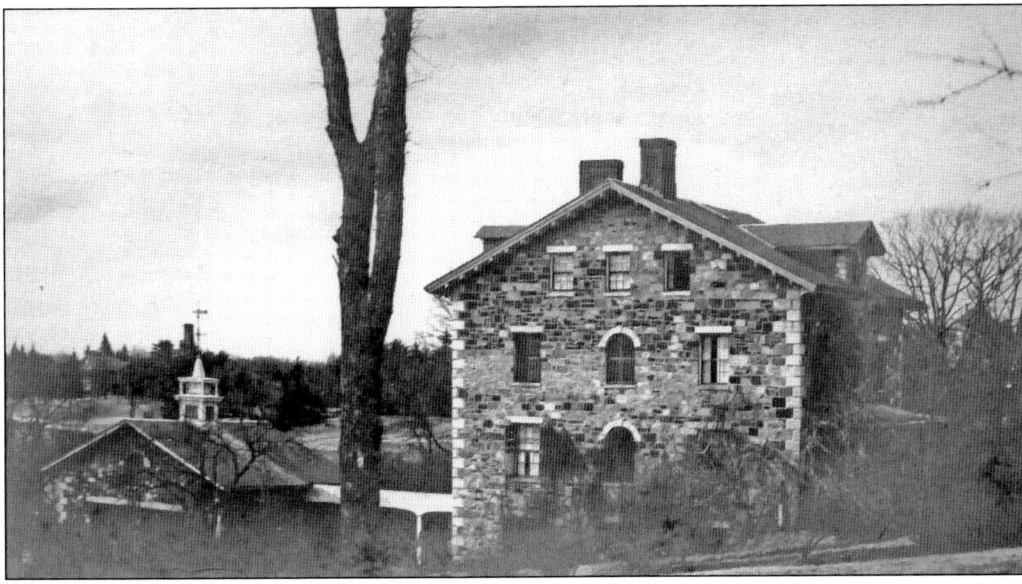

This view of James Eaton's stone mansion was taken looking north about 1899. The Botume House, now used as a visitors' center, is visible beyond the carriage house at the far left. A prominent merchant from Malden, Eaton, along with William Foster, bought 120 acres along Spot Pond's eastern shore in 1846. This mansion was one of four in Stoneham designed by William Bailey Lang in the late 1840s. The Botume House is the only mansion still standing. (Courtesy of DCR Archives.)

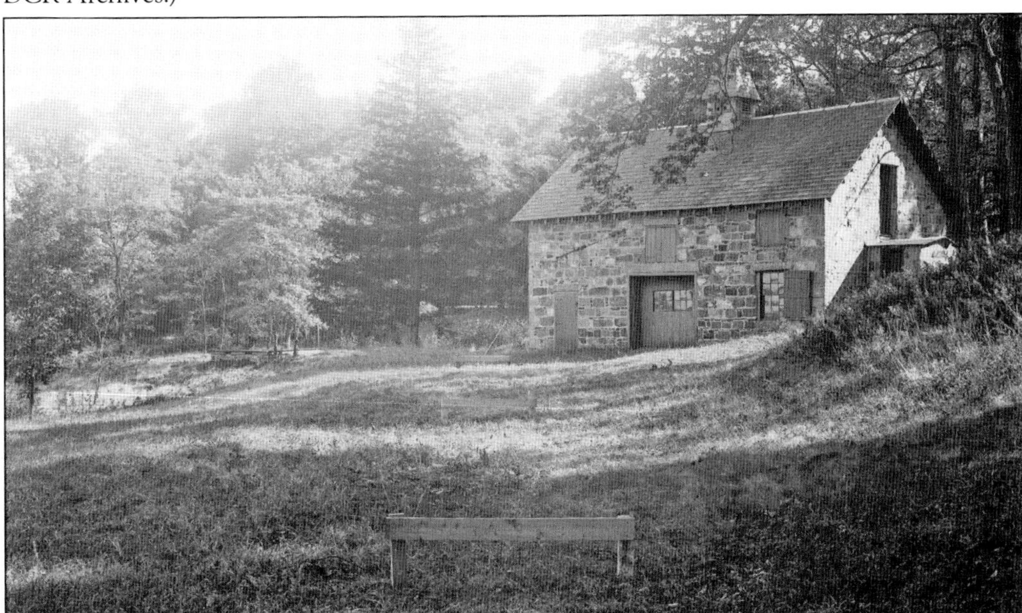

Oliver Tryon, photographer for the Massachusetts Water and Sewerage Board, took this image of the Tudor Barn on October 11, 1915. This barn and the nearby Botume House are the only 1840s stone buildings remaining in the Fells. After years of neglect and waiting for the state to rebuild the barn, Friends of the Middlesex Fells donated $15,000 to DCR, which added state funds, and the barn was restored in 2006. (Courtesy of Massachusetts State Archives.)

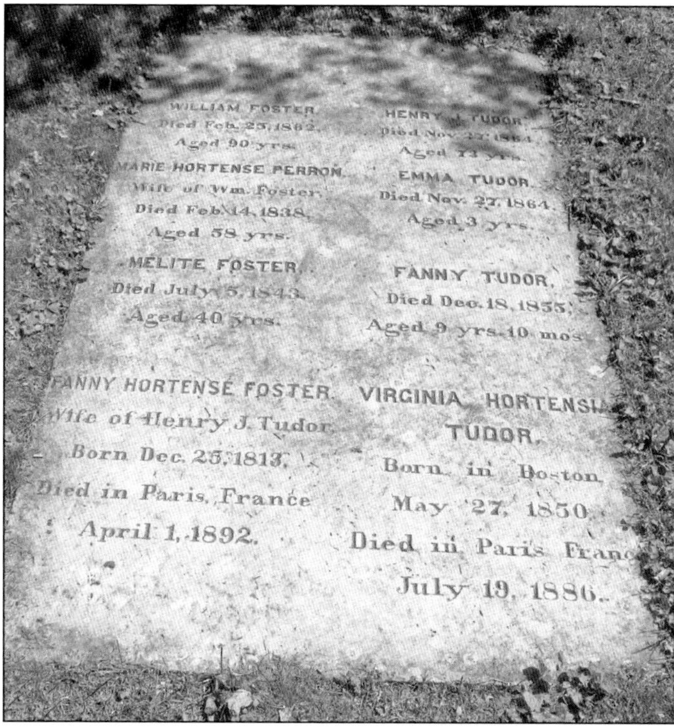

William Foster and his family are buried in Mount Auburn Cemetery in Cambridge (designated as a National Historic Landmark in 2003). All but two of the family members buried here were moved from the Trinity Church cemetery in Boston in 1881. Both Virginia Tudor and her mother, Fanny, died in Paris and were returned to the United States, probably by steamship, in 1886 and 1892, respectively. (Authors' collection.)

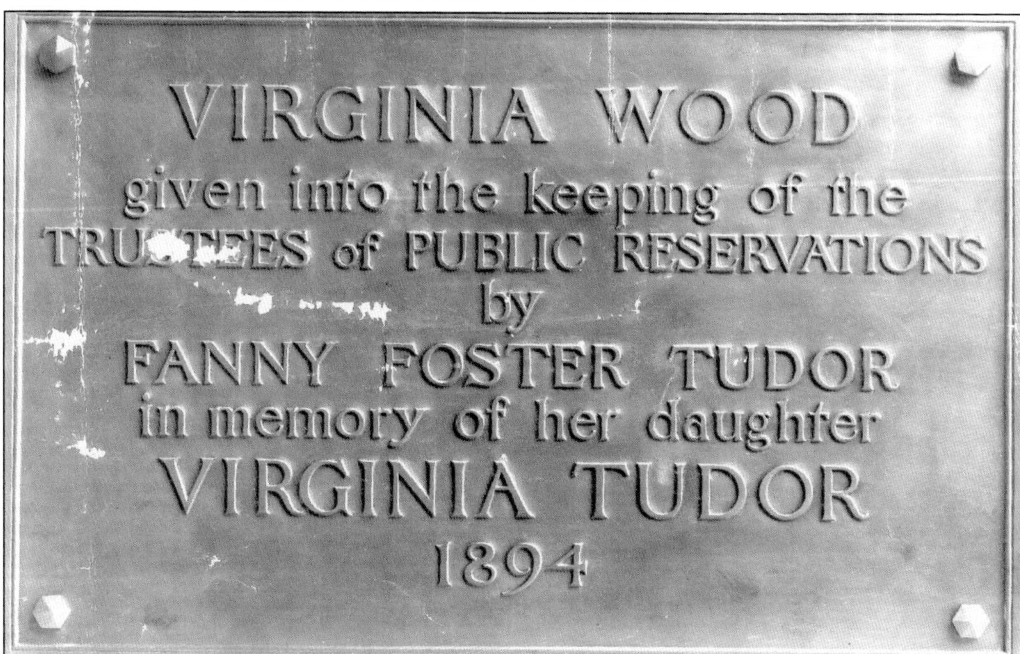

In February 1892, Fanny Tudor gave the Trustees of Public Reservations their first property, a 20-acre parcel called Virginia Wood. Two months later, she died in Paris. About 1905, the Trustees set this bronze plaque, made by Murdoch Parlor Grate Company of Boston, onto a bedrock outcrop in Virginia Wood. The parcel is now part of Middlesex Fells. (Photograph by Arthur A. Shurtleff, courtesy of the National Park Service, ONHS.)

These images show a milldam and waterfall on Spot Pond Brook (located at "Present Pool" on lower map on page 29). A mill operated at this location from at least 1792. In 1891, the Appalachian Mountain Club built this footbridge over the dam to allow public access to both sides of the brook. The view at right is from a postcard dated 1905. The view below shows the site after the bridge and dam were rebuilt by the Work Progress Administration in the late 1930s. (Both, courtesy of DCR Archives.)

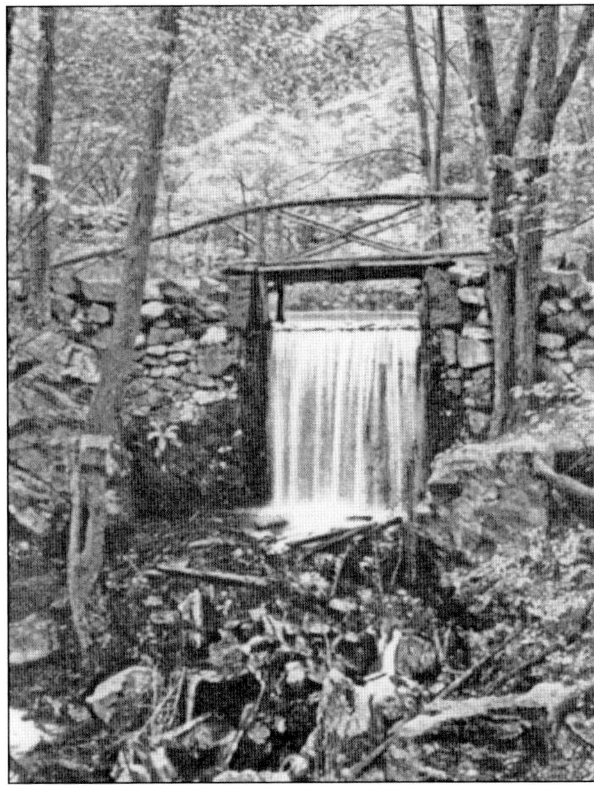

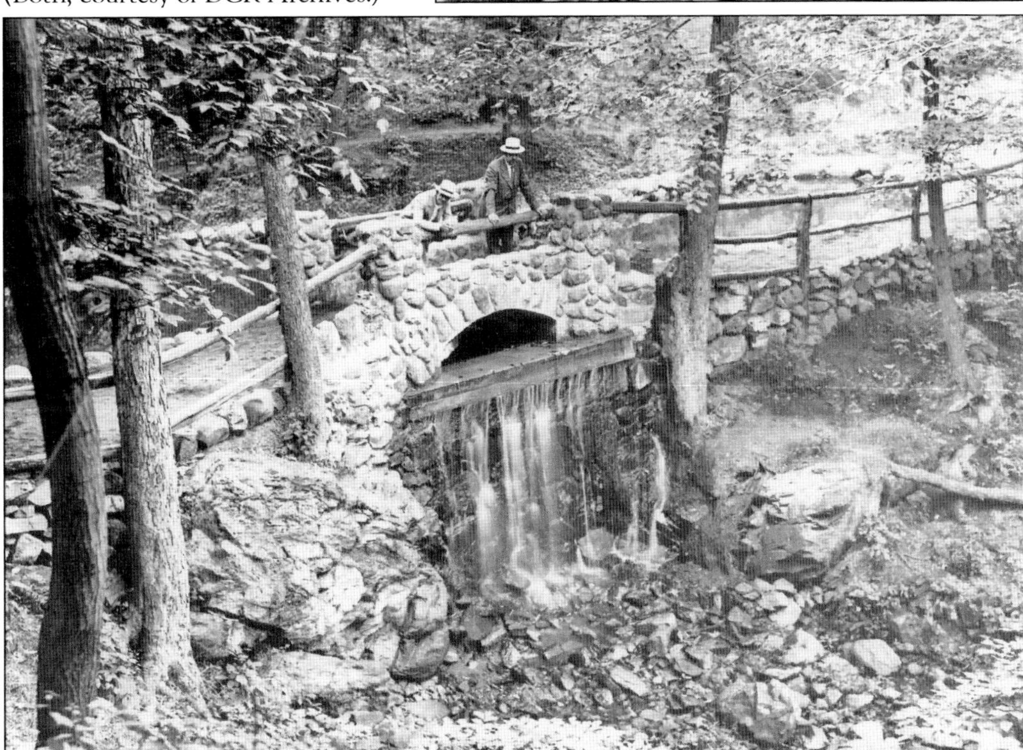

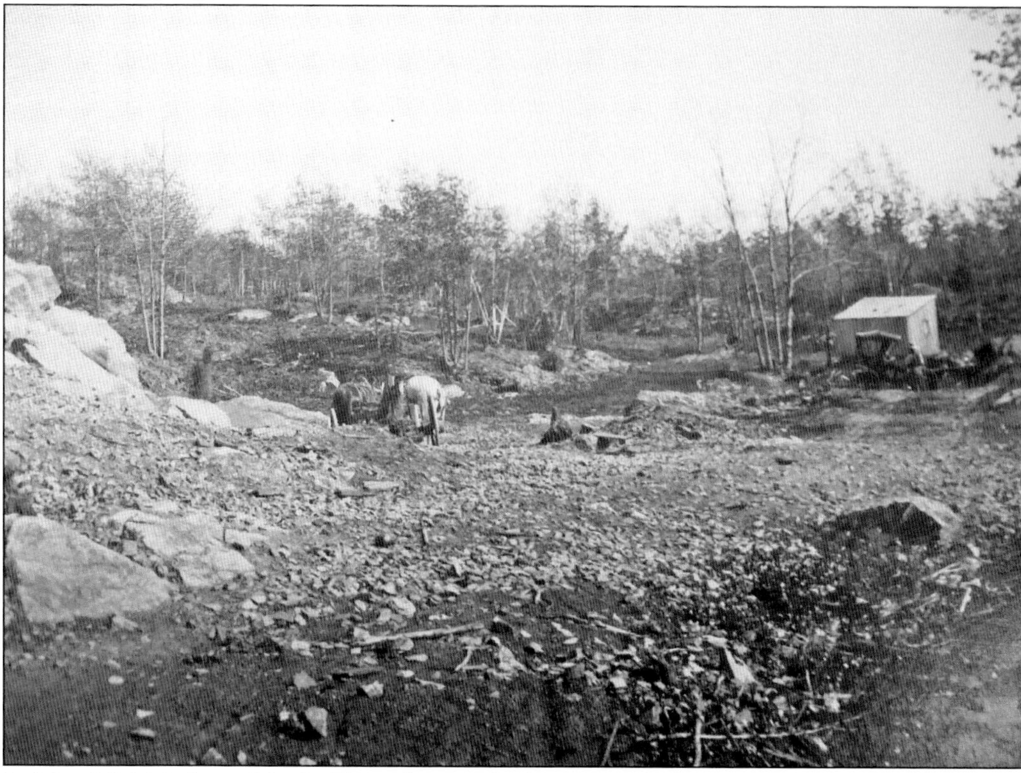

In May 1894, Nathaniel L. Stebbins, known for his nautical photographs, took these images of the Quigley Quarries with views looking southeast (above) and northwest (below). The granite quarries, located north of Pine Hill, were mined from the 1830s to the 1880s for building-stone and gravel for walkways on the Boston Common and Public Garden. This granite was used to build the 1840s mansions along the eastern shore of Spot Pond, and, in 1880, to build Medford's Cradock Bridge over the Mystic River. (Both, courtesy of Massachusetts State Archives.)

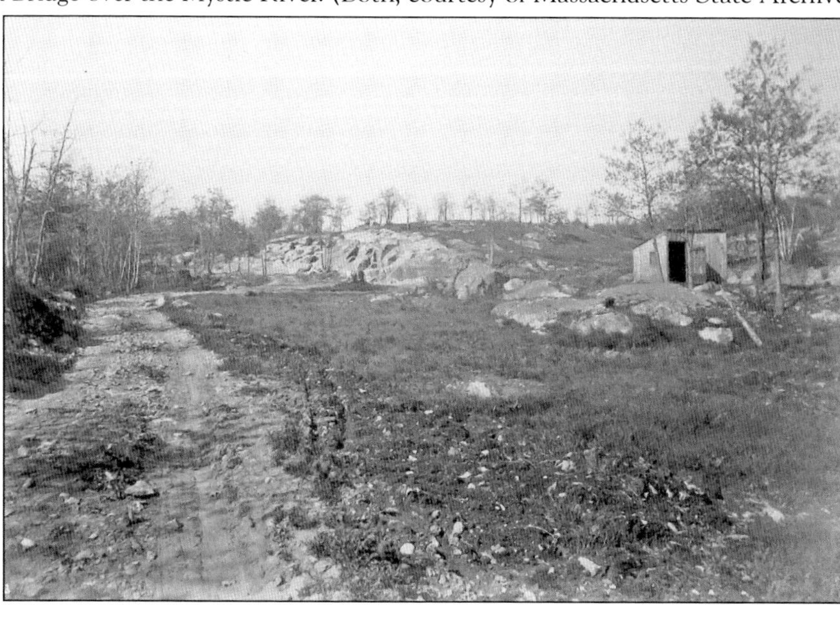

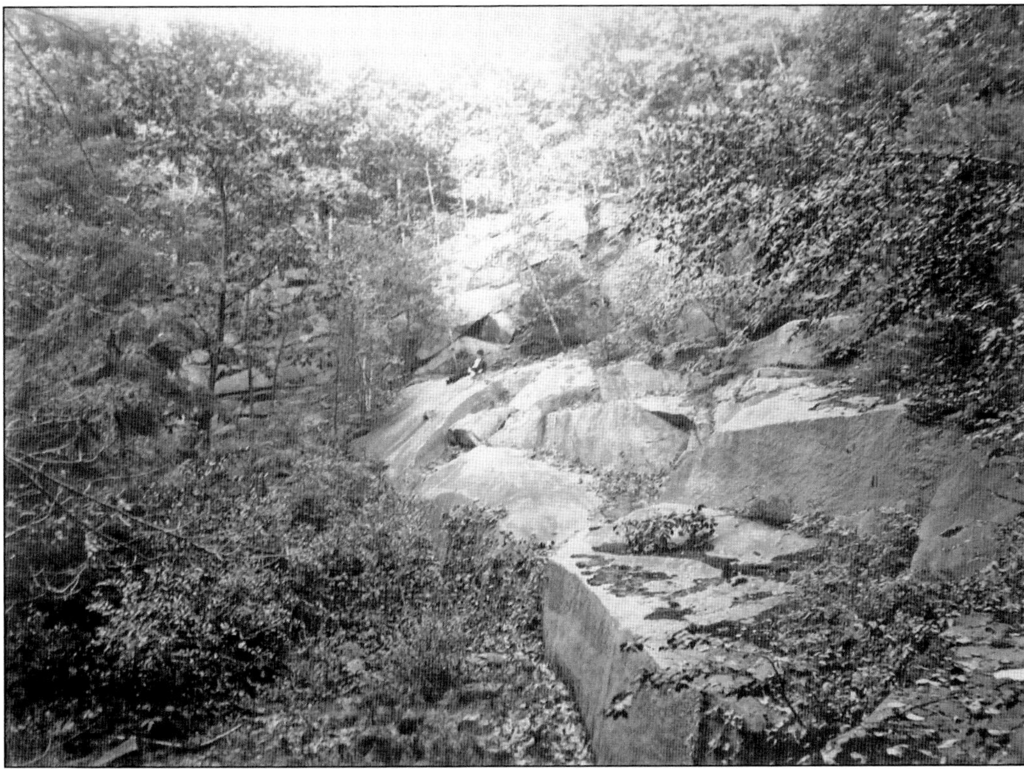

Above, Nathaniel Stebbins photographed one of the granite quarries on September 1, 1894. The man reclining on the rocks may be in the photograph to provide scale. The view below shows the scene as it appeared in early 2014, largely unchanged after 120 years. The quarries are located beside Quarry Road, which begins at the Bellevue Pond parking lot on South Border Road in Medford. (Above, courtesy of Massachusetts State Archives; below, authors' collection.)

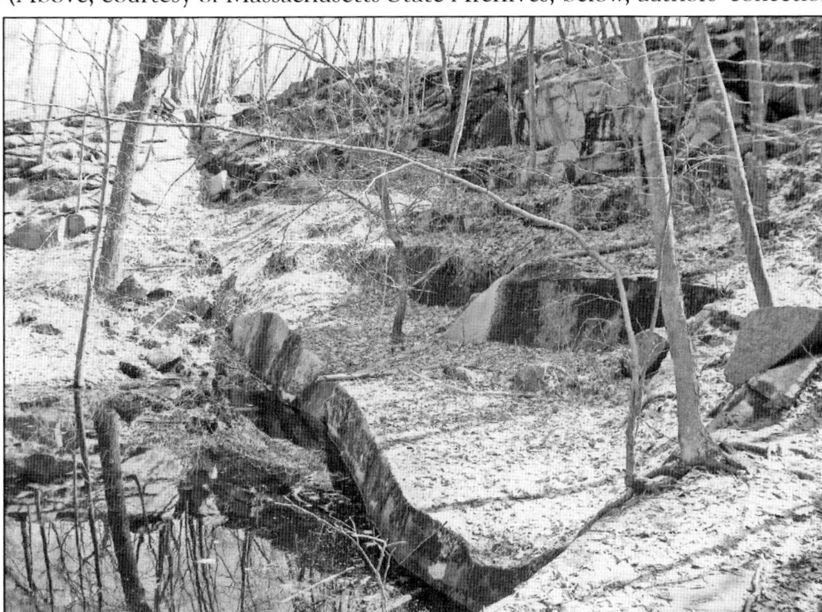

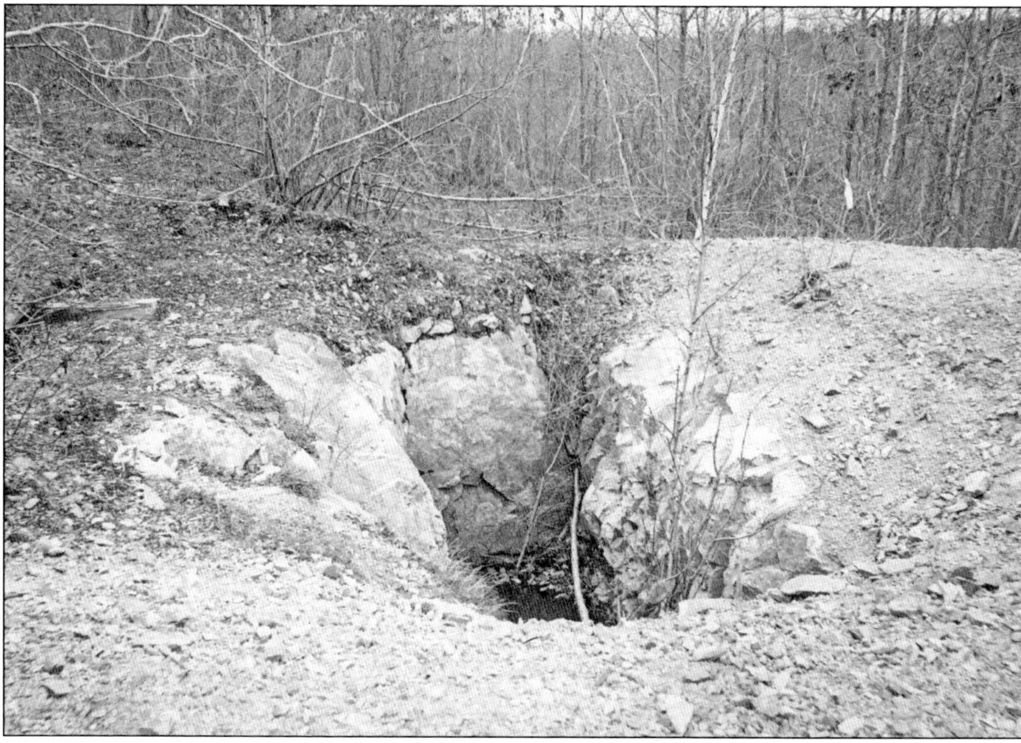

This silver mine operated from 1881 to 1883 and produced minor amounts of silver, gold, and copper. In 1881, Francis William Morandi, an accountant from Malden, noted an area of rock east of Turkey Swamp (now the Winchester reservoirs) that he believed was ore grade. Morandi bought the land and hired workers to dig a shaft. The first assay yielded a value of $18 a ton for silver and $4 a ton for gold, and the ore yielded as much as $50 per ton, mostly of copper. After digging 85 feet and spending $10,000, Morandi abandoned the mine. The shaft was still open in April 1894, as seen above. The photograph below, taken in April 1934, shows the mine after the MDC closed it for public safety. (Above, courtesy of Historic New England; below, courtesy of Massachusetts State Archives.)

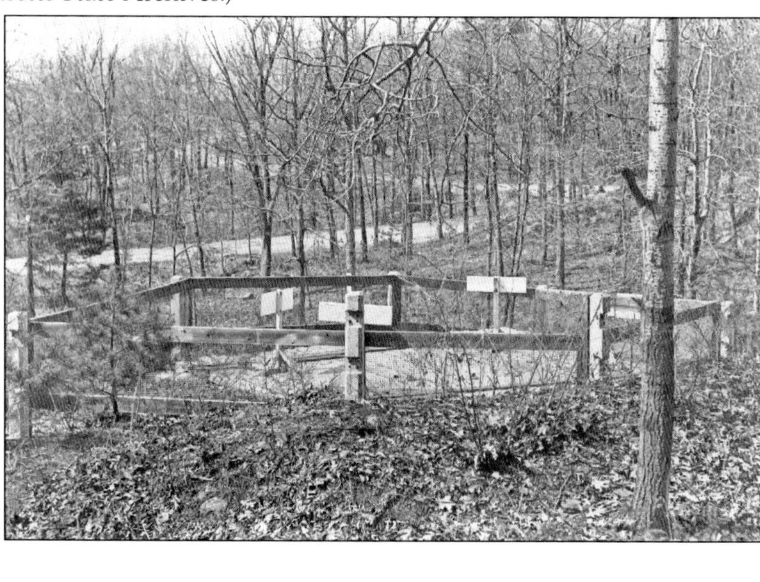

The complex pattern of land ownership in the Haywardville area is evident on this 1874 map by G.M. Hopkins of Philadelphia. At that time, Theodore Weeks owned the mill buildings clustered along Spot Pond Brook near the center of this image. Much of the land to the west of the mills was owned by Fanny Tudor, then living in France. Land to the east of the mills was owned by the Lynde family. (Courtesy of Stoneham Public Library.)

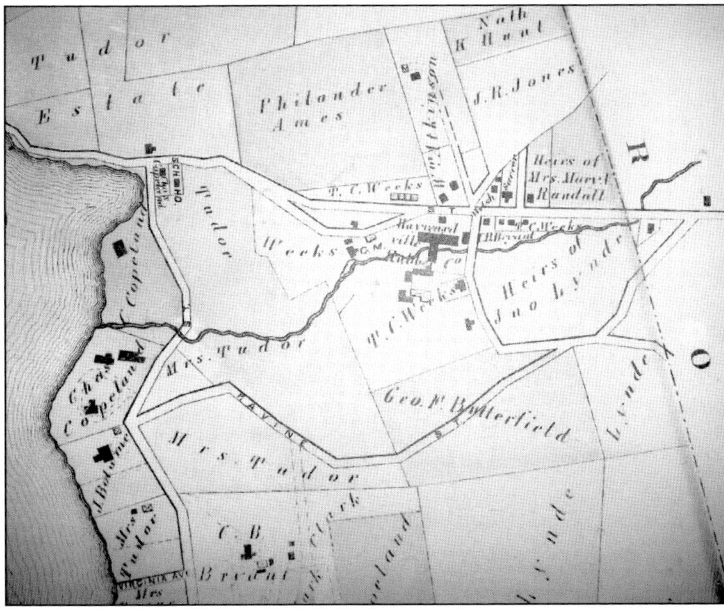

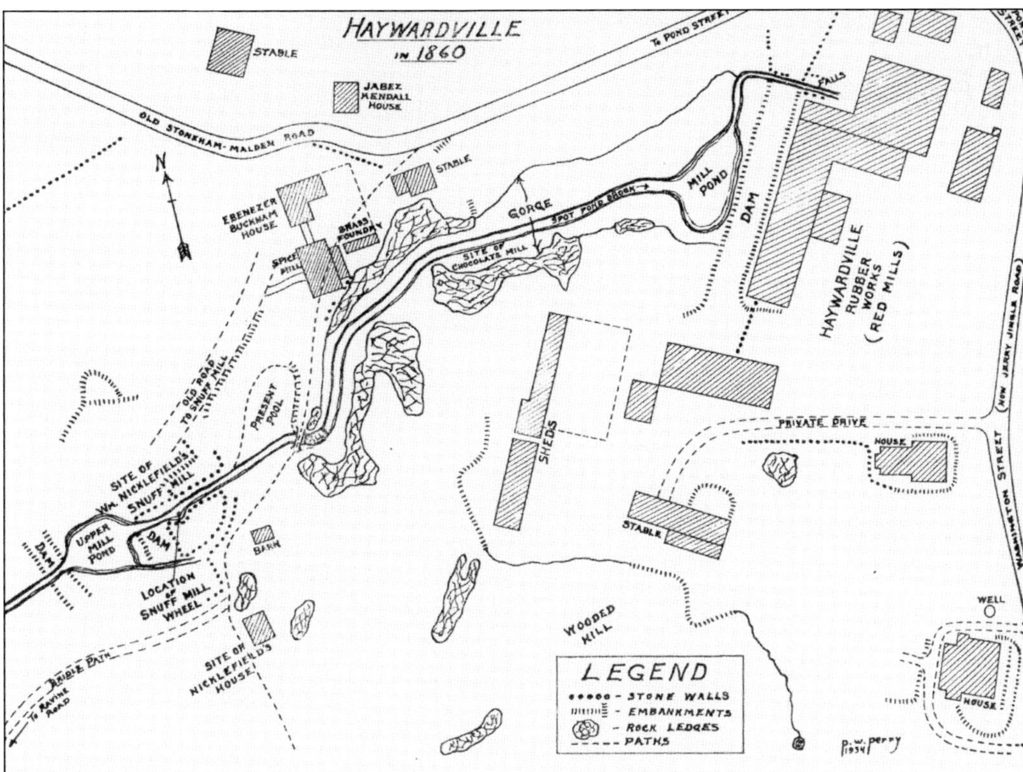

Based on extensive research, this 1934 map by Parker W. Perry shows Haywardville in 1860 at the height of mill operations. The flow in Spot Pond Brook is west to east. Until 1846, the Old Stoneham-Malden Road, perhaps an old Indian trail, was the main road connecting those two towns. In 1846, part of the old road was replaced by Pond Street (north of map), and the old road became a secondary road. (Courtesy of Stoneham Public Library.)

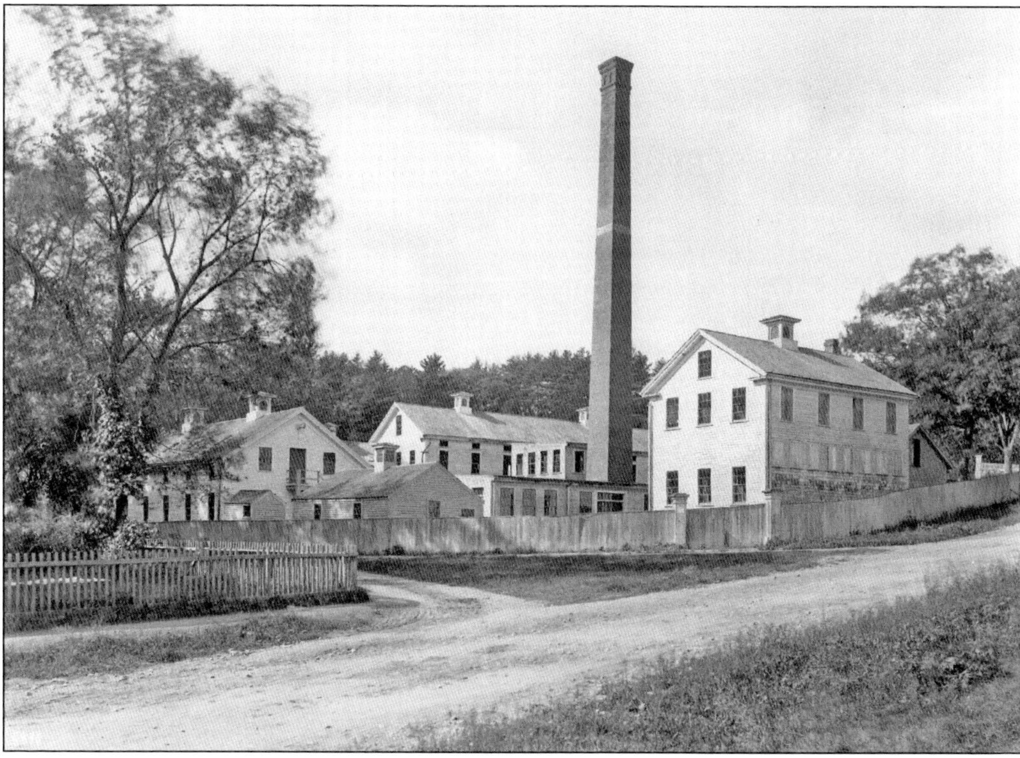

Nathaniel Stebbins took these photographs of Haywardville in October 1895 (above) and in May 1894 (below). In 1858 and 1859, Nathaniel Hayward, an inventor of rubber vulcanization, bought all the mill property (except the Grundy brass mill) along Spot Pond Brook and the area became known as Haywardville. In 1865, Hayward's son-in-law Theodore Weeks bought Hayward's rubber factory. By then, the factory was mostly powered by eight steam engines and employed 30 men at $33 a month and eight women at $15 a month. (Both, courtesy of Massachusetts State Archives.)

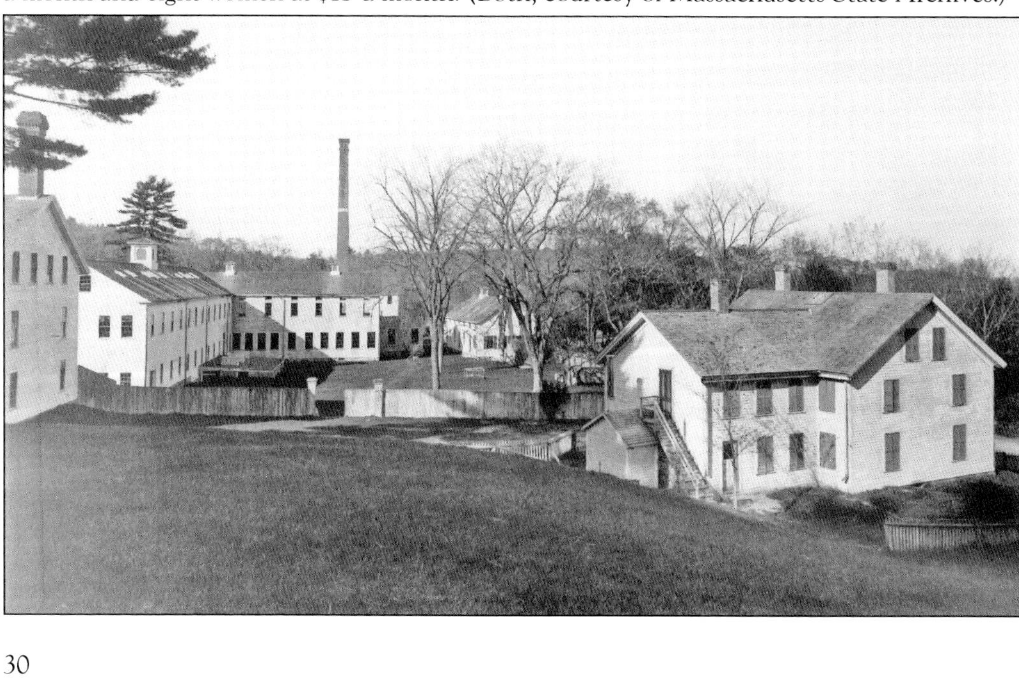

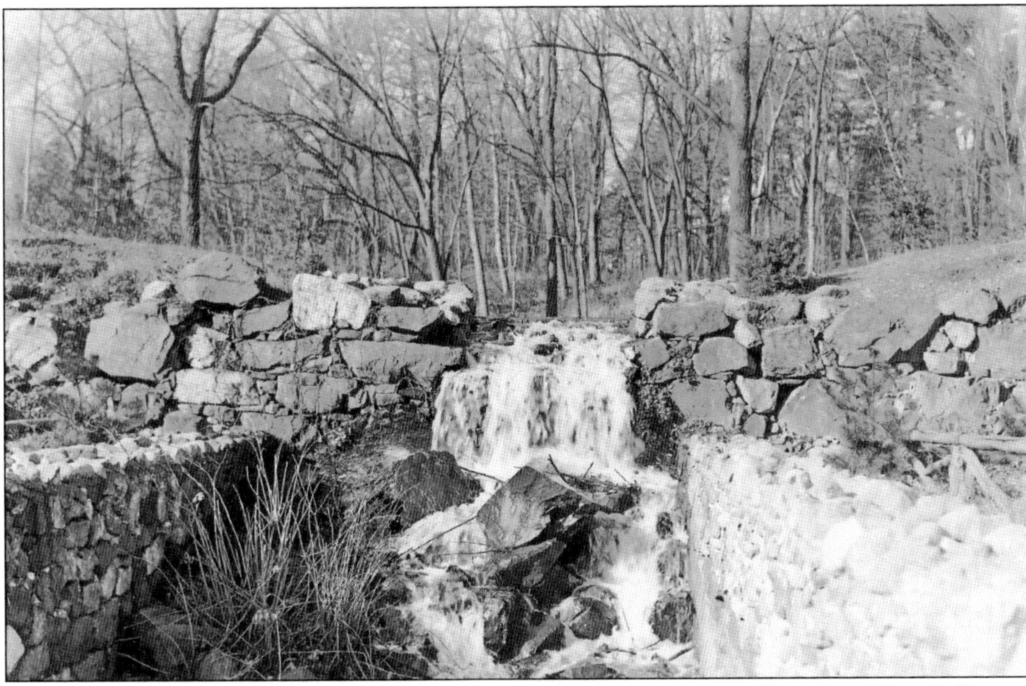

This March 1935 photograph by Albert C. Dove of the MDC shows Spot Pond Brook flowing over the milldam, which at one time had provided waterpower to Hayward's rubber factory. The earth and fieldstone dam is 248 feet long and 32 feet wide. Today, the dam still exists, but the brook has been diverted into a culvert that starts near the dam and flows under Fellsway East. (Courtesy of DCR Archives.)

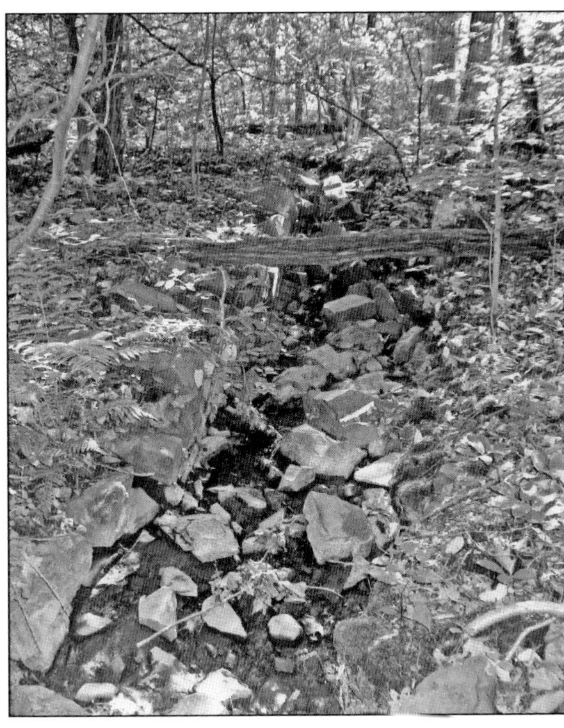

A typical mill along Spot Pond Brook had a waterwheel beside or beneath the mill and an upstream dam to divert flow into a headrace that fed water into the mill. In 1707, Daniel Green built this stone-lined headrace in Spot Pond Brook east of Woodland Road for a sawmill. Some of the mills (those that were water powered) along Spot Pond Brook could no longer operate after Spot Pond Water Company diverted water from Spot Pond Brook in 1869. (Authors' collection.)

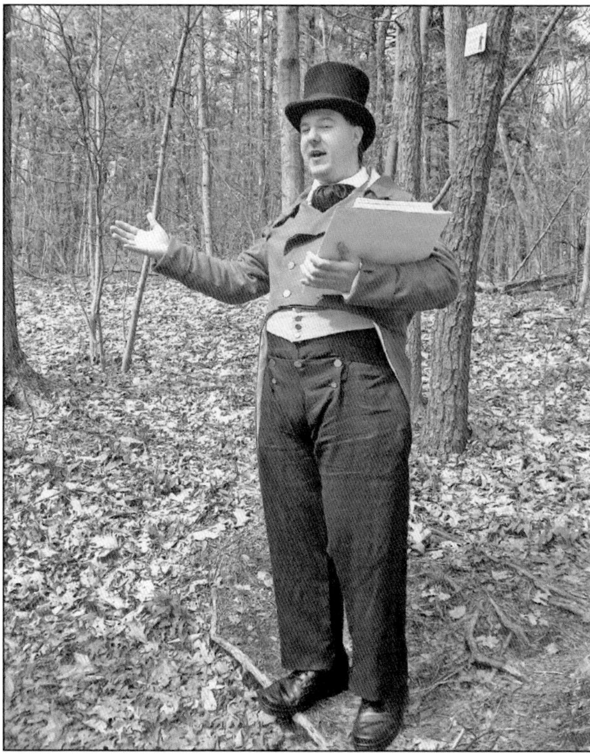

Preservationist Ryan Hayward (no relation to Nathaniel Hayward) brings Virginia Wood and Haywardville back to life during his tours for the public. Hayward uses historical maps and photographs and his knowledge of history to recreate 19th-century daily life along Spot Pond Brook. (Authors' collection.)

Marie McCusker stands in front of the Ebenezer Bucknam House on Ravine Terrace in Melrose. This house was built in Haywardville in the late 18th century at the location shown on the lower map on page 29. In 1879, Bucknam, a mill owner, sold the house to ice merchant Charles C. Jones, who owned the home until 1891. The structure was moved, along with several other Haywardville residences, to Ravine Terrace about 1896. McCusker and her husband, Edward, bought the house in 1966. (Authors' collection.)

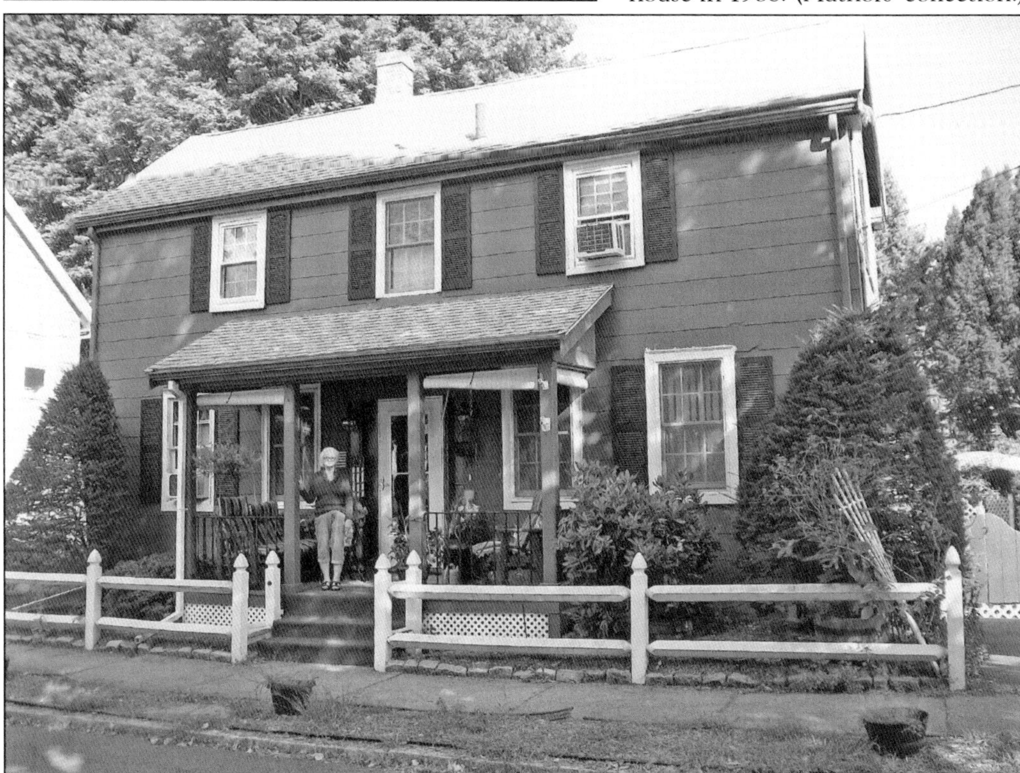

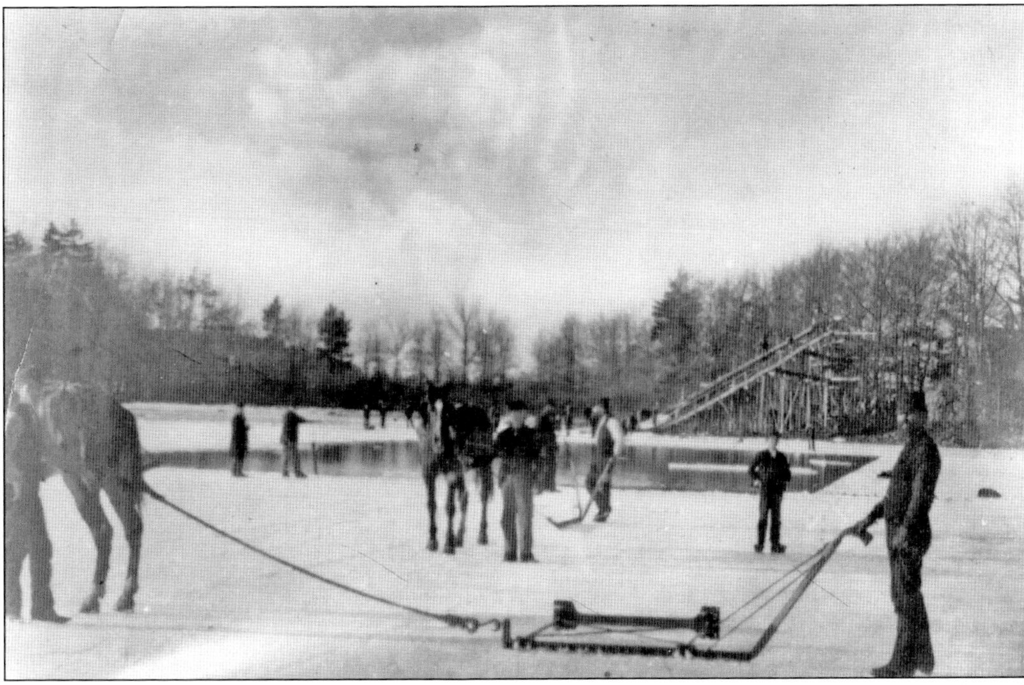

"Ice King" Frederic Tudor harvested ice from Boston-area ponds, including Spot and Doleful Ponds in the Fells, and shipped it to the Caribbean and as far as India. During the 1860s, Tudor owned an icehouse near Pickerel Rock on Spot Pond. Other icehouses, owned by Charles Copeland and Charles Jones, were located on Spot Pond's northeastern shore. This 1890s photograph shows Jones's employees cutting ice on Spot Pond. Ice was stored in Jones's icehouses (below) on Pond Street near Bold Point. In 1891, the Spot Pond Water Company took the property and Jones moved to New Hampshire. In 1900, most of Bold Point was submerged during reconstruction of Spot Pond. (Above, courtesy of SHS; below, courtesy of Ryan Hayward.)

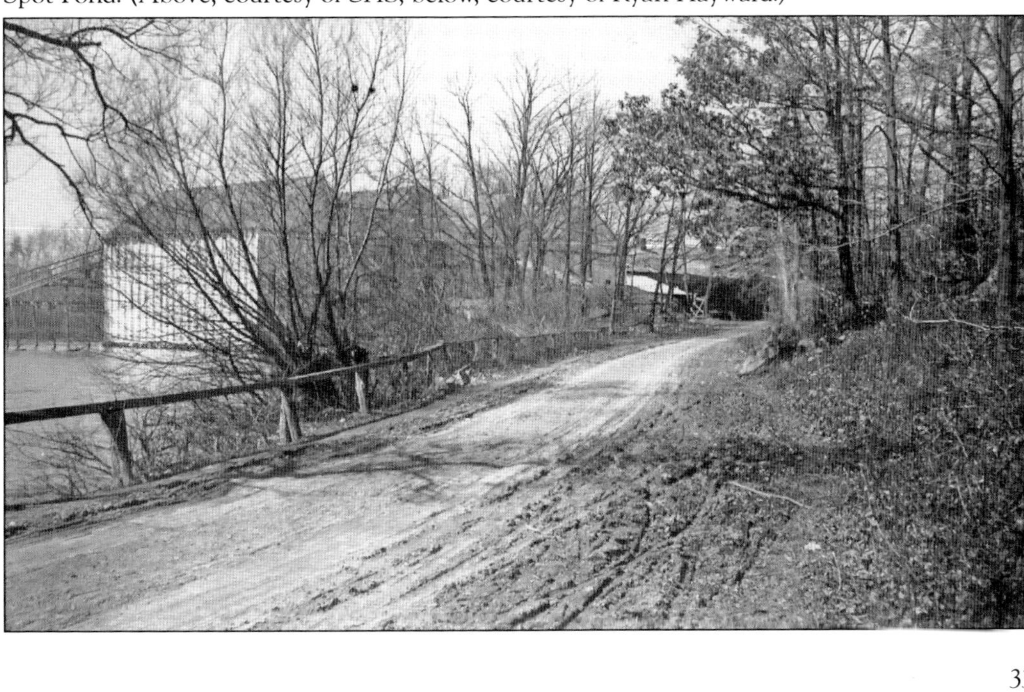

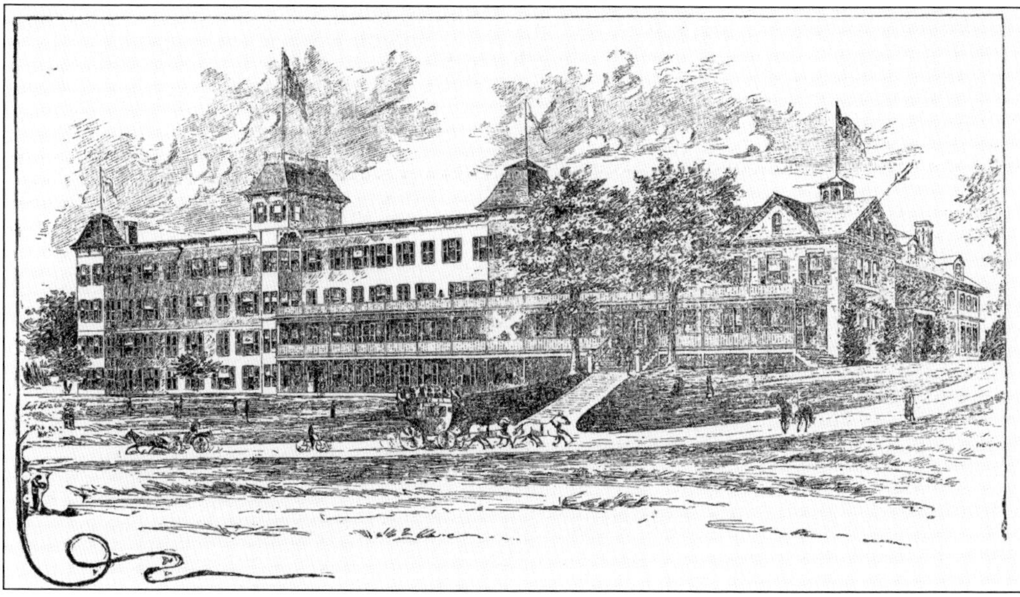

In the late 1840s, William Bailey Lang built a stone mansion west of Woodland Road. George F. Butterfield bought the mansion in 1878 and, with Jonathan Munyan of Worcester, spent nearly $200,000 to convert it to the Langwood Hotel, shown above in a c. 1901 drawing. The photograph below was taken during a fire on April 1, 1902, caused by a defective chimney flue. Most of the hotel was destroyed, but firemen saved the mansion (far right). In 1903, the owners sold the 42-acre property to the New England Sanitarium and Benevolent Society. Another fire on New Year's Day 1905 damaged the dormitory for nursing students, but it was rebuilt. In March 1967, the name of the sanitarium was changed to New England Memorial Hospital. In August 1967, the buildings were demolished and replaced by a new hospital, which is now closed. (Both, courtesy of SHS.)

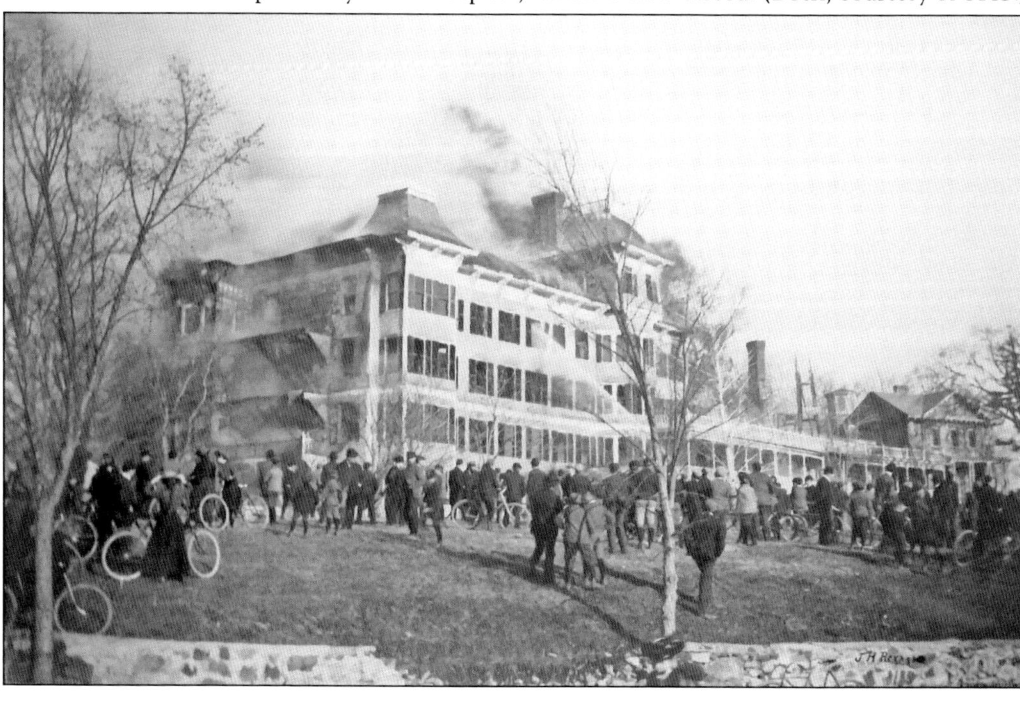

Three

WATERWORKS

If the whole of the water which falls on the Middlesex Fells . . . can be saved, it will be sufficient not only to nourish the densest forest of pines but to furnish . . . to a million of people, for every day of the year, four imperial gallons of pure water apiece.

—Elizur Wright, 1895, "Appeals for the Middlesex Fells and the Forests"

In the early 19th century, Boston was faced with water-supply problems. As early as 1825, Daniel Treadwell recommended Spot Pond for Boston's use, but engineers concluded that the pond was too small for the growing city. Boston selected Lake Cochituate in Framingham instead, and it was not until 1898 that Boston tapped Spot Pond as a source of drinking water.

Meanwhile, cities and towns near Spot Pond were also looking for supplies. At that time, each household had a private supply, usually a well, and sometimes a cistern to hold rainwater gathered from the roof. In 1867, businessmen from Medford, Malden, and Melrose formed the Spot Pond Water Company to develop a public supply and built a pumping station for each city. In 1891, the three cities bought the land bordering Spot Pond as an antipollution measure.

In January 1898, control of Spot Pond passed to the Metropolitan Water Board (MWB), which hired Olmsted Brothers landscape architects to develop plans to enlarge Spot Pond as a reservoir as part of the Boston's northern distribution system while retaining its natural beauty. By 1901, the state had replaced the three city pumping stations with a pumping station with two large steam engines and pumping capacity of 30 million gallons a day. The MWB spent almost $542,000 to drain and excavate Spot Pond. Shallow areas were deepened and the water level was raised by nine feet.

West of Spot Pond was the great Turkey Swamp. This was the home of the area's last Native American, Hannah Shiner, who died in 1820. In 1873, Moses Herrick, Winchester's water commissioner, proposed using the swamp for a water supply. A dam was completed in 1874, and water flowed into the reservoir (now called North Reservoir). In 1890, the town inundated the southern end of the swamp to create South Reservoir. The following year, Middle Reservoir was created between the existing reservoirs.

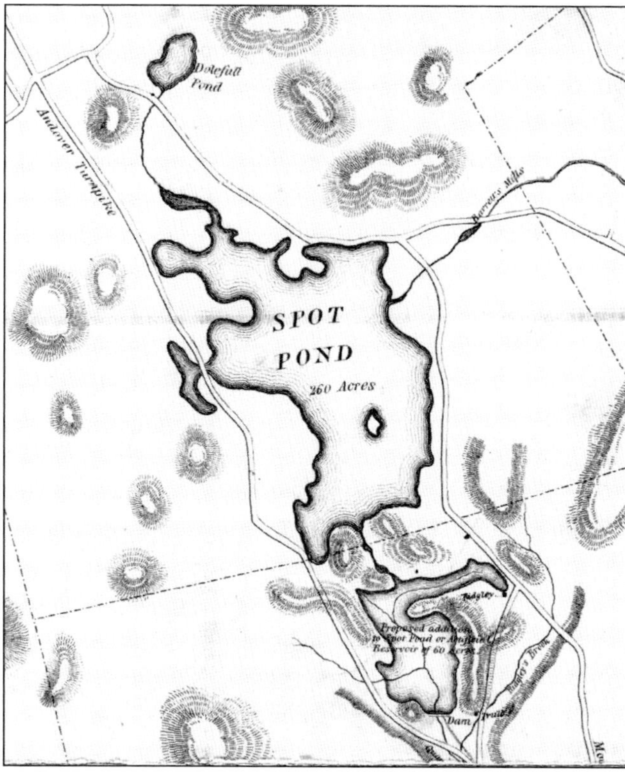

In 1825, Daniel Treadwell proposed using Spot Pond as a water supply for Boston. In 1836, Robert Henry Eddy published this map, entitled "Map of the Water Region of the County of Middlesex Exhibiting the Mode of Supplying Boston and Charlestown with Soft Water from Spot and Mystic Ponds." Treadwell also proposed to build a 60-acre reservoir south of Spot Pond. This smaller pond (Wright's Pond) was created after 1862 and was also used for harvesting ice. (Courtesy of Boston Public Library.)

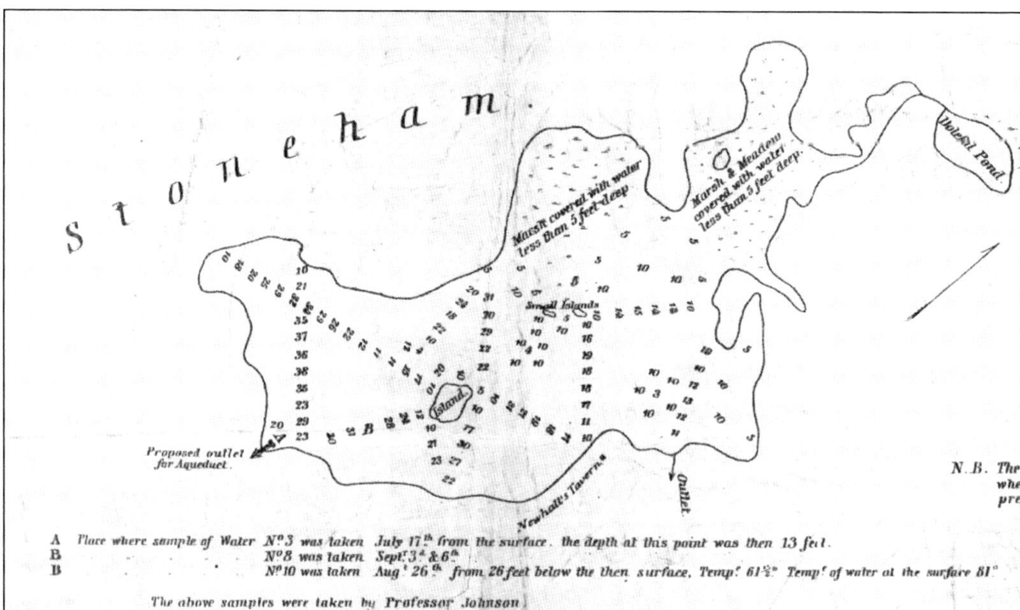

In 1845, the state legislature commissioned John Jervis, Walter Johnson, and Henry Tracy to map the depth of Spot Pond to assess its potential as a reservoir for Boston. This map shows that pond depth ranged from less than five feet in the northwest to 38 feet at its southern end. Long Pond (Lake Cochituate) in Framingham was selected instead. It was 53 years before Boston revisited Spot Pond for its reservoir potential. (Courtesy of Boston Public Library.)

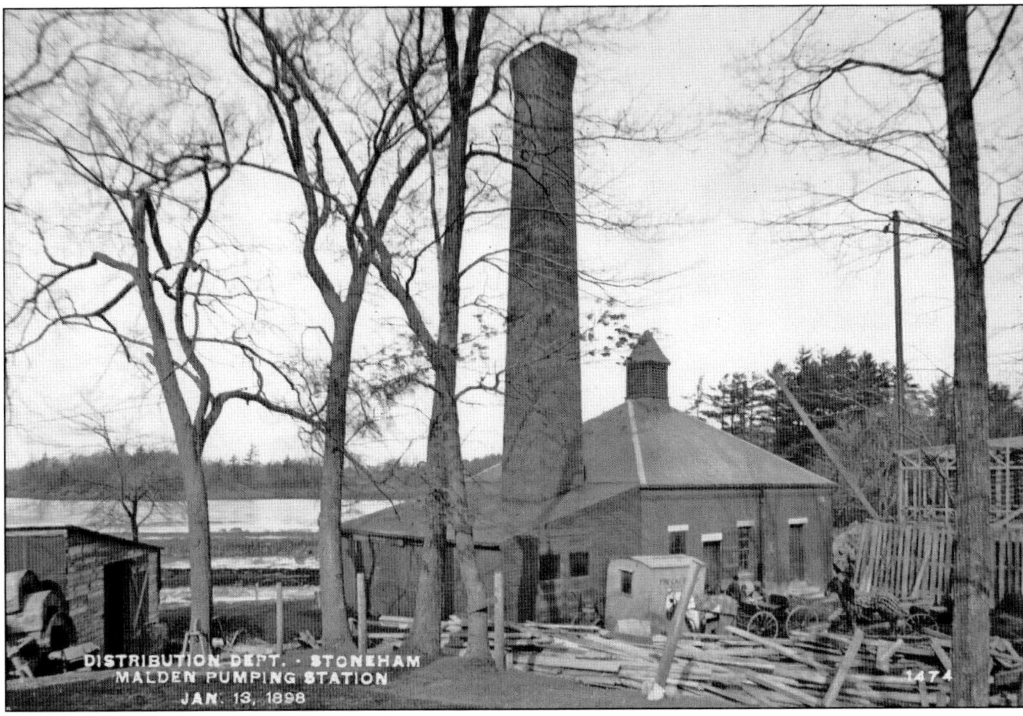

In 1867, the state legislature incorporated the Spot Pond Water Company, allowing the towns of Malden, Medford, and Melrose to pump water from Spot Pond. Two years later, Malden built a coal-fired, steam-powered pumping station near the outlet of Spot Pond Brook. This 1898 photograph was taken less than two years before the station was razed and replaced with a larger pumping station for the MWB. (Courtesy of Massachusetts State Archives.)

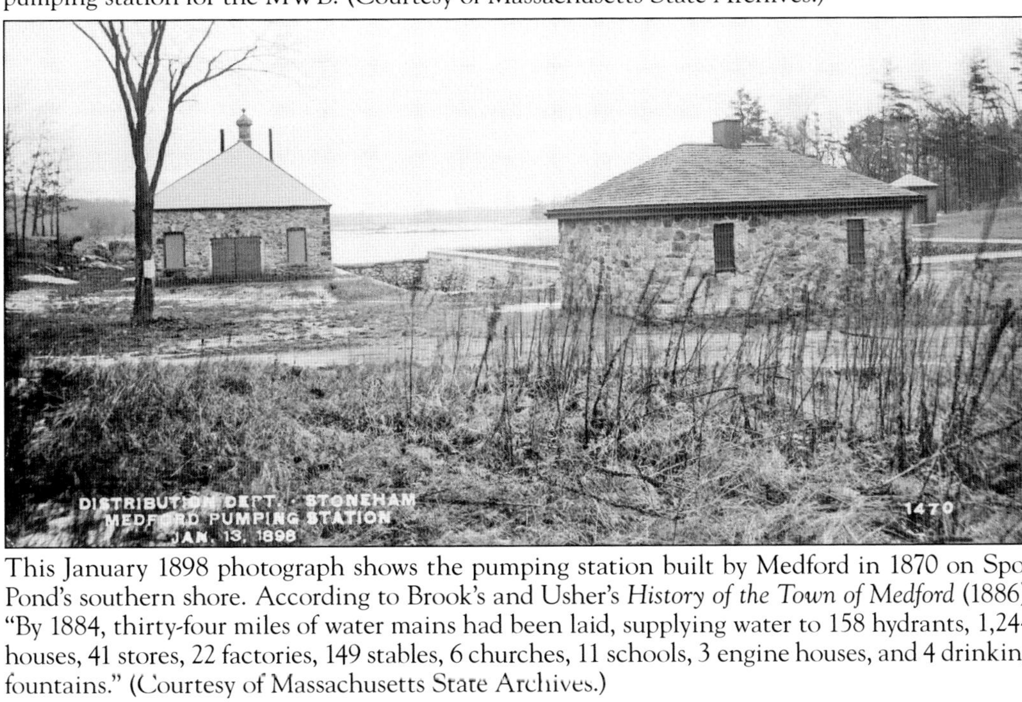

This January 1898 photograph shows the pumping station built by Medford in 1870 on Spot Pond's southern shore. According to Brook's and Usher's *History of the Town of Medford* (1886), "By 1884, thirty-four miles of water mains had been laid, supplying water to 158 hydrants, 1,244 houses, 41 stores, 22 factories, 149 stables, 6 churches, 11 schools, 3 engine houses, and 4 drinking fountains." (Courtesy of Massachusetts State Archives.)

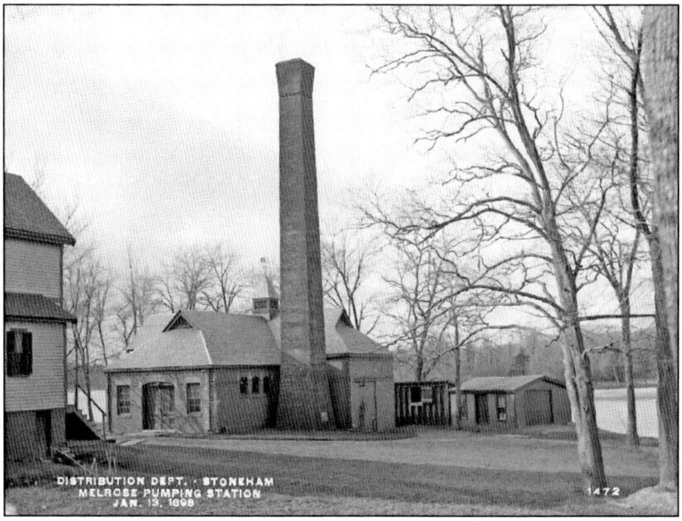

In 1870, Melrose built a pumping station on Spot Pond's eastern shore (south of the Botume House) and, by March 1871, had laid about 13 miles of water pipe. This view of the station was taken in January 1898, two years before it was razed by the MWB as part of its project to incorporate Spot Pond into Boston's water system. (Courtesy of Massachusetts State Archives.)

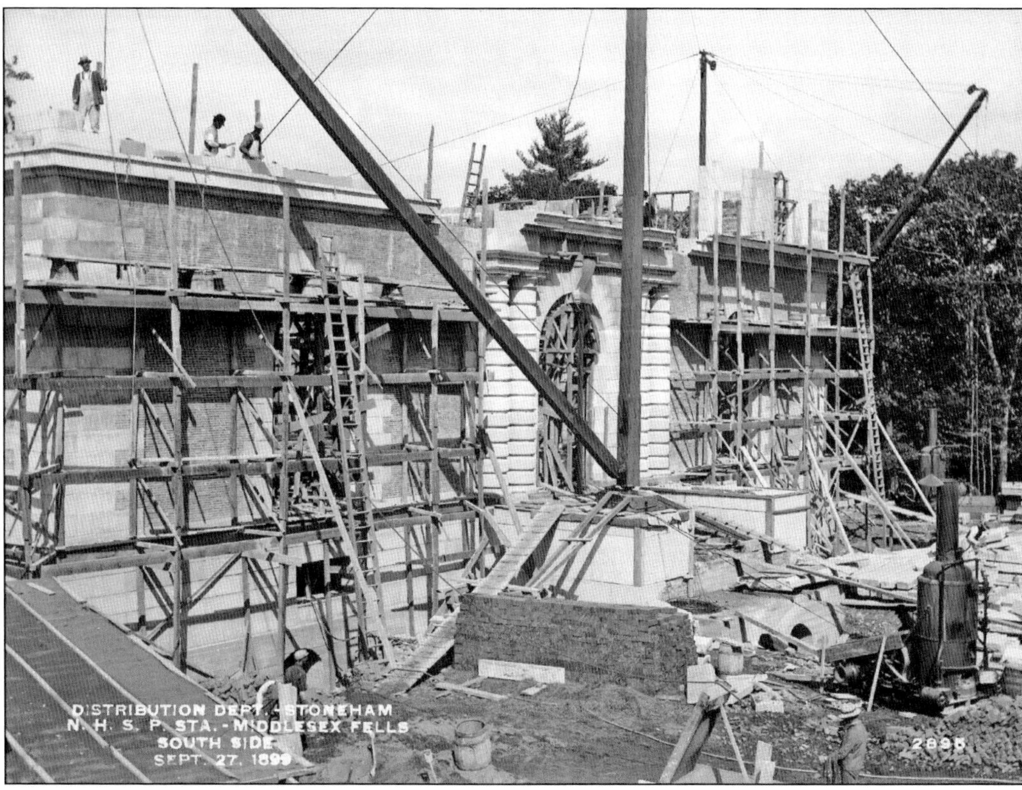

Shepley, Rutan and Coolidge, the architectural firm that designed Boston's South Station, Harvard University Medical School, and the Chestnut Hill Pumping Station, designed this Renaissance Revival pumping station at the east side of Spot Pond. The station was built by McNeil Brothers for about $120,000 between 1899 and 1900. The steam-powered winch and derrick were used to lift blocks of Milford pink granite and limestone. (Photograph by John Hildreth, courtesy of Massachusetts State Archives.)

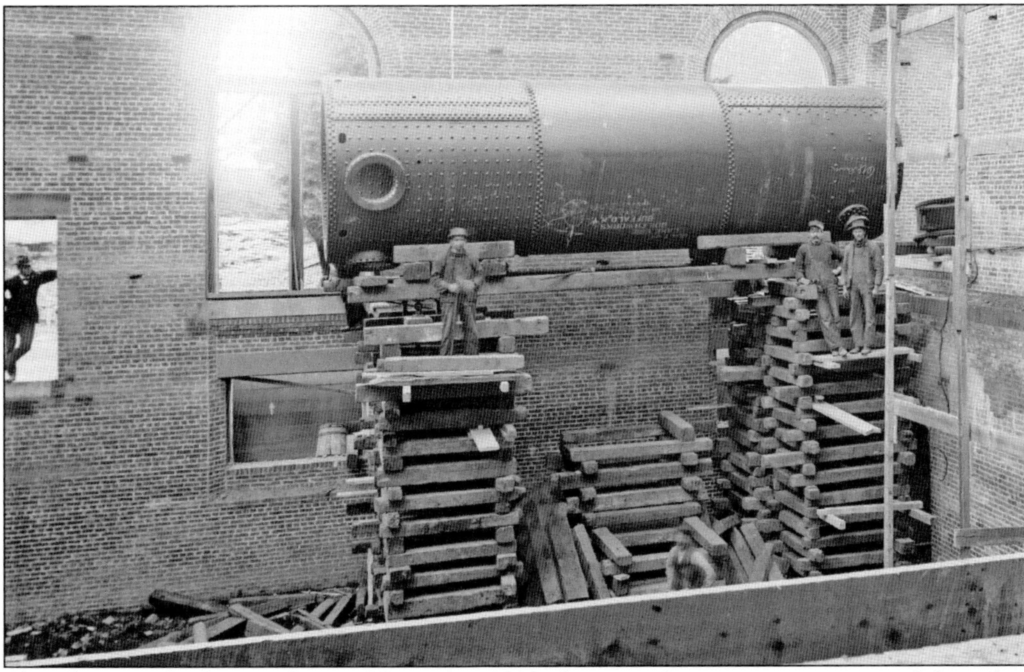

The photograph above, taken in November 1899, shows workmen mounting one of three fire-tube boilers in the new Spot Pond pumping station. The Atlantic Works Company installed the coal-fired boilers, which provided steam to power two enormous water pumps. The Spot Pond pumping station used a Leavitt engine with a 10 million-gallons-per-day (mgd) capacity, and a vertical triple-expansion Holly Engine, shown below in November 1900, with a 20 mgd capacity. The Holly Manufacturing Company and N.F. Palmer Jr. and Company manufactured the engines and pumps, transported them in pieces on railroad cars and horse-drawn wagons, and assembled them on-site. The cost of the boilers, engines, and pumps was $108,244. (Both, courtesy of Massachusetts State Archives.)

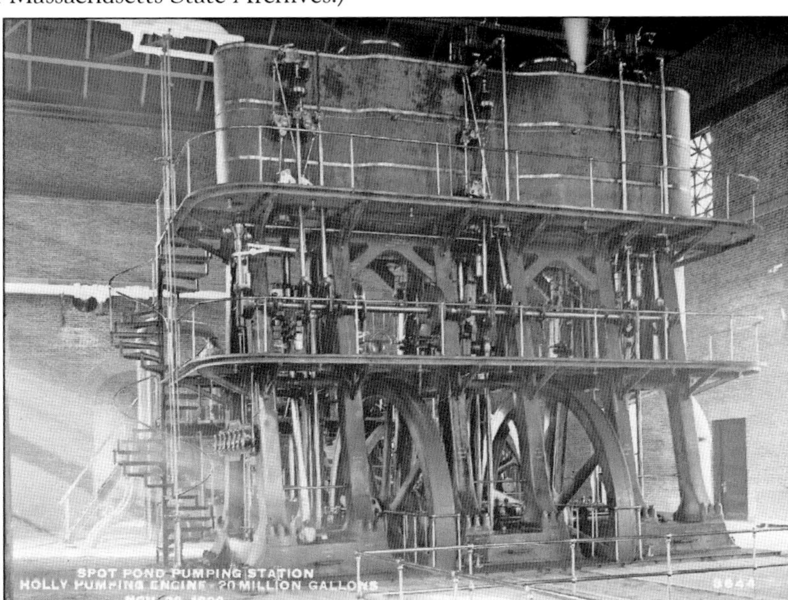

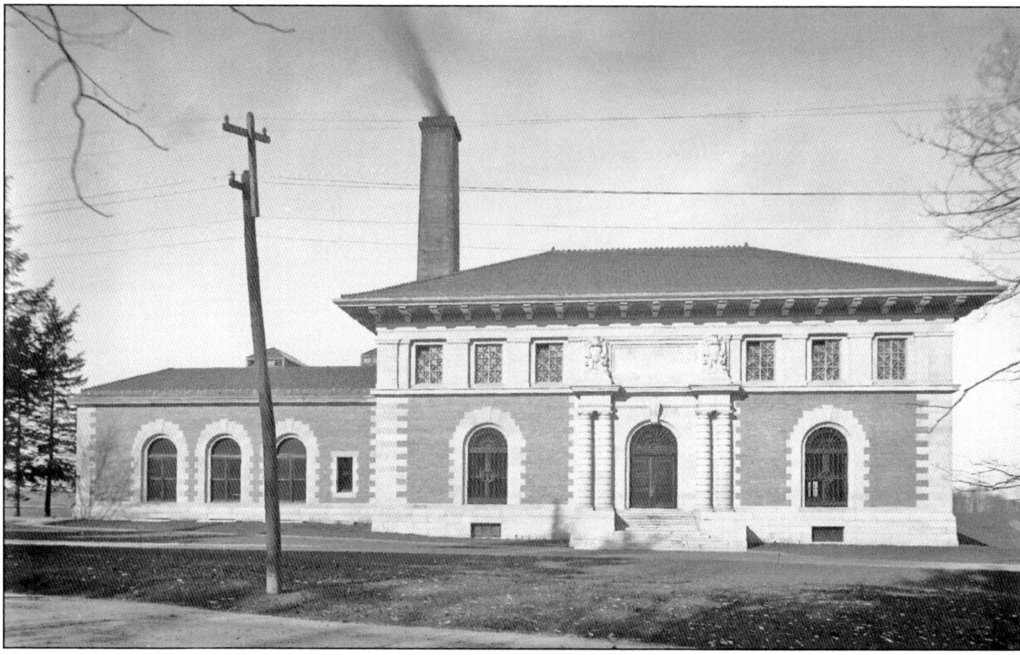

This photograph, taken in November 1900, shows the new pumping station for Spot Pond. The station operated with its original coal-fired steam engines until the early 1960s when they were replaced with diesel engines. In 1997, the Massachusetts Water Resources Authority restored the building and installed new, fuel-efficient pumps. (Courtesy of Massachusetts State Archives.)

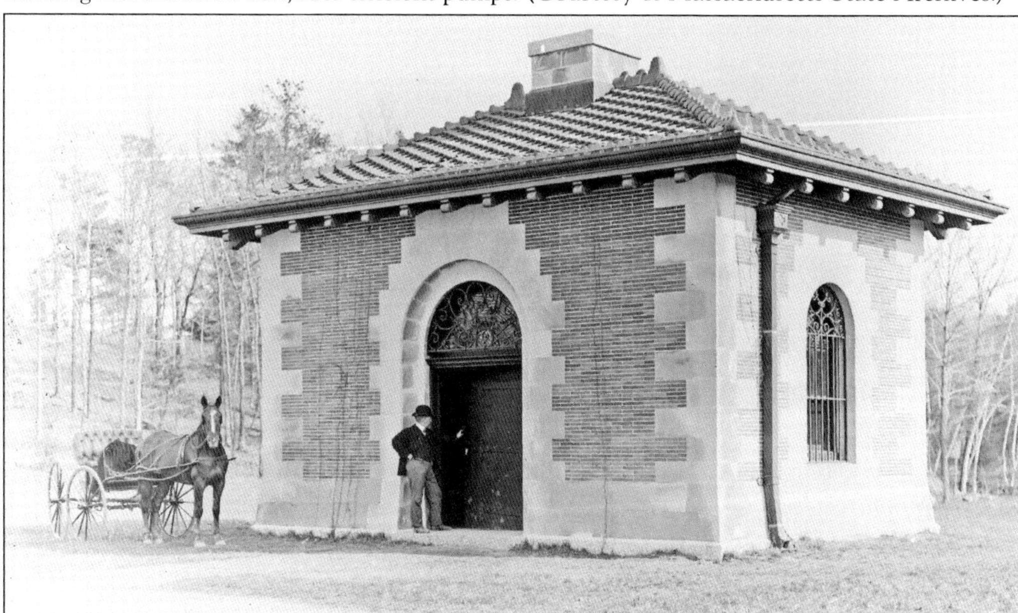

This 1900 gatehouse at the southern end of Spot Pond was built for $4,400 with Roman brick and Bedford sandstone by John S. Jacobs and Son. It contains two 60-inch hydraulic sluice gates for controlling flow to and from the Chestnut Hill Reservoir in Brighton. The photograph shows the gatehouse in May 1903, but it appears the same today. (Courtesy of Massachusetts State Archives.)

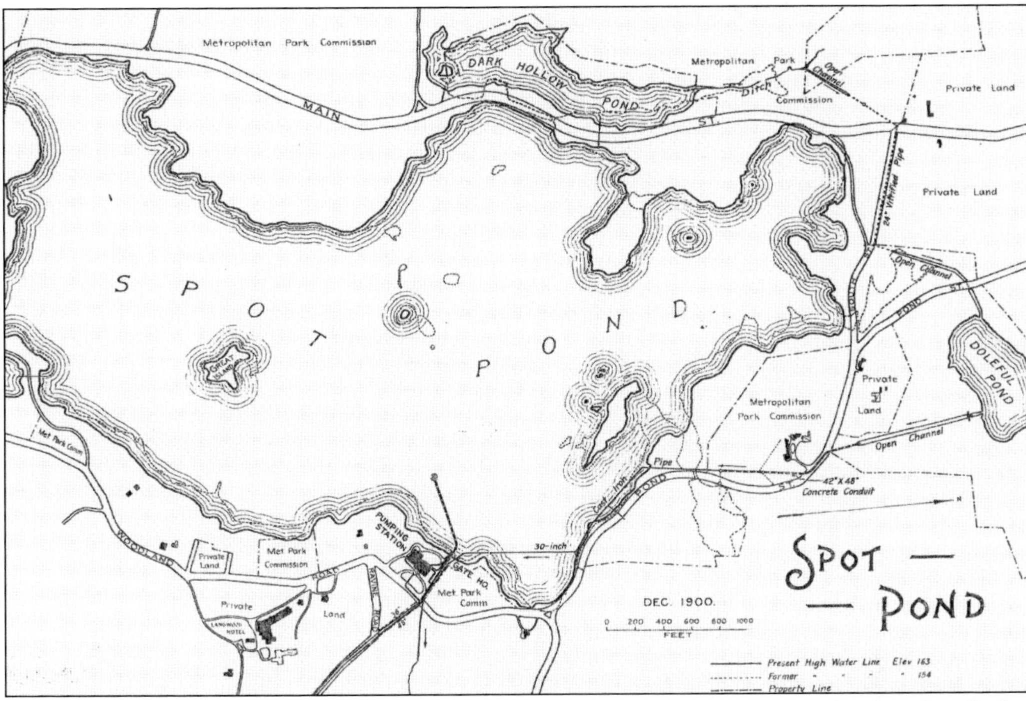

This 1900 map of Spot Pond by George H. Walker & Co. of Boston shows the shoreline before 1898 (dashed line) and after the pond level was raised by nine feet. It also shows ditches, channels, and pipelines that diverted water from Dark Hollow and Doleful Ponds into Spot Pond Brook (see page 43) to avoid contaminating Spot Pond. (Courtesy of Massachusetts State Archives.)

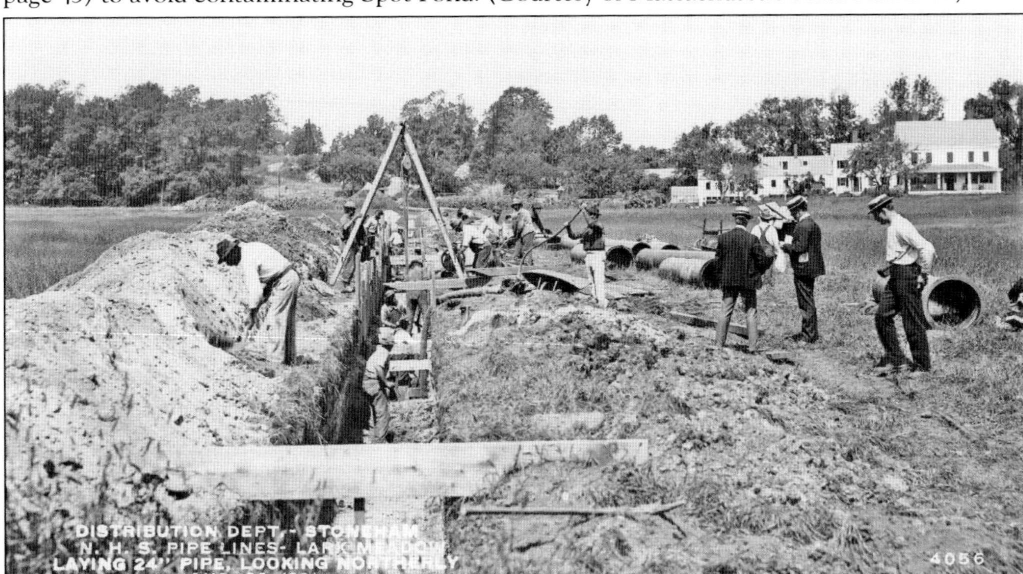

This August 1901 photograph shows workers laying a 24-inch-diameter pipe from Lark Meadow north of Spot Pond to the Bear Hill Reservoir. The work was supervised by the first Fells superintendent, Charles Price, who lived in the old Gould-Frost Farm (upper right), which was acquired by the MPC in 1894. Price had a collection of local wildlife, which eventually expanded into the Middlesex Fells Zoo (see chapter 6). (Courtesy of Massachusetts State Archives.)

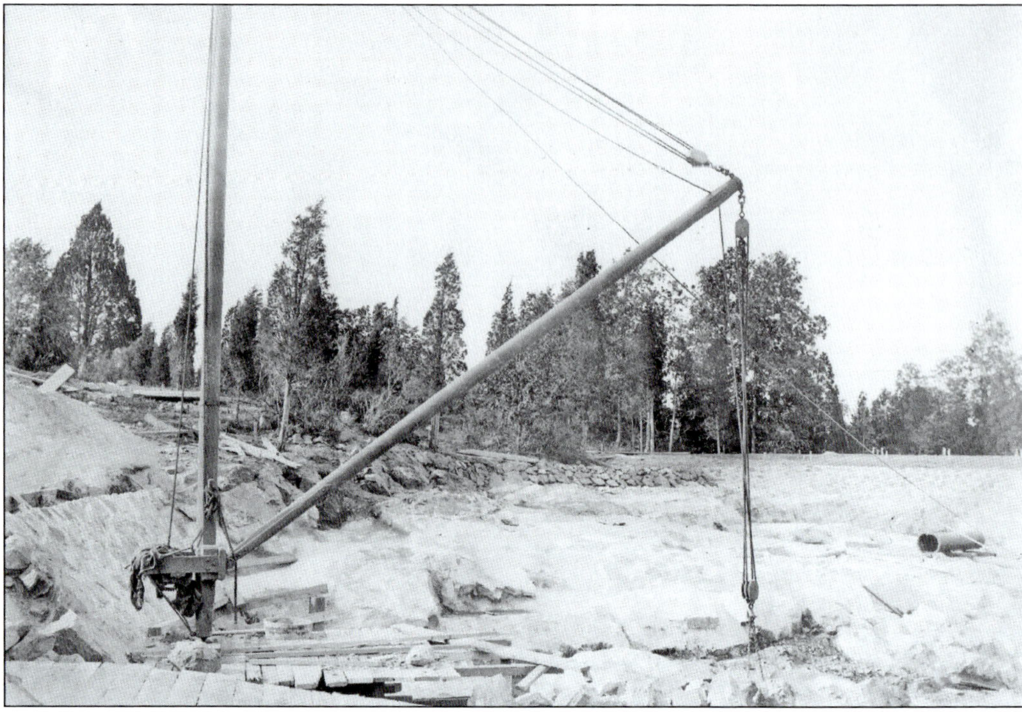

The MWB built Bear Hill Reservoir to supply water to Stoneham at a higher pressure than was available from the Fells Reservoir. The 1900 photograph above shows a derrick used to position rocks along the reservoir shoreline. The 1903 image below shows the gatehouse and reservoir, which had a capacity of almost 2.5 million gallons. Bear Hill Reservoir was later replaced by a large covered tank. In 1893, the Appalachian Mountain Club built a wooden observation tower (visible behind trees at left) to encourage people to visit the Fells. In 1910, the MPC replaced this with a concrete tower (see page 78). (Above, courtesy of the National Park Service, ONHS; below, courtesy of Massachusetts State Archives.)

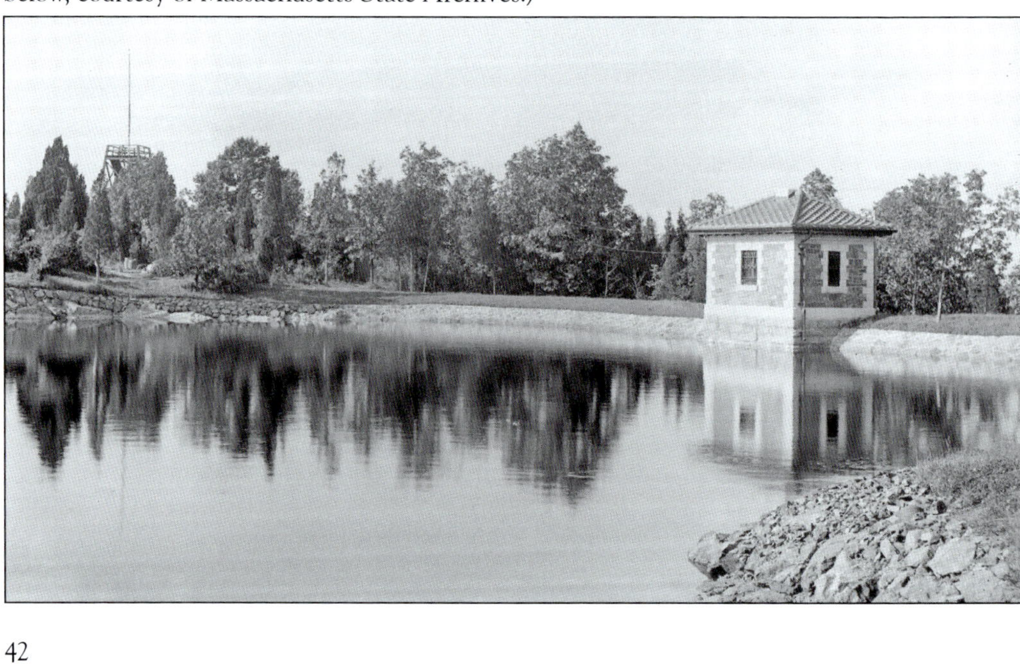

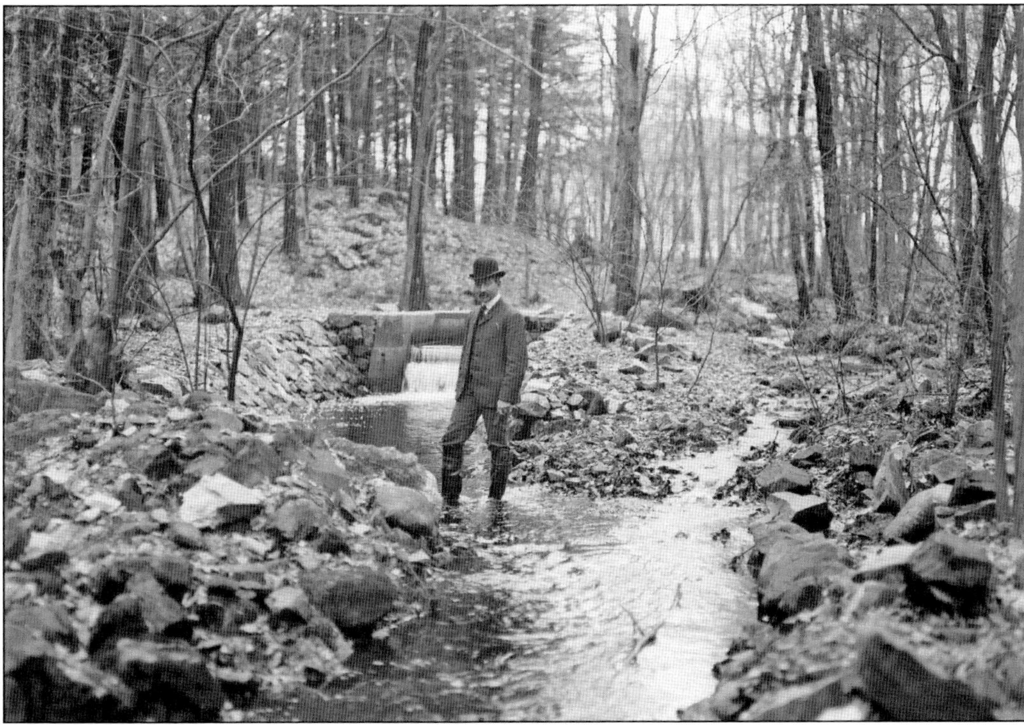

In October 1898, before emptying Spot Pond, engineers installed pipes, channels, and a drainage weir to divert water from Dark Hollow and Doleful Ponds into Spot Pond Brook. These 1904 photographs show a Metropolitan Water and Sewerage Board engineer measuring the height of water passing over a weir built to calculate flow into Spot Pond Brook. Although no longer functional, the weir still exists in Virginia Wood east of the pumping station on Woodland Road. (Both, courtesy of Massachusetts State Archives.)

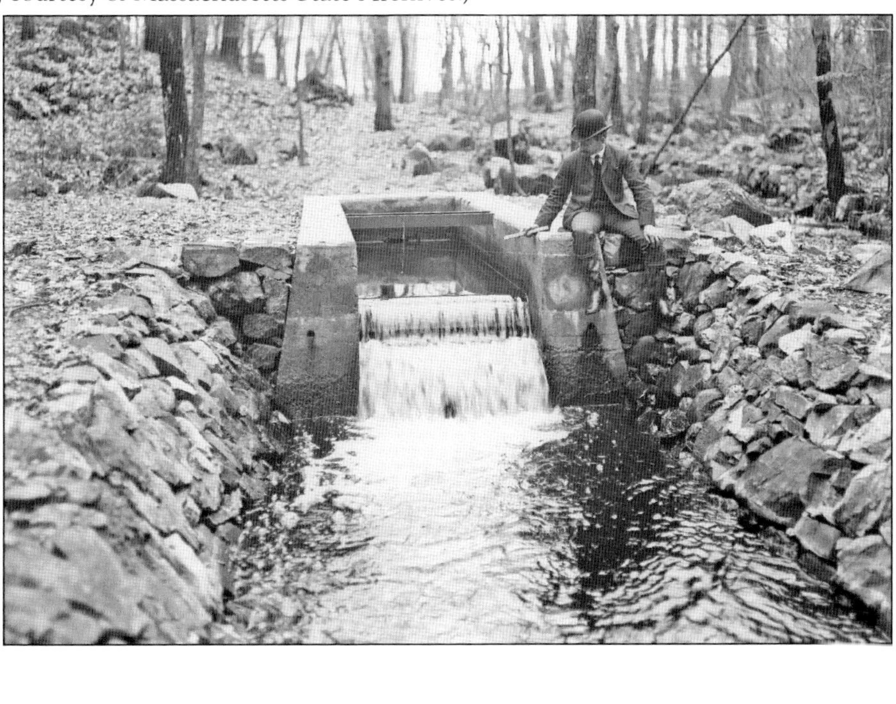

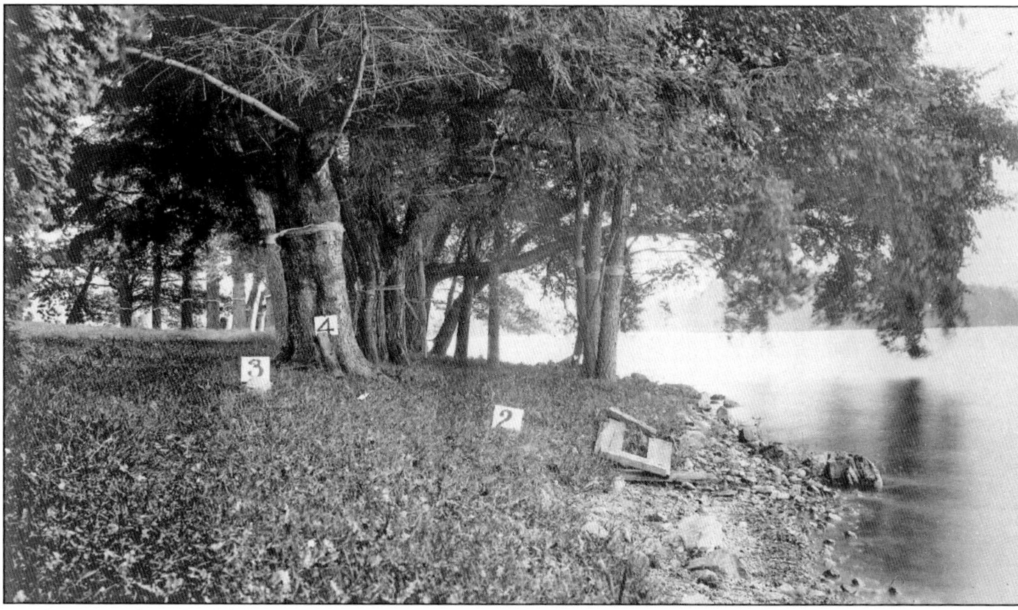

Arthur A. Shurtleff (changed in 1930 to Shurcliff) took this photograph in July 1898 showing elevation markers in feet along the shore of Old Pepe's Cove (see map on page 10). Olmsted Brothers surveyed the shoreline of Spot Pond to determine which areas would be flooded with a nine-foot increase in water level. The burlap wrapping around tree trunks was used to trap gypsy moths (see chapter 5). (Courtesy of the National Park Service, ONHS.)

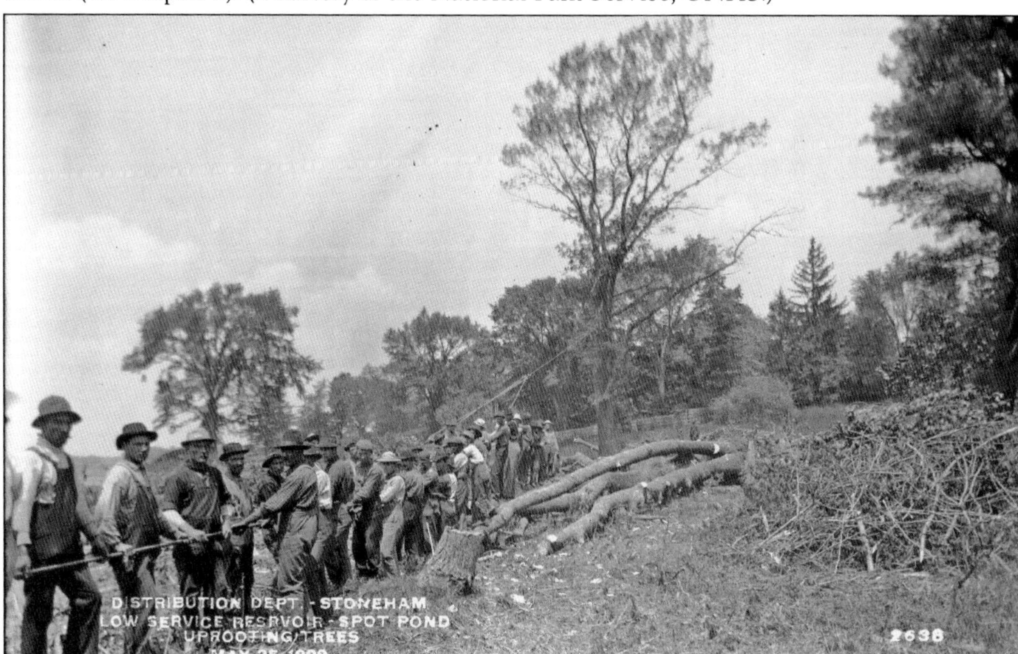

This image, taken on May 25, 1899, shows men felling trees and clearing brush along Spot Pond's shoreline in preparation for raising the water level by nine feet. Under the direction of Olmsted Brothers, men cleared about 80 acres, cut over 1,000 cords of wood, and burned huge piles of brush. (Courtesy of Massachusetts State Archives.)

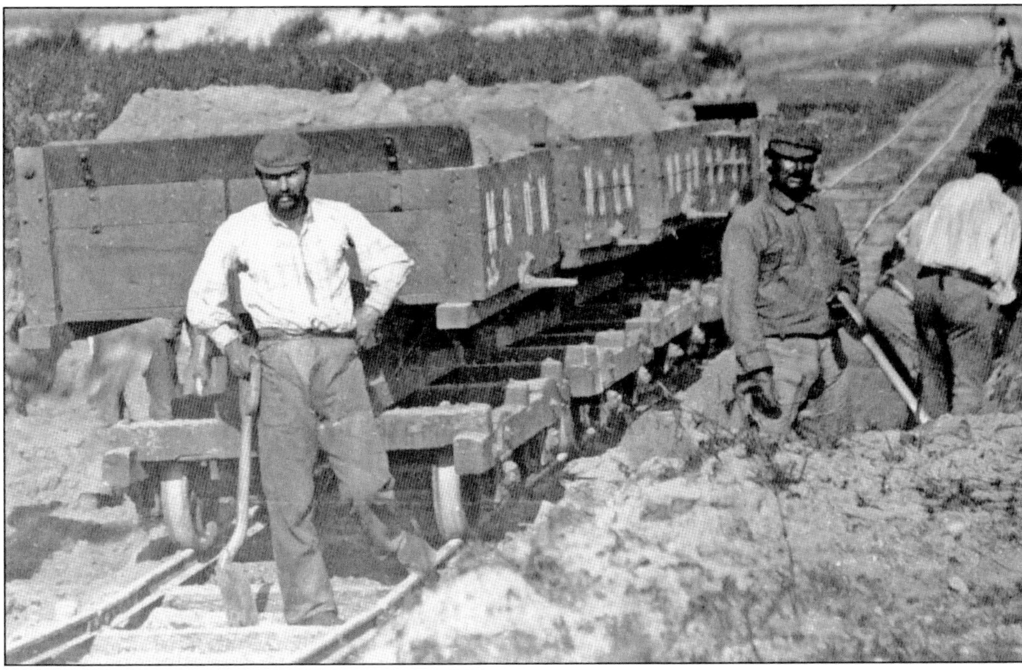

James S. Pray, a landscape architect with Olmsted Brothers, captured this image in September 1899 of men shoveling mud and sand onto a "mud train" to deepen Spot Pond by 15 feet. The train was hauled by cable and a steam-powered winch to an area north of the pond, and the material was later used to grade roads and build embankments. (Courtesy of the National Park Service, ONHS.)

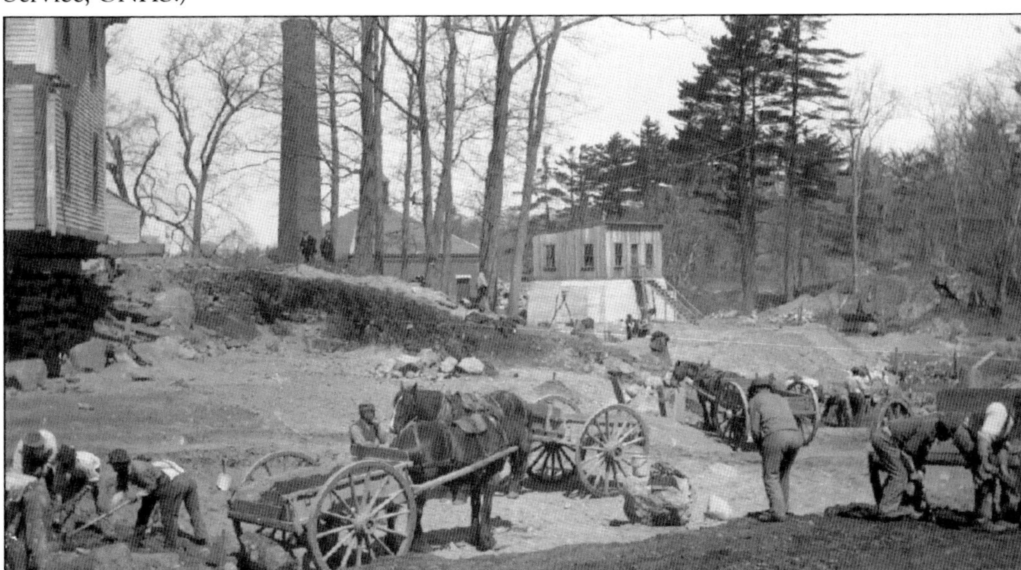

Workers employed by McNeil Brothers of Boston are digging the foundation for the Northern High Service pumping station on Spot Pond. Their office is on the raised platform in front of the Malden pumping station. At left, the house that had been used by the Malden station engineer is ready for removal off-site. (Photograph taken in April 1899 by John L. Hildreth, courtesy of Massachusetts State Archives.)

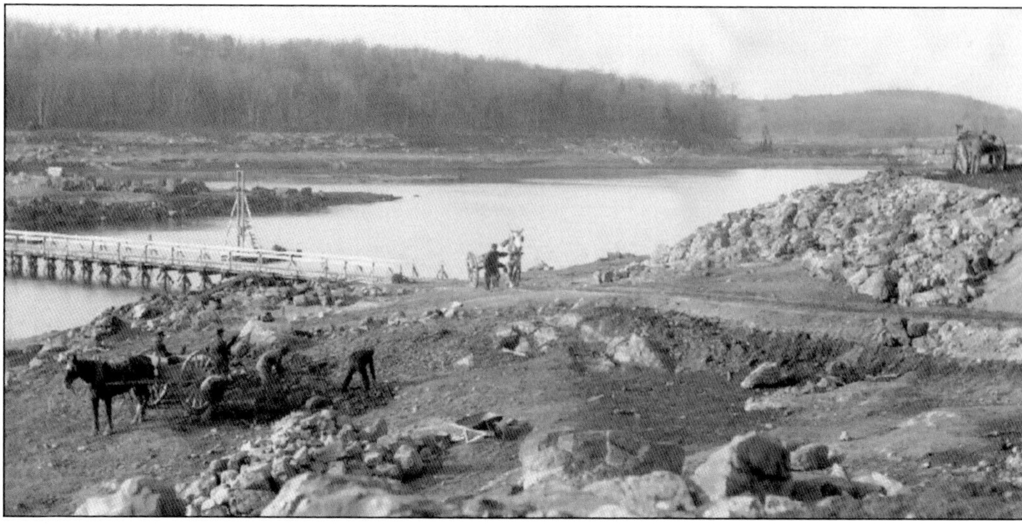

In this November 1899 image, workers lay riprap and soil on Great Island to raise its elevation above the heightened Spot Pond water level. To provide access for men, horses, and wagons, a 170-foot-long wooden bridge was built between the island and Spot Pond's western shore. (Photograph by John L. Hildreth, courtesy of Massachusetts State Archives.)

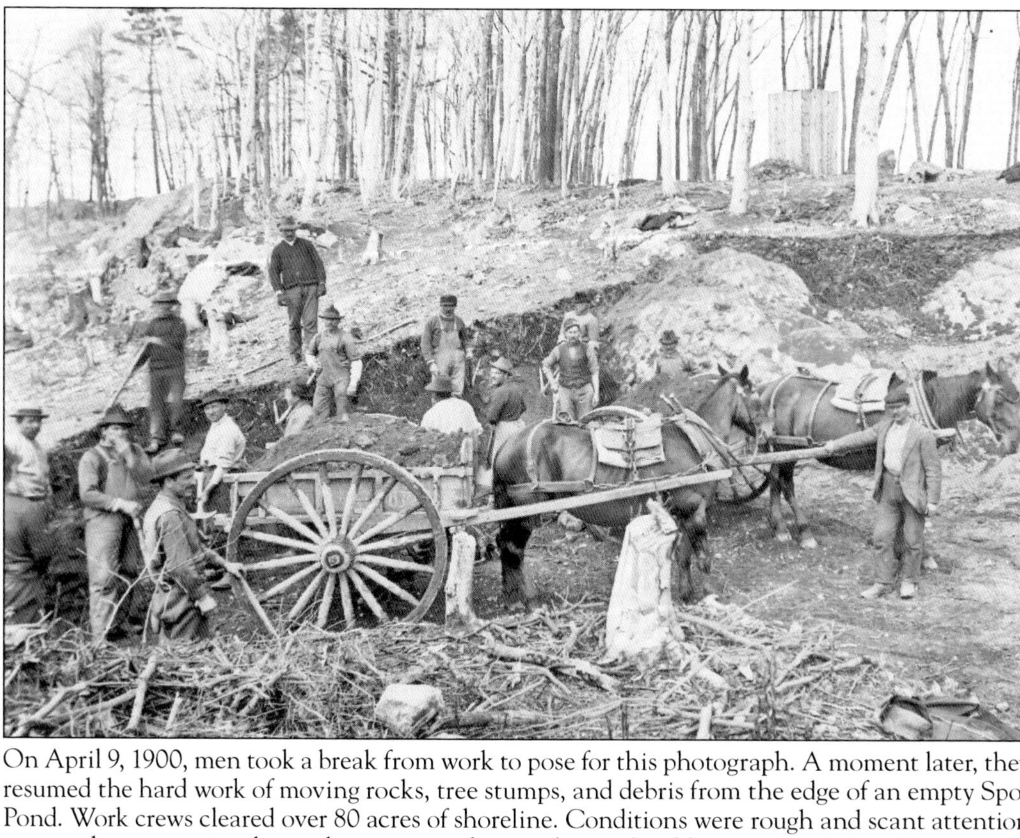

On April 9, 1900, men took a break from work to pose for this photograph. A moment later, they resumed the hard work of moving rocks, tree stumps, and debris from the edge of an empty Spot Pond. Work crews cleared over 80 acres of shoreline. Conditions were rough and scant attention was paid to sanitation beyond provision of an outhouse (visible at upper right). (Courtesy of Massachusetts State Archives.)

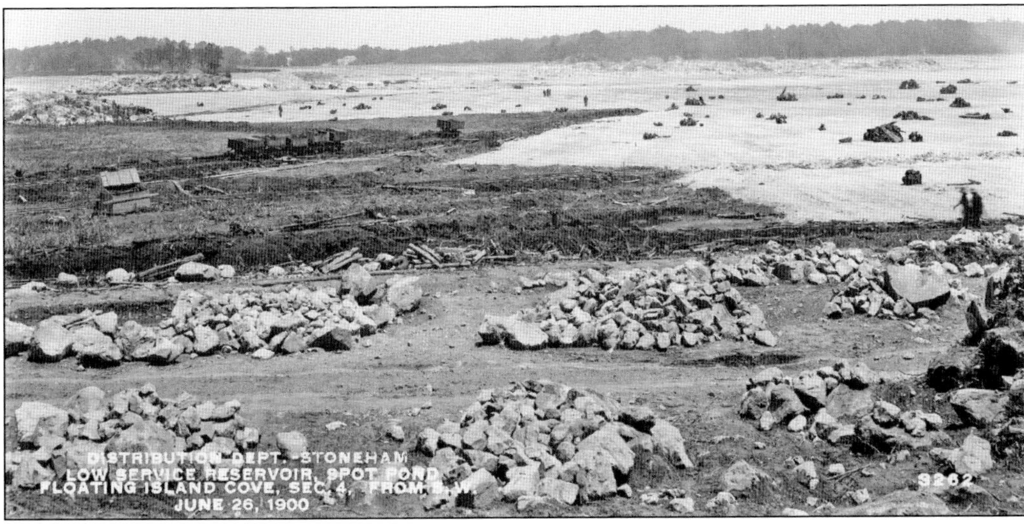

This photograph shows southwestern Spot Pond on June 26, 1900. Men hired by Moulton and O'Mahoney created these rock piles to use as riprap along the shoreline of a redesigned Spot Pond. Rock came from the pond bottom, and as reported by the MWB, also from old stone walls near the pond. The light area in the distance is sand, which the men spread over the muddy bottom. (Courtesy of Massachusetts State Archives.)

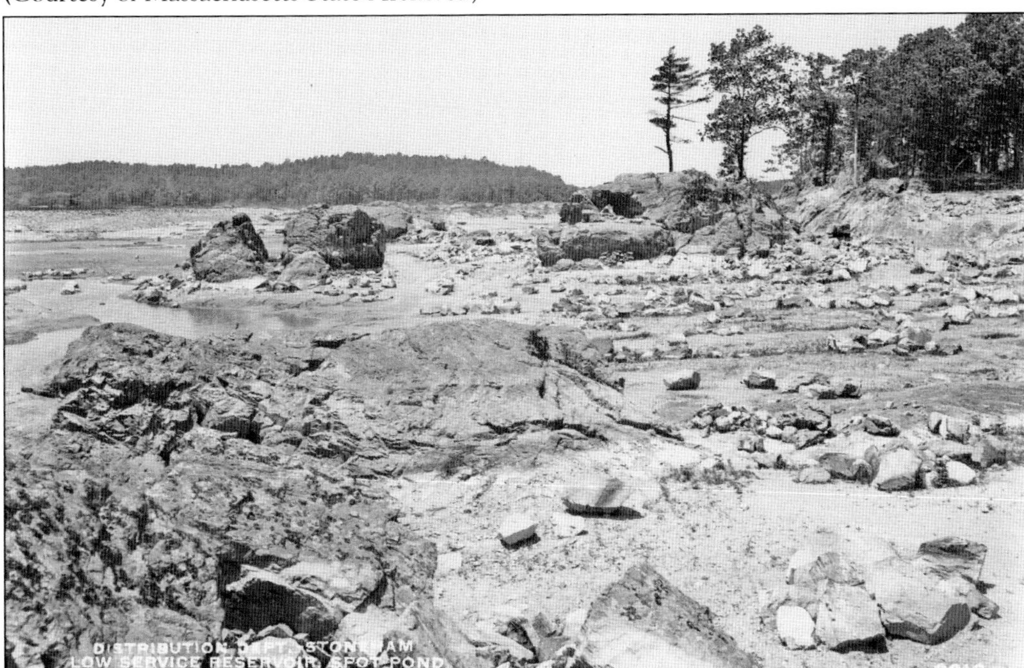

This July 1900 photograph shows Bold Point before it was transformed into a small island when Spot Pond was refilled. Bold Point had been a prominent peninsula on the pond's northeast side with a series of owners—including Ephraim Buttrick, William Foster, Fanny Foster, Charles Jones, and Sherman Cass—before it was taken in 1891 by the Spot Pond Water Company. Jones operated icehouses near this point during the 1880s (see page 33). (Courtesy of Massachusetts State Archives.)

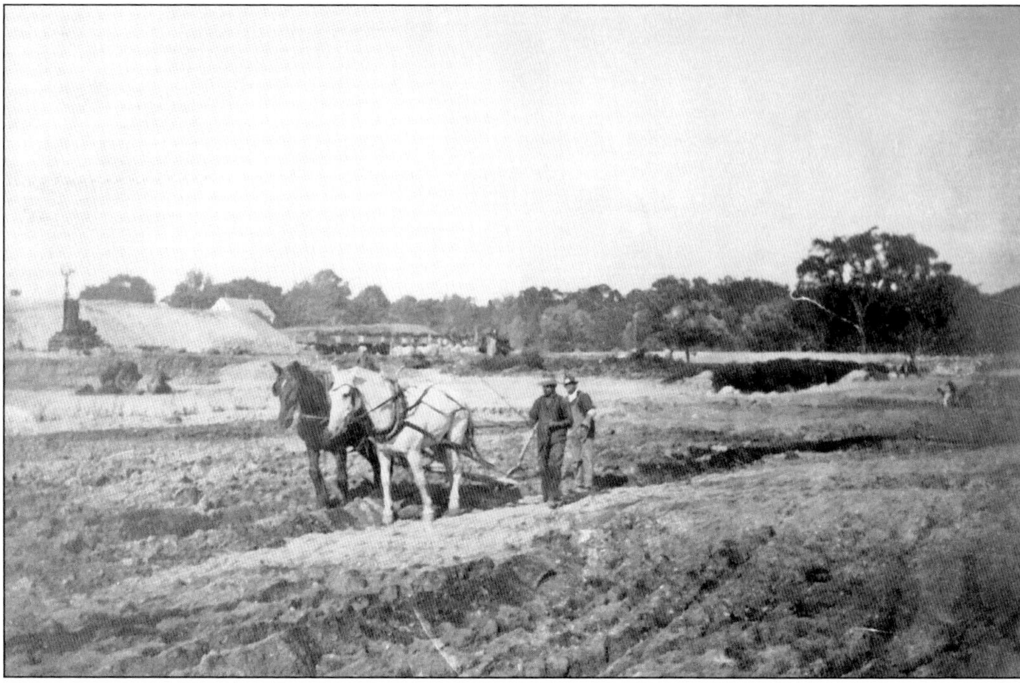

James S. Pray took this photograph in September 1899 of men using a horse-drawn plow to break up Spot Pond's dried lake bottom. These bottom materials were then shoveled into a mud train (see page 45) and deposited in large piles like the one visible on the left side of the image. (Courtesy of the National Park Service, ONHS.)

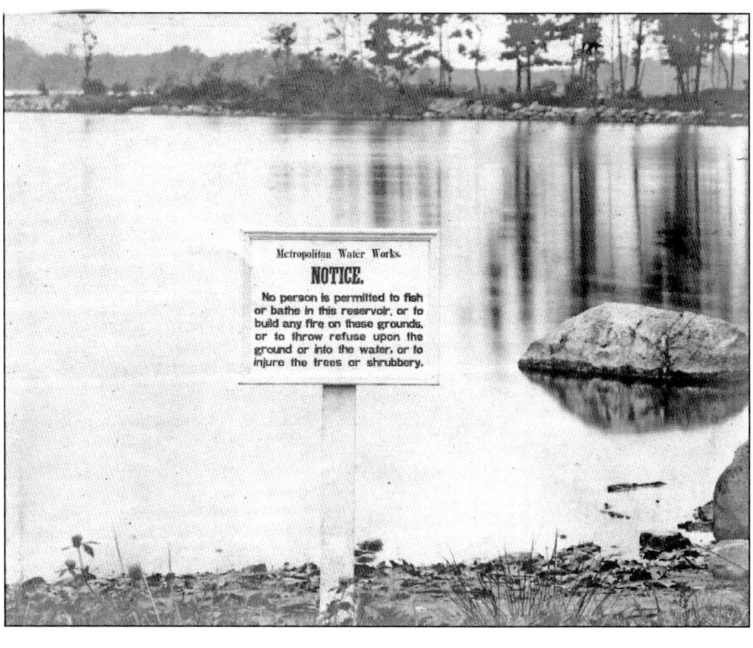

Priorities of the Metropolitan Water Board included maintaining drinking-water quality and enforcing antipollution rules. The board posted several signs in Spot Pond's watershed that read: "No person is permitted to fish or bathe in this reservoir, or to build any fire on these grounds or to throw refuse upon the ground or into the water, or to injure the trees or shrubbery." (Courtesy of Massachusetts State Archives.)

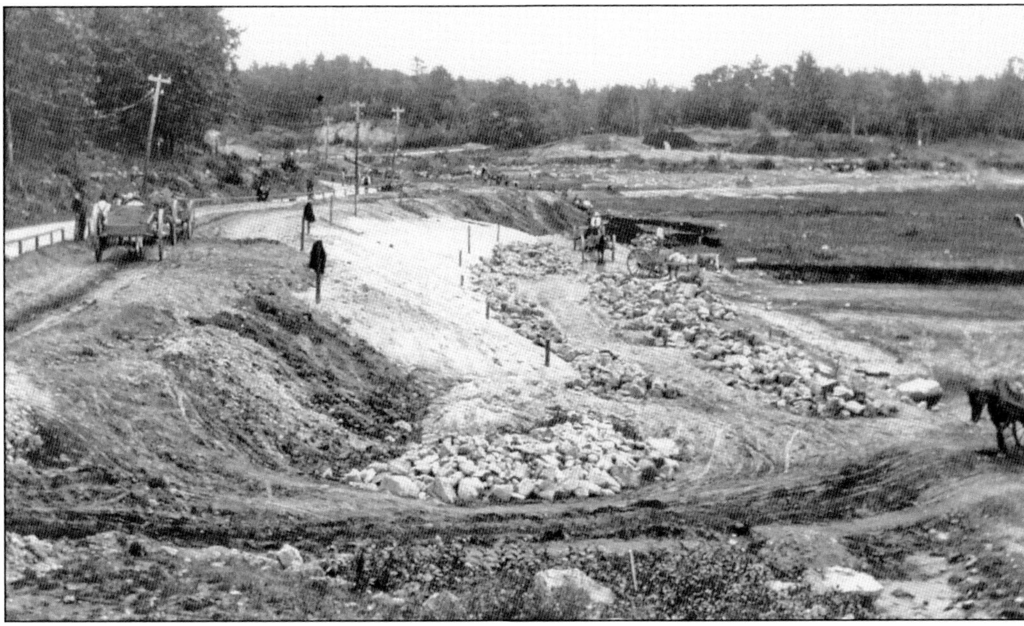

Using wagons and horsepower, workmen haul loads of sand and clay along Pond Street from the north end of Spot Pond on August 14, 1899. Much of this material was used to raise the roads around the pond to accommodate a higher water level in Spot Pond after it was refilled in 1900. The rocks shown in the photograph were collected for use as riprap along the shoreline. (Courtesy of Massachusetts State Archives.)

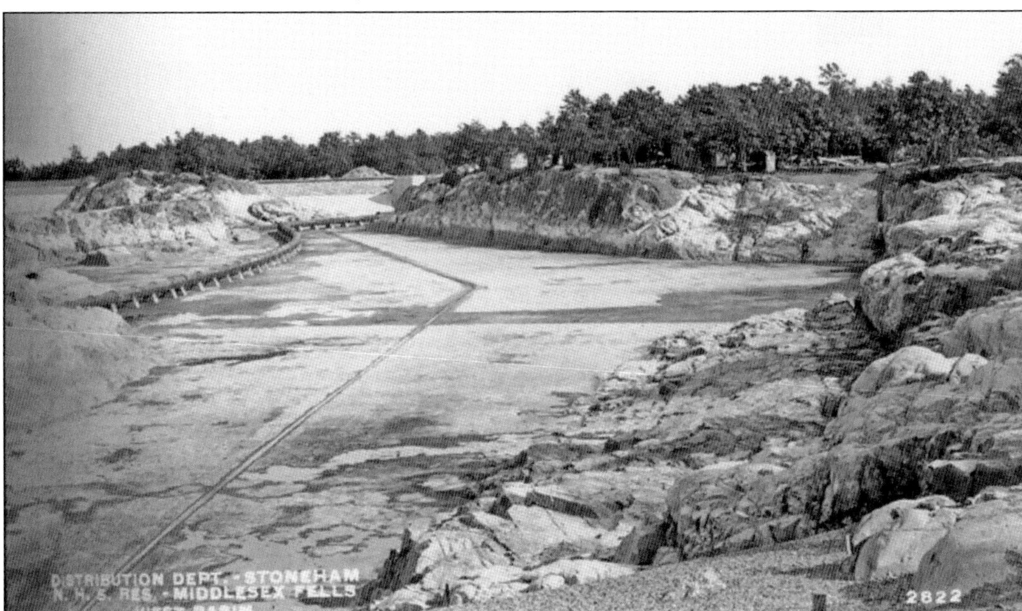

The MWB built the Fells Reservoir about 2,500 feet southeast of Spot Pond in an alder swamp. On May 20, 1898, T.W. Kinser and Sons began construction by clearing trees and shrubs. It excavated soil to a uniform depth of 21 feet and poured concrete to seal the bottom. The eight-acre reservoir was built to have a capacity of 38.5 million gallons. (Courtesy of Massachusetts State Archives.)

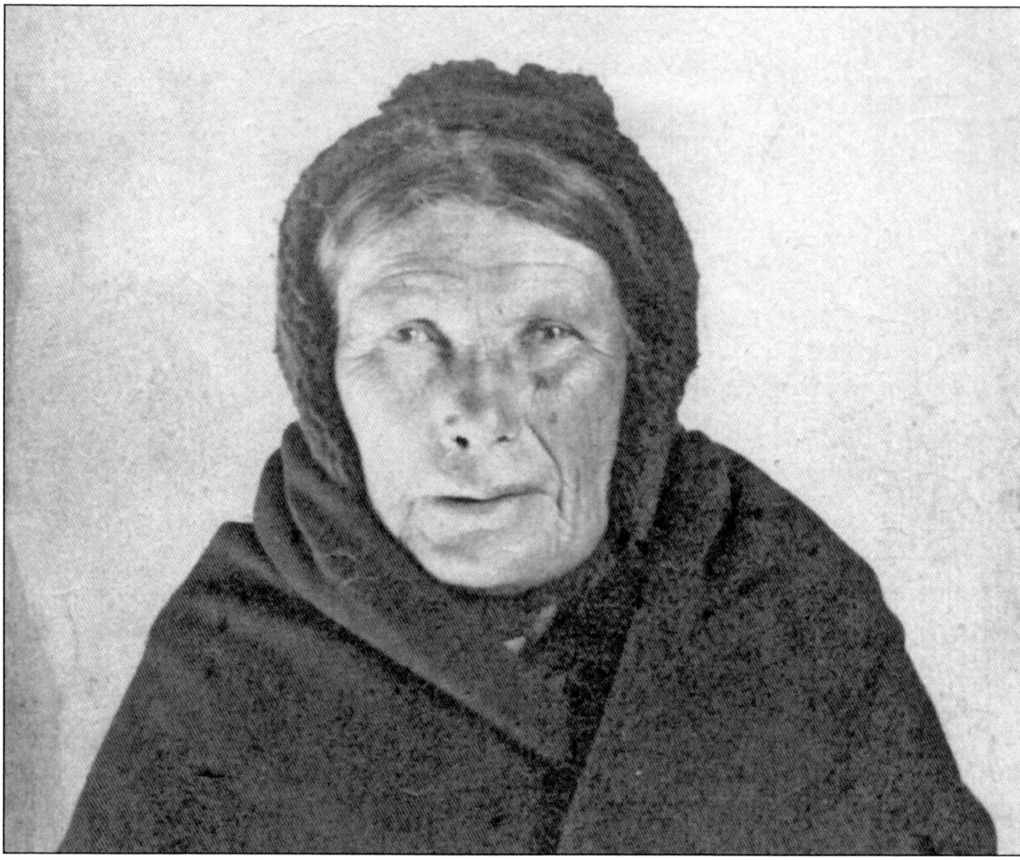

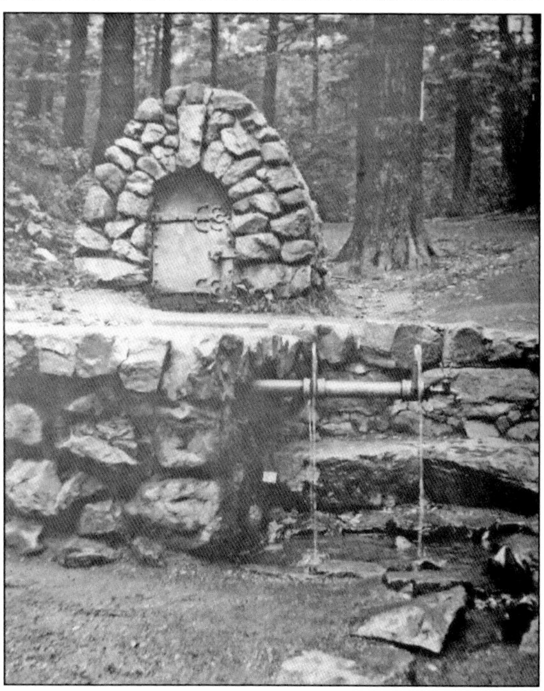

Walter F. Brackett of Winchester took this photograph of Molly Connor about 1890. Born in Ireland about 1820, Molly lived in Winchester for several decades. She was well known enough to have a spring and road named after her. Molly's Spring and Molly's Spring Road are located west of Winchester's South Reservoir. (Courtesy of Winchester Massachusetts Archival Center.)

This image shows Crystal Spring, located north of Pond Street, in August 1931. Patients and workers from the nearby New England Sanitarium filled buckets from this spring in the 1920s and 1930s at times when Spot Pond water had a "fishy taste" due to algae blooms. The stonework for Crystal Spring still exists, but the spring no longer flows. (Courtesy of Massachusetts State Archives.)

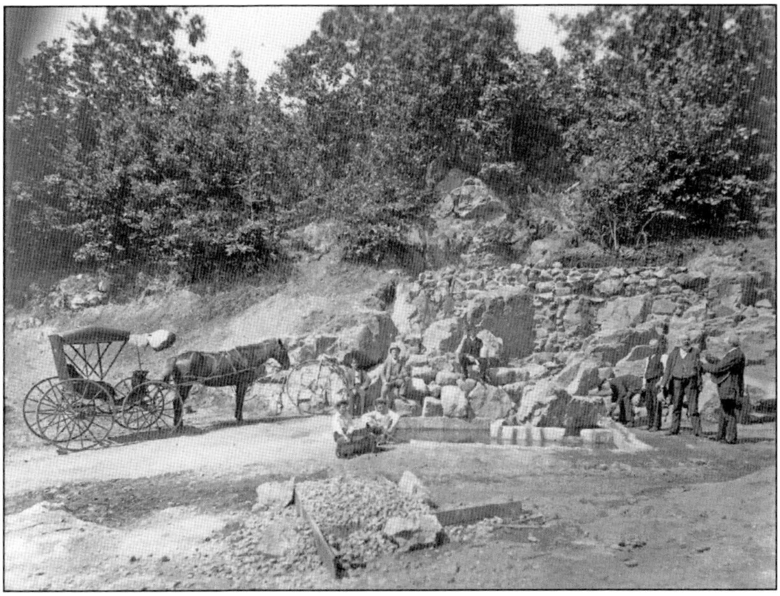

This c. 1885 photograph shows people gathered at the Middlesex Mount Spring, located near Fulton Spring Road and east of Pine Hill. The water was reportedly pure enough to be bottled and sold in Medford Square. Note the horse trough at center right. (Courtesy of Medford Historical Society and Museum.)

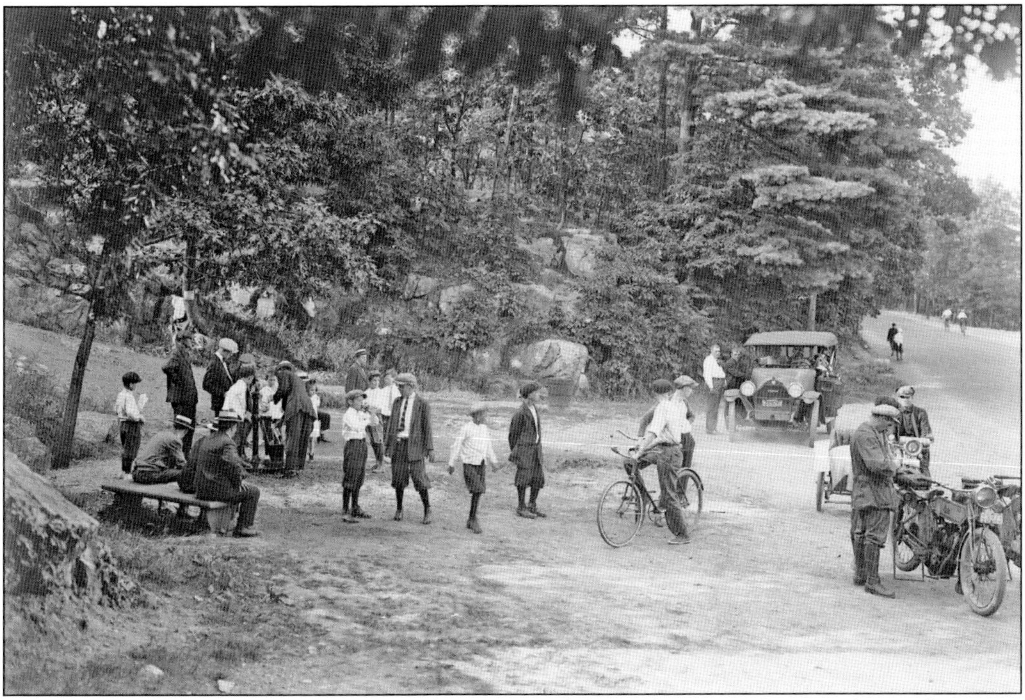

On August 27, 1916, a crowd of people gathered around the well at Porter Cove in the southwestern part of Spot Pond. Forest Street (now Route 28) is on the right. Five days later, the Metropolitan Water and Sewerage Board shut down the well after testing by the Department of Public Health showed that the water "was unfit for human consumption." (Photograph by Oliver Tryon, courtesy of Massachusetts State Archives.)

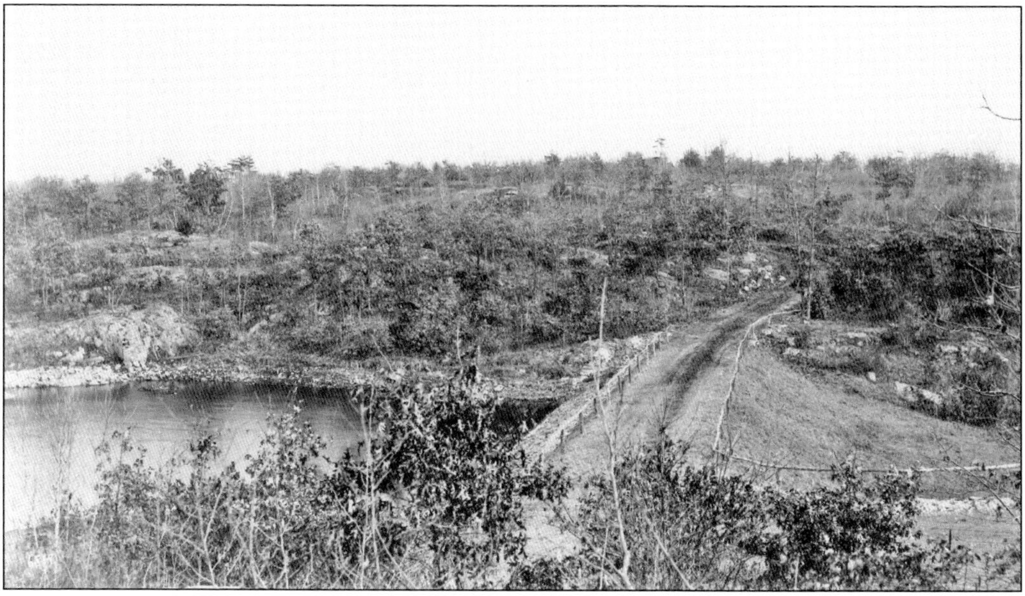

In 1896, Nathaniel Stebbins took these photographs of Winchester's reservoirs while working for Olmsted Brothers, the MPC's landscape architects. The image above shows the dam, built in 1891, separating Middle Reservoir (at left) from South Reservoir. The image below shows South Reservoir, created in 1890, in a view looking south from the dam. (Both, courtesy of Massachusetts State Archives.)

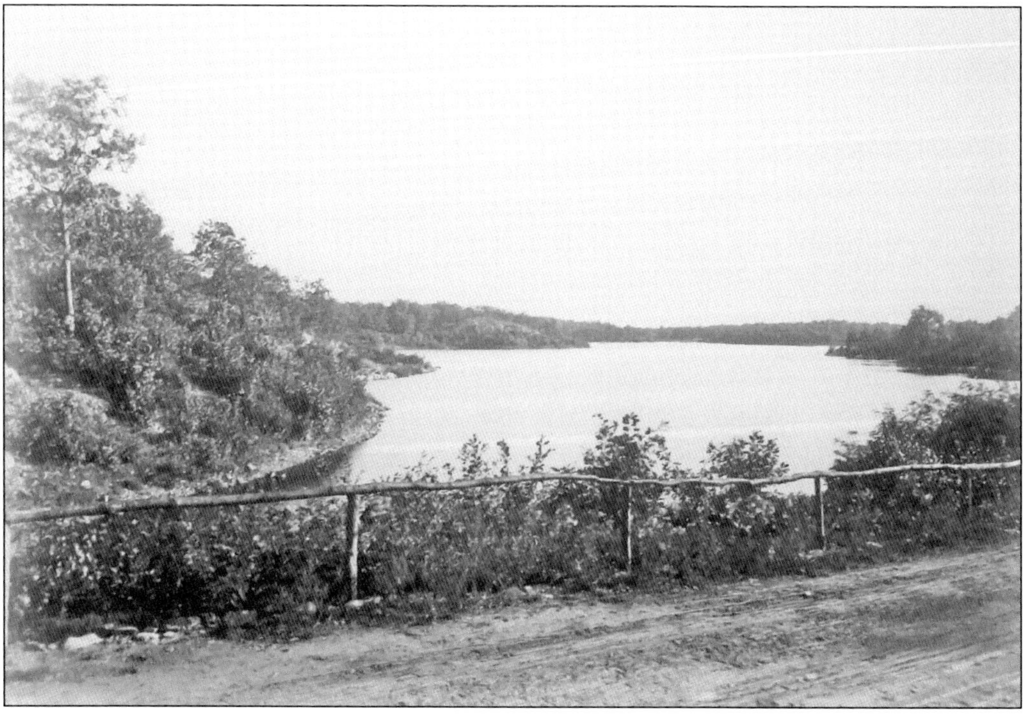

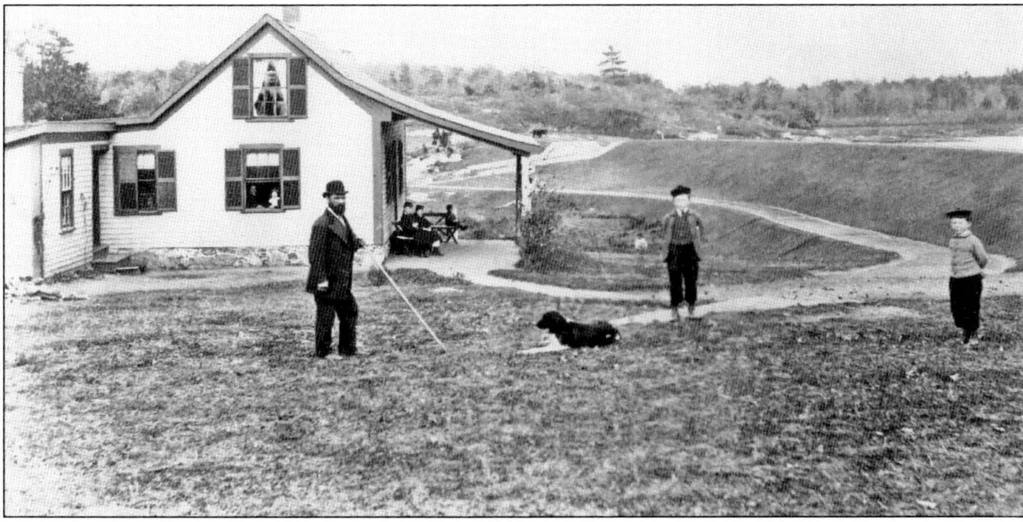

William Dotten (1843–1925), first superintendent of Winchester's Highland Water Works, poses with his family next to the North Reservoir about 1878. Dotten and his wife, Adelaide, moved to Winchester from Nova Scotia in 1872. Two years later, the reservoir was filled and water flowed to Winchester residents. To the right of Dotten are the family's dog Gip and sons James and William Jr. (Courtesy of Winchester Massachusetts Archival Center.)

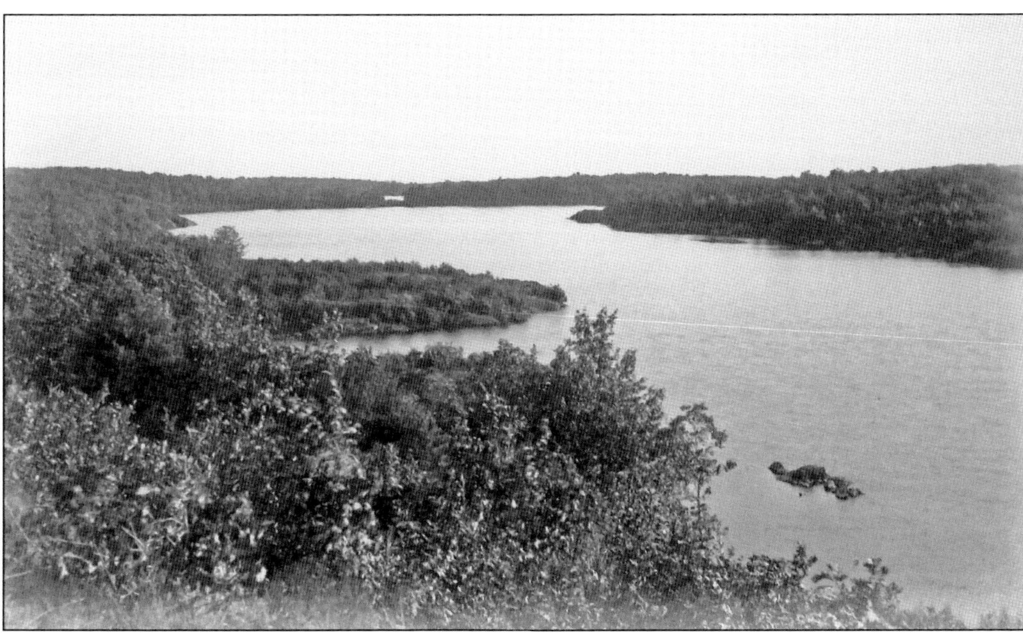

Nathaniel Stebbins took this photograph of Middle Reservoir in Winchester, with a view looking south from Wanapanakin Hill, in October 1895. This scene remains virtually unchanged. (Courtesy of Massachusetts State Archives.)

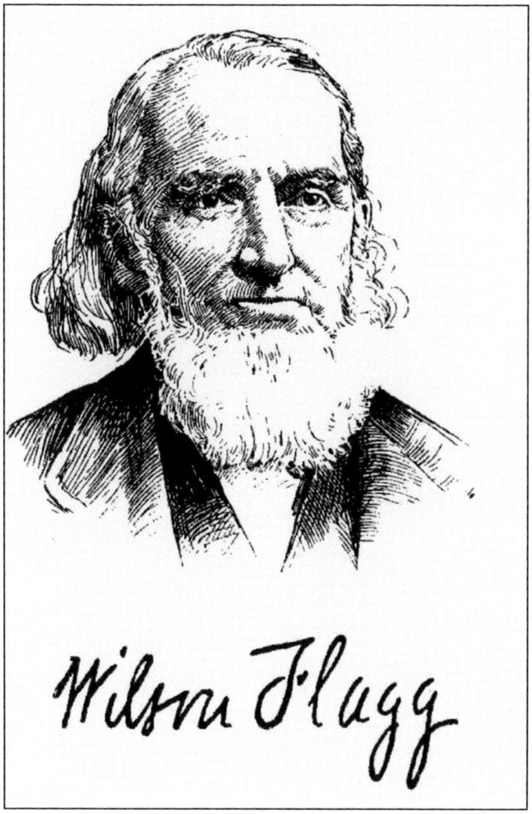

Wilson Flagg (1805–1884), born in Beverly, Massachusetts, wrote articles and books about horticulture and botany. In 1856, he was the first person to call for protection of the Fells. In 1872, he wrote, "We feel, while rambling under these lofty trees, and over this carpet of leaves and mosses, that nothing which art has accomplished will compare with the primitive works of nature. There is no architecture so sublime as that of a forest; there are no gardens like the little paradises to be found here." Flagg was well known to the public through his writings, which express a true admiration for nature. (Courtesy of Mike Ryan.)

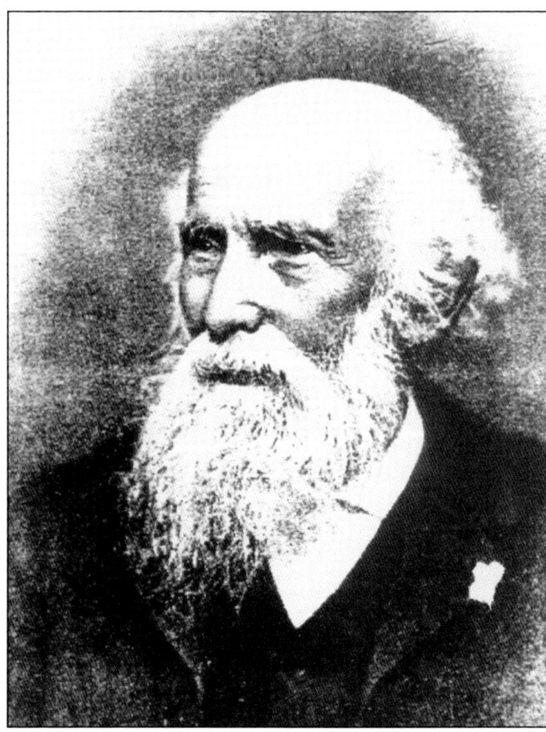

Elizur Wright (1804–1885) was a mathematician, abolitionist, and conservationist. He was active in the American Anti-Slavery Society and later became interested in life insurance. As the first insurance commissioner of Massachusetts, he convinced the state legislature to require insurance companies to hold reserves, thus stopping policies, especially those of the poor, from lapsing. Wright helped ensure passage of the Massachusetts Forest Law of 1882 (or Public Domain Act), and many consider him "Father of the Middlesex Fells." (Courtesy of Medford Historical Society and Museum.)

Four

Creation of the Fells

In 1856, Wilson Flagg advocated setting aside "the wild region extending from Stoneham to Salem, for the purpose of one or more preserves." In 1869, Elizur Wright published a pamphlet urging the state to designate the Five Mile Wood as Mount Andrew Park. In an 1879 *Boston Herald* article, Sylvester Baxter calls the area the Middlesex Fells for the first time.

In 1880, Wright and Flagg founded the Middlesex Fells Association, which pushed for legislation to enable towns to preserve land. The following year, George Butterfield, owner of the Langwood Hotel, clear-cut the Ravine Road hemlock groves (now in Virginia Wood). In a glass-slide lecture, George Davenport decried the calamity of replacing noble hemlocks with "acres of unsightly stumps." This destructive act became a rallying cry to preservationists and helped lead to passage of the Public Domain Act in 1882.

Charles Eliot and Sylvester Baxter had lead roles in advocating for a state commission to oversee a regional park system. In 1890, Eliot wrote a letter to the editor of *Garden and Forest* entitled "The Waverly Oaks: A Plan for their Preservation for the People," which was really a plan for preserving scenic areas near Boston. Eliot was concerned that these areas were being destroyed by developers or bought by the wealthy. With help from the Appalachian Mountain Club (AMC), Eliot and Baxter worked with Gov. William E. Russell and the legislature to pass an act in 1891 creating the Trustees of Public Reservations, the world's first conservation land trust. (In 1895, Britain's National Trust was created using the Trustees as a model.)

Eliot and Baxter realized they needed a state commission to overcome barriers created by inconsistent town regulations. In spring 1892, the legislature authorized a temporary Metropolitan Park Commission (MPC), with Eliot as its landscape architect and Baxter as its secretary. Based on reports by Baxter and especially Eliot, the commissioners endorsed creating a metropolitan district, including 36 cities and towns and securing Middlesex Fells, the Blue Hills, and other areas. In 1893, the legislature passed the Park Act, which created a permanent MPC.

The MPC's first takings included Blue Hills (3,953 acres), Middlesex Fells (1,583 acres), Stony Brook (475 acres), and Beaver Brook (Waverly Oaks) (59 acres). Including reservoirs, the Middlesex Fells encompassed some 3,000 acres. In 1893, Charles Eliot joined Frederick Law Olmsted's firm and brought with him the commission to plan the Metropolitan Park System.

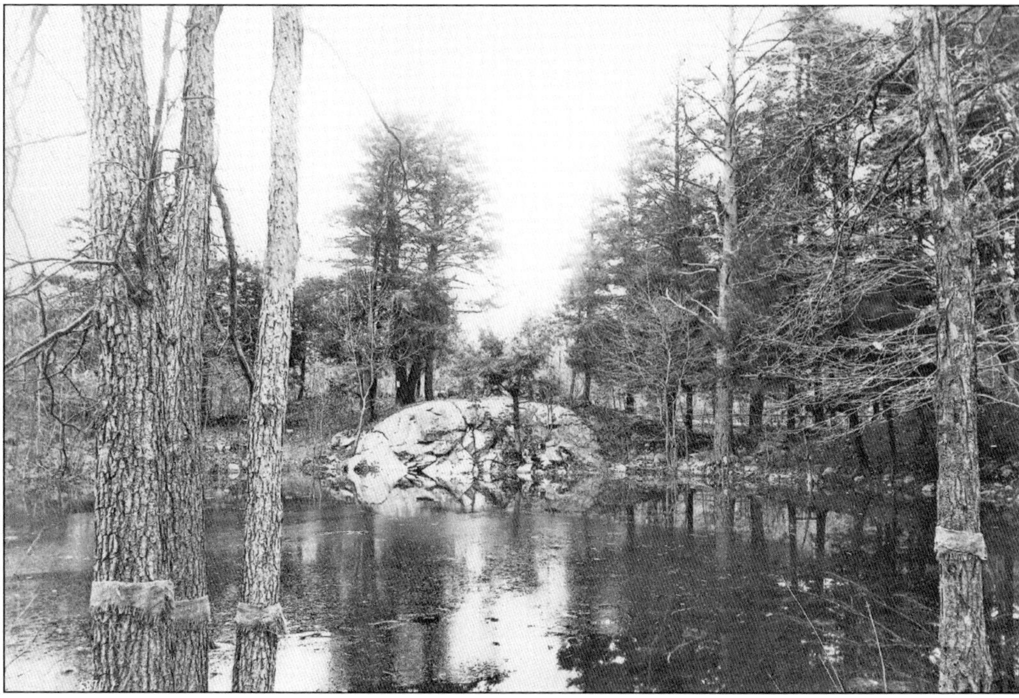

Hemlock Pool, a small pond in the southeastern part of the Fells, is shown here in 1896. The rugged terrain around this pool protected it from development in the decades leading up to the creation of Middlesex Fells Reservation. (Courtesy of DCR Archives.)

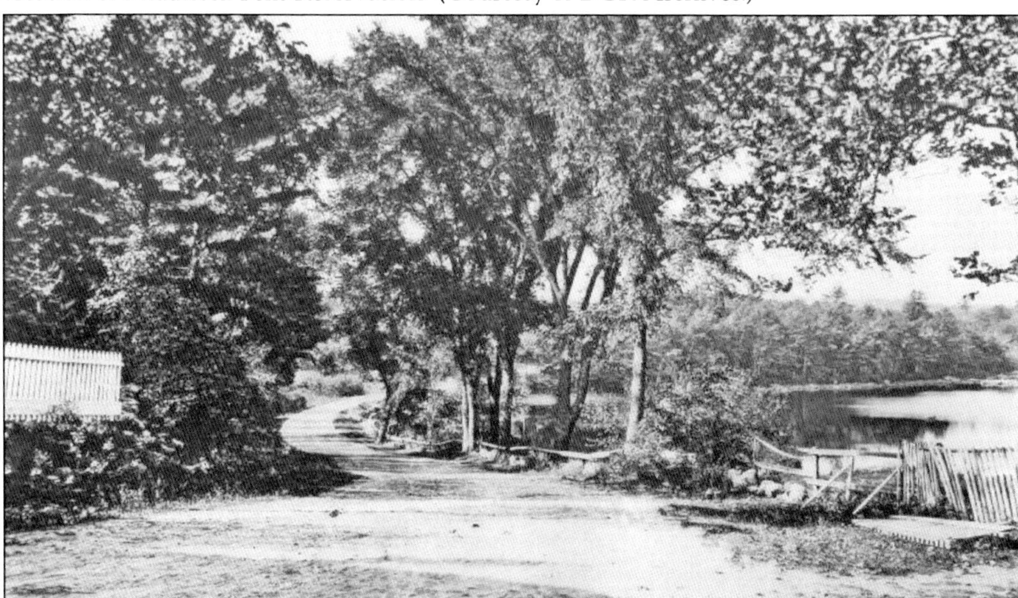

Wilson Flagg took this photograph of Spot Pond and included it in his 1875 book *Birds and Seasons of New England*. Flagg's caption reads, "Old road, as seen from the hill leading to Spot Pond on the route from Medford to Stoneham." This road was laid out in 1806 along the west side of Spot Pond, and, over the years, has been known as Forest Street, the Andover and Medford Turnpike, and Route 28. (Courtesy of Mike Ryan.)

This photograph shows Meeting House Brook, which now flows from Winchester's South Reservoir (formerly Turkey Swamp) to the Mystic River. The brook was first named Marble Brook after Thomas Marble, who lived nearby. It became known as Meeting House Brook when Medford's second meetinghouse was built beside it in 1727. (Courtesy of Massachusetts State Archives.)

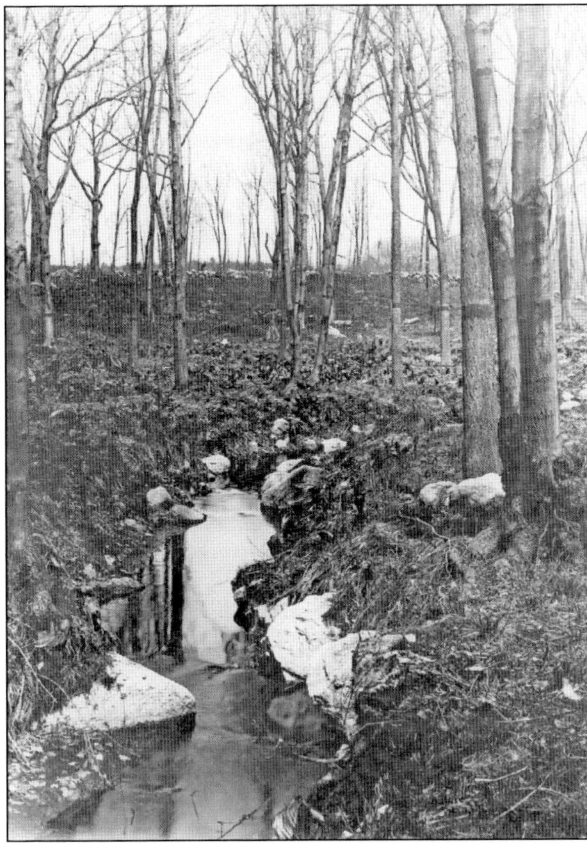

Nathaniel Stebbins took this photograph of Hemlock Pool Road in December 1896 and wrote on its margin, "Near Shiner Pool." George Davenport explained how Shiner Pool got its name: "a short distance to the north is Shiner Pond, where those astute historians, the boys, who are generally well initiated into all the mysteries of the woodlands, within any reasonable distance of their homes, say they used to go fishing for the little fish called 'shiners.'" (Courtesy of DCR Archives.)

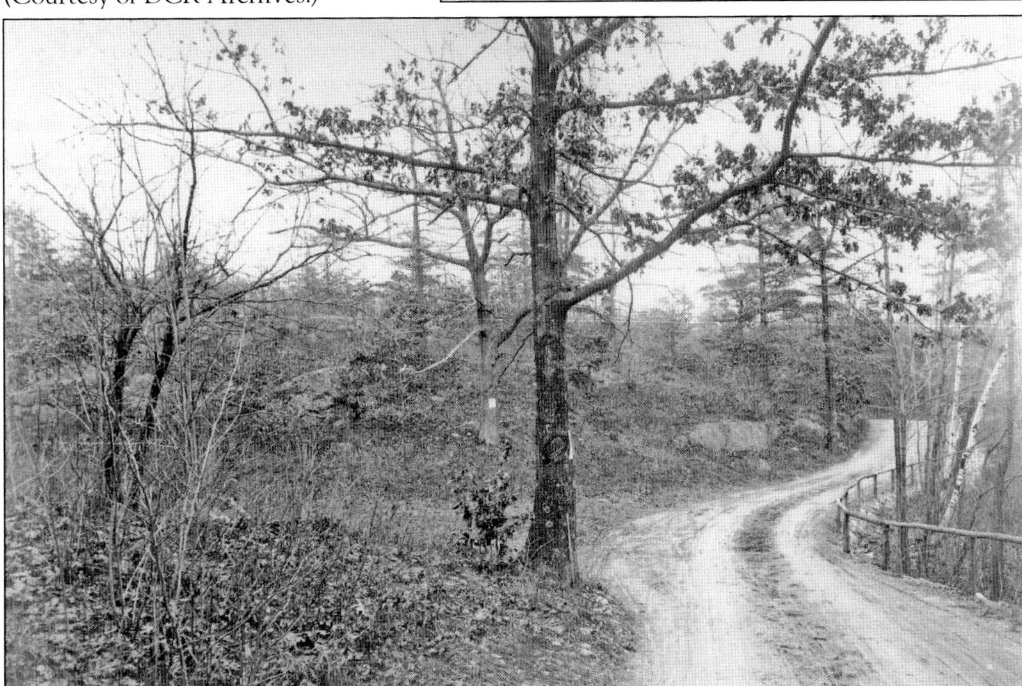

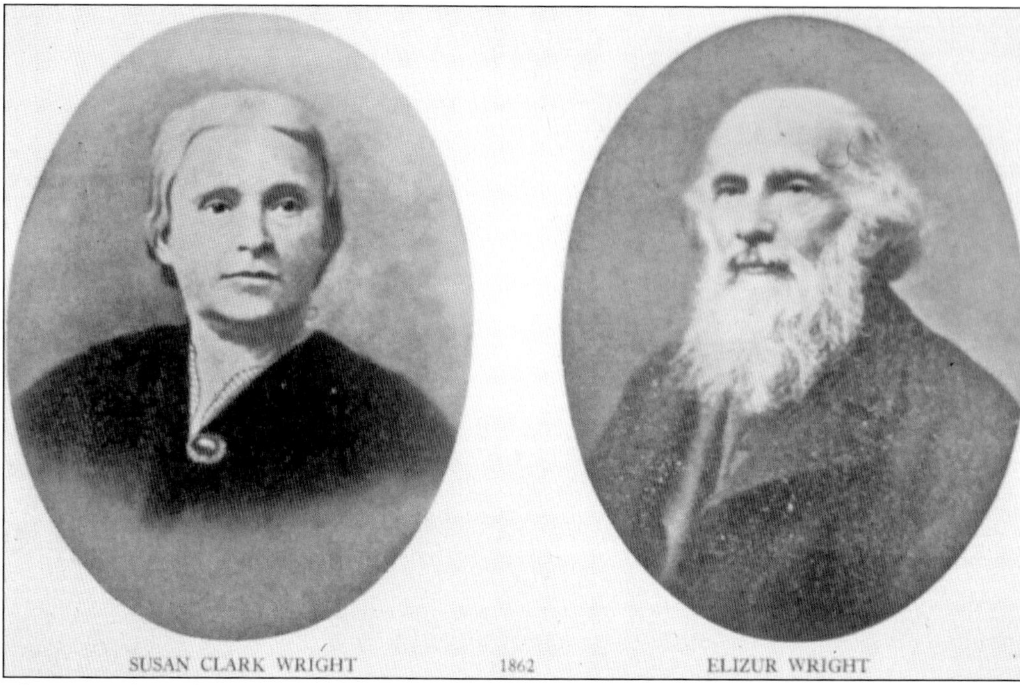

The image above shows Elizur Wright and his wife, Susan (Clark), in 1862. They met in 1826 when Clark was attending Groton Academy. While there, Clark met Margaret Fuller, famed women's rights advocate. In 1829, Clark and Wright got married and eventually had 10 children. In 1864, the Wrights moved into an expansive 1853 house next to Pine Hill, pictured below. In July 1896, their children Ellen and Walter donated Pine Hill and more than 20 acres to the MPC "to keep the [Middlesex Fells] Reservation . . . in the interest of the forest as well as the people." Wright's house was razed before 1924 and, in 1959, Interstate 93 was built across the property. (Above, courtesy of Mike Ryan; below, courtesy of DCR Archives.)

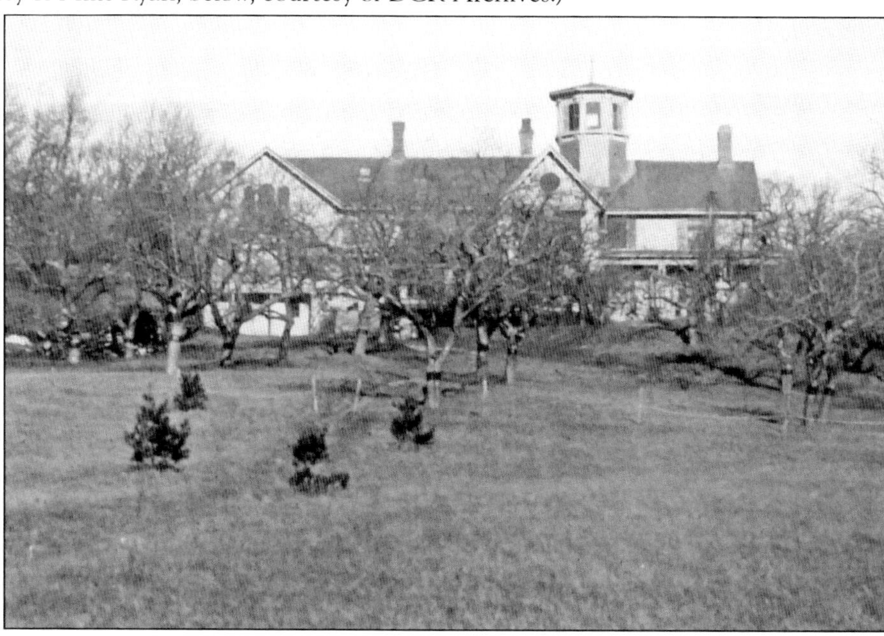

Sylvester Baxter (1850–1927), pictured here in 1893, was a journalist for the *Boston Herald* and the *Boston Evening Transcript* and secretary of the first (temporary) MPC. In the December 6, 1879, issue of the *Boston Herald*, he proposes the name Middlesex Fells, writing that "the nature of this region cannot better be characterized than by the application of the old Saxon designation 'fells' – a common enough word in England, meaning a tract of wild stone hills." (Photograph by Elmer Chickering, courtesy of DCR Archives.)

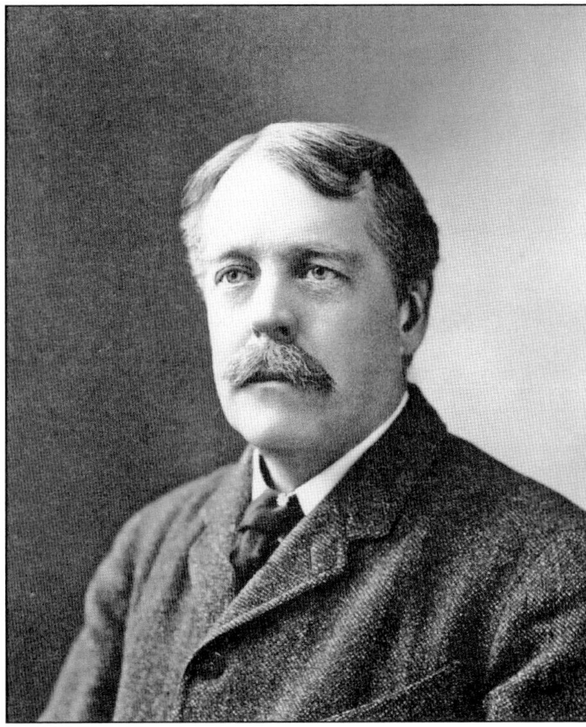

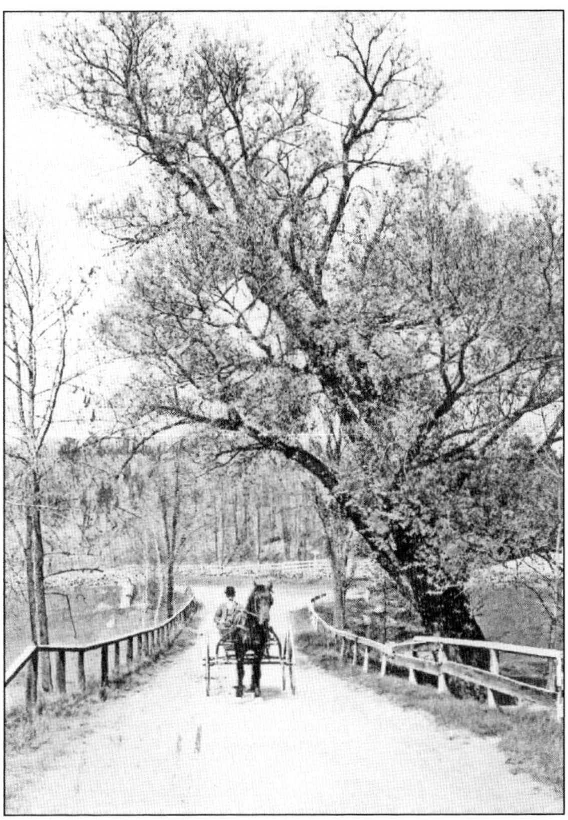

This c. 1905 postcard of a man riding through the Fells was published by New England News Company of Boston and printed in Germany. Postcards of the Fells were mainly produced from 1905 to 1912 and some, including this one, were hand-colored. In the early 20th century, postcards were both souvenirs and a popular means of correspondence. (Courtesy of DCR Archives.)

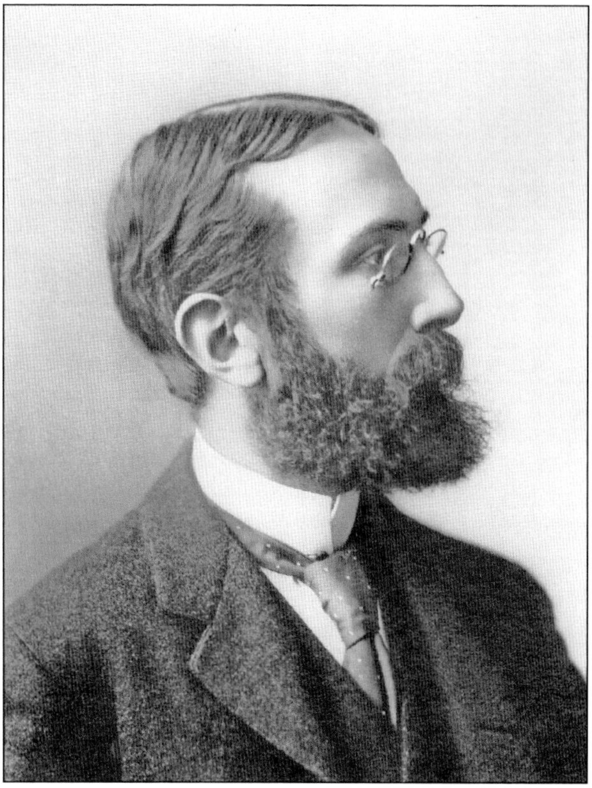

Charles Eliot (1859–1897) apprenticed with renowned landscape architect Frederick Law Olmsted and was a key figure in establishing the Metropolitan Park System., including Middlesex Fells. Eliot was the consulting landscape architect for the MPC. At Eliot's 1906 memorial service at Blue Hills, William B. de las Casas said, "Charles Eliot loved the woods and rocky hills; he knew their bounds and innermost recesses, and he knew the refreshment which they held for the tired souls of those who must live for the most part in the noisy ugliness of towns." (Photograph by Elmer Chickering, courtesy of DCR Archives.)

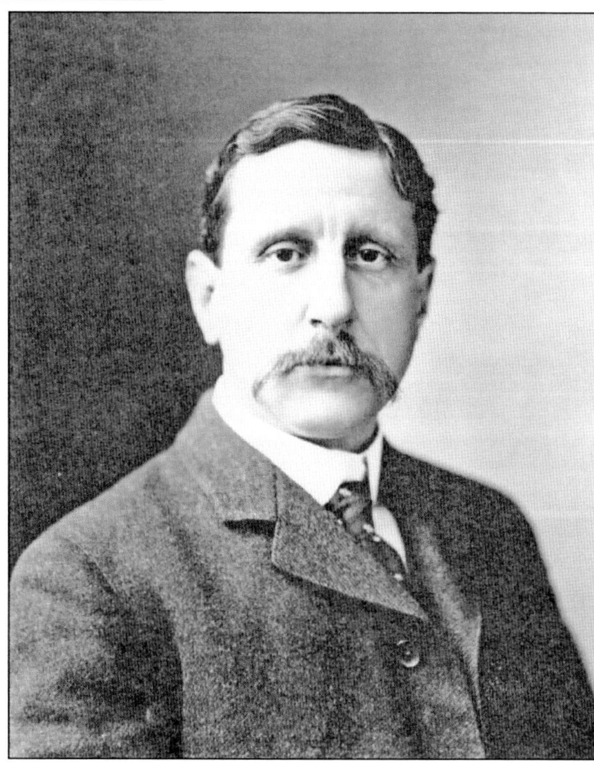

William B. de las Casas (1857–1930) was the second chairman of the board of the Metropolitan Park Commission from 1895 to 1919. In the 1898 article "The Middlesex Fells," he writes: "The scenery of the Fells has been much affected by human life within and about it, working sometimes to its preservation and sometimes to it destruction. Moreover, the efforts made to preserve this region as a public park have given us the entire metropolitan park system." (Photograph by Elmer Chickering, courtesy of DCR Archives.)

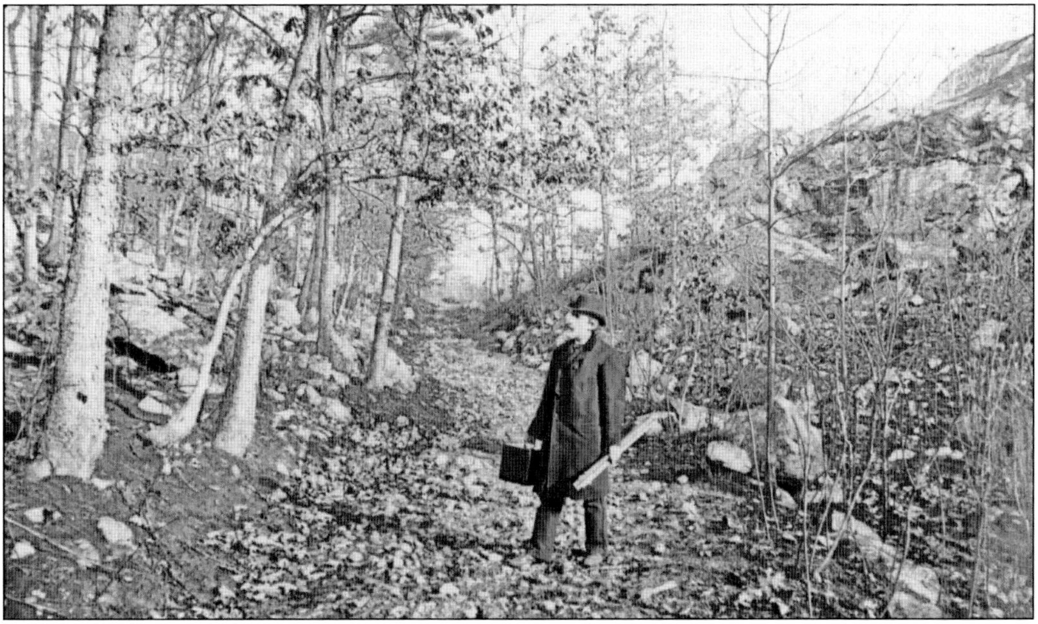

In a c. 1889 image, George E. Davenport (1833–1907) carries his camera and tripod along Jerry Jingle Road on his way to the Bears Den, a rock formation located in the southeastern part of the Fells. The road, named after an itinerant peddler from Melrose, lies between the Bears Den and Pinnacle Rock. Davenport's grandson Alfred may have taken this photograph. The recent photograph below shows that Jerry Jingle Road has changed very little in over 120 years. (Above, courtesy of Medford Historical Society and Museum; below, authors' collection.)

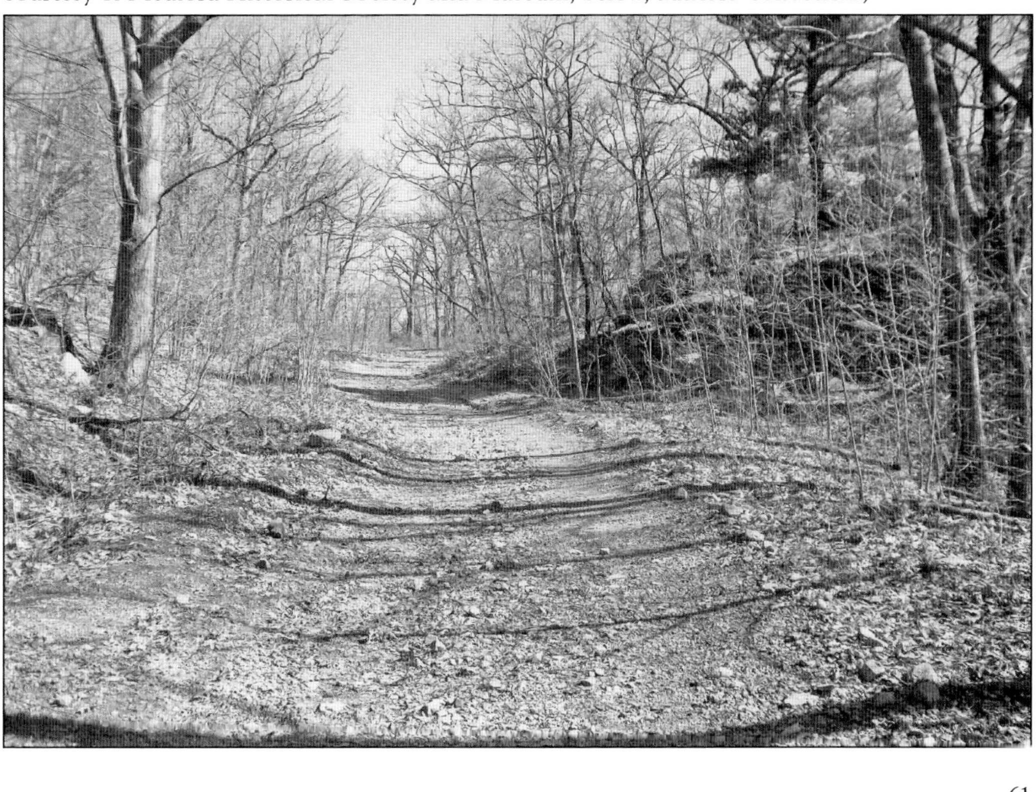

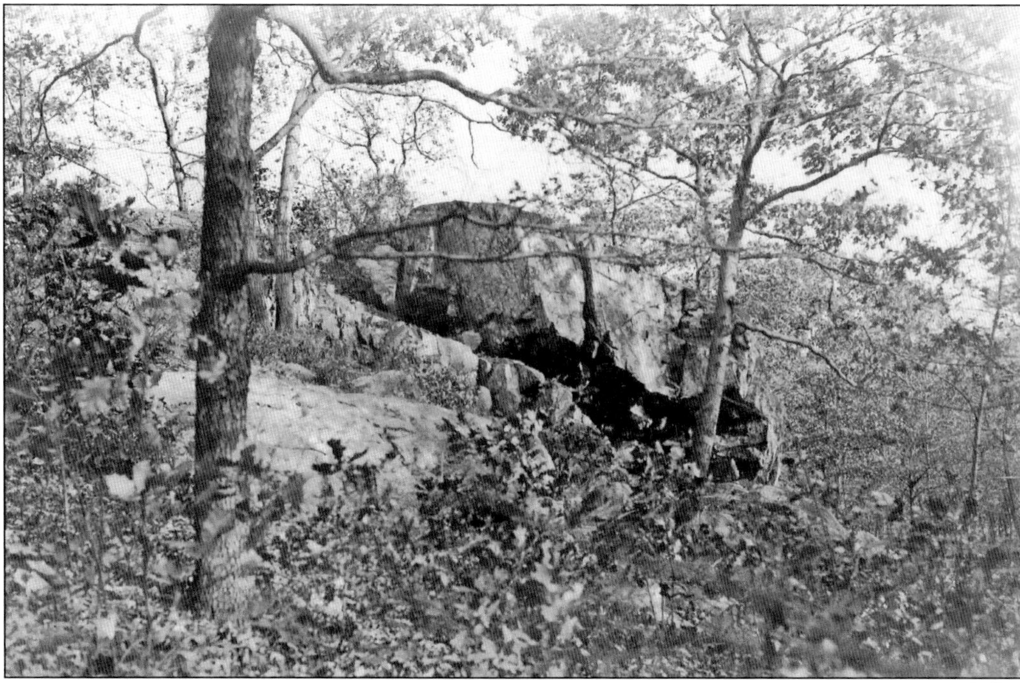

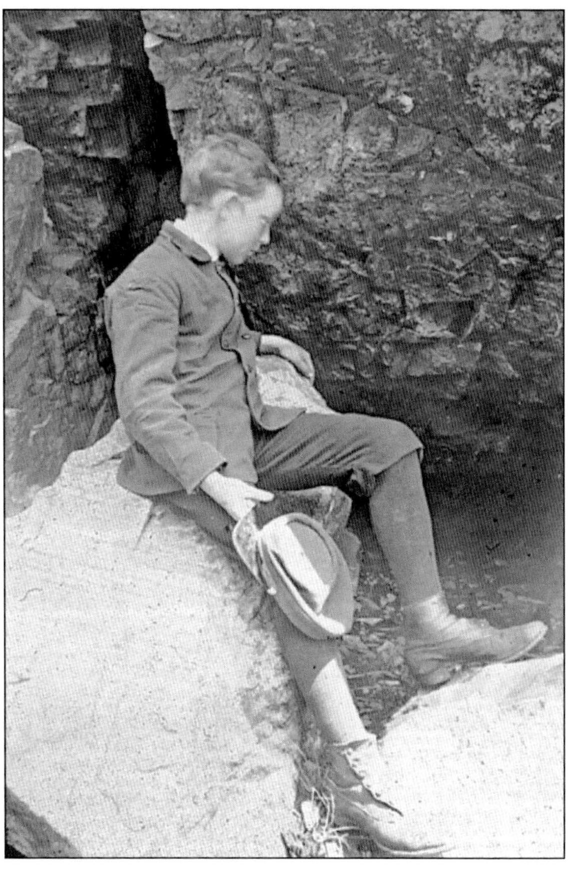

George Davenport took these images of the Bears Den near Boojum Rock about 1889. At left, Davenport's eldest grandson, Alfred, poses at the den's entrance. Alfred Davenport (1879–1937) became an insurance broker in Boston, president of the Boston Board of Fire Underwriters, and a state representative for Malden. In 1914, he wrote the Davenport Bill, giving control of railroads to the state. (Both, courtesy of Medford Historical Society and Museum.)

George Davenport took this photograph of his wife, Mary Cronin, and daughters at their Valley Street home in Medford about 1890. From left to right are (first row) Alice, Mary, and Florence; (second row) Laura, Elizabeth, Ella and Annie. Alice and Florence often joined their father on walks through the Fells. (Courtesy of Tom McCarthy.)

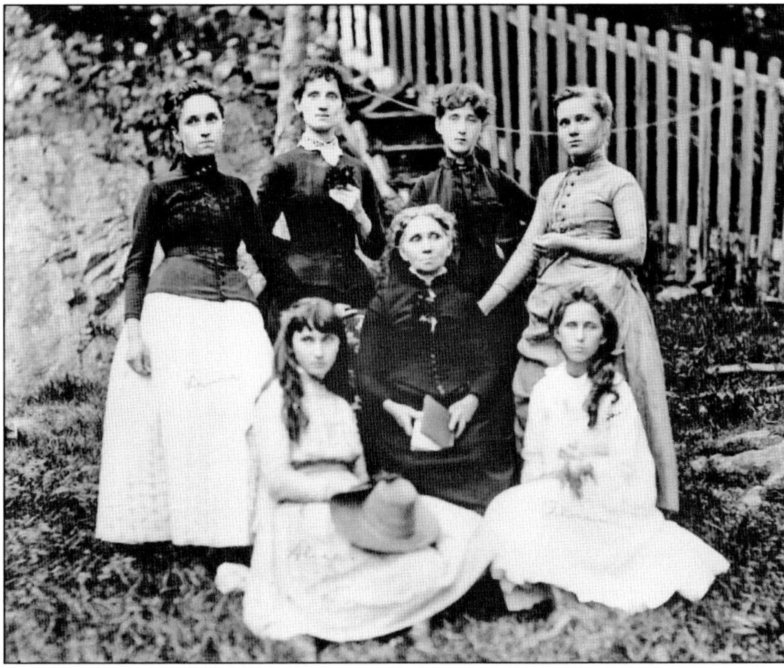

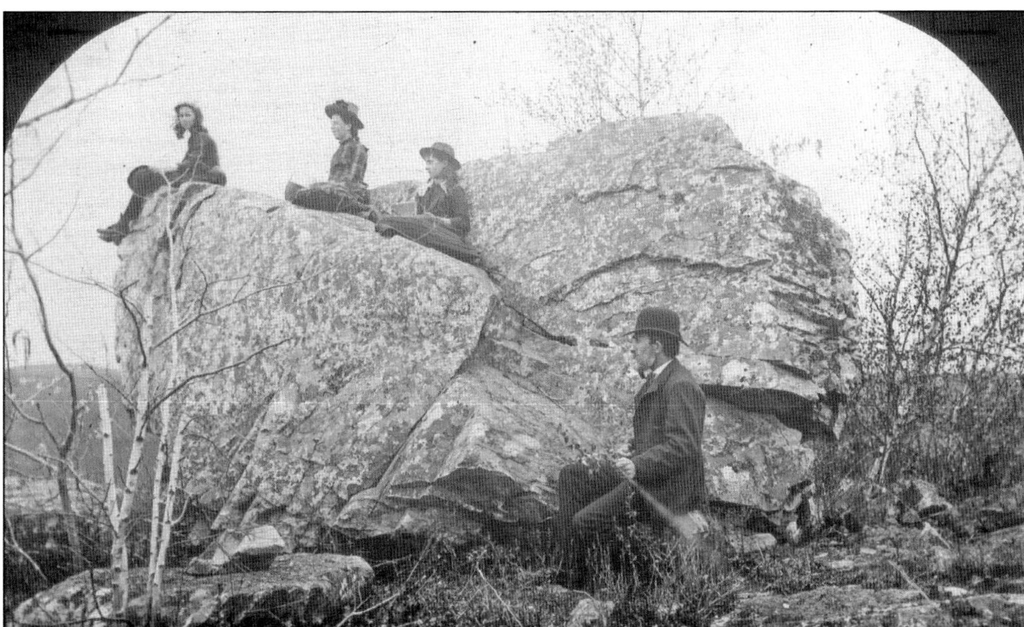

George Davenport took this portrait of himself and his daughters (from left to right) Florence, Laura, and Alice at Druidical Rock by pulling a string to trip the camera shutter. This 1880s photograph was one of many lantern slides Davenport used in public presentations. The rock was probably destroyed in 1896 during the construction of East Border Road. (Courtesy of Medford Historical Society and Museum.)

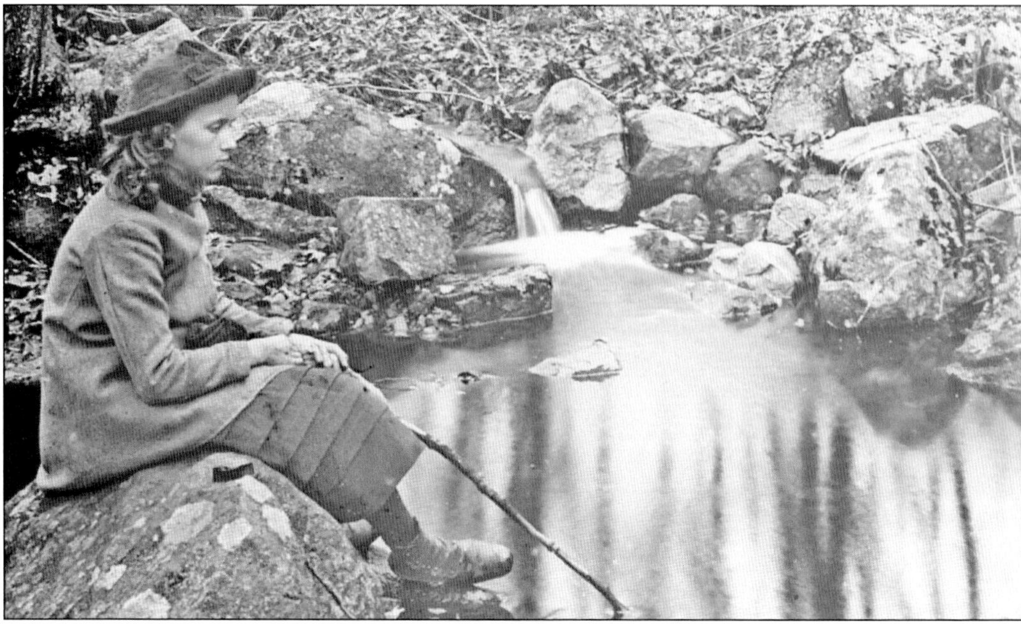

Florence E. Davenport (1871–1937) poses for her father beside a stream in Middlesex Fells about 1888. Born in Boston, Florence married Indiana native Walter Jackson. They had two children in Florida before moving to Quincy, Massachusetts. Florence's sister Alice moved to Nova Scotia, where Florence visited her in 1926 and 1930. (Courtesy of Medford Historical Society and Museum.)

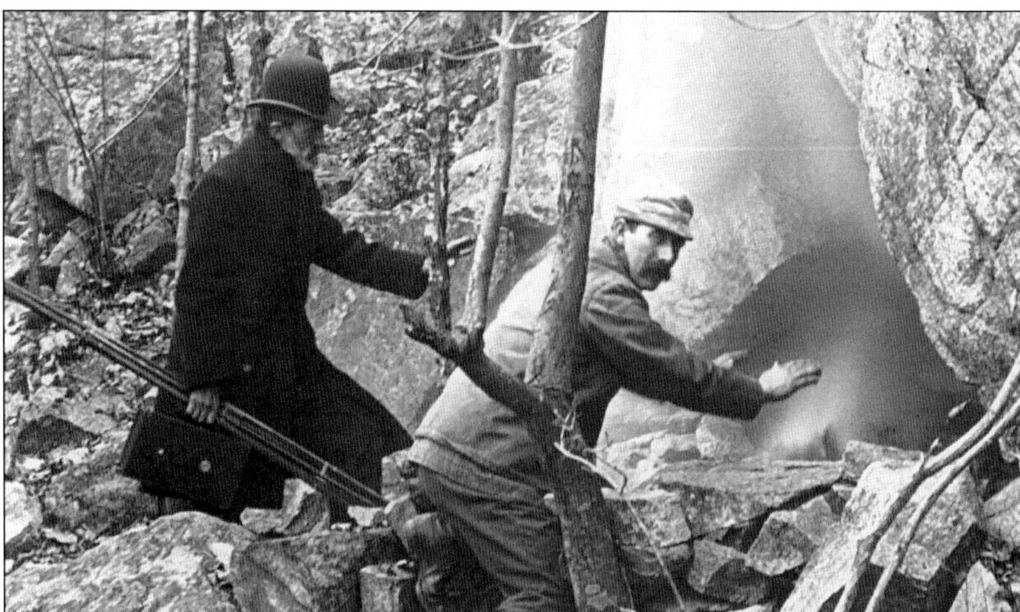

George Davenport and a friend warm their hands beside a fire on a cold day in the Fells. Davenport, a botanist and photographer, was a founding member of the Mystic Camera Club and a gilder of picture frames. Starting in 1889, the club took many photographs in the Fells, and Davenport helped advocate for creation of the park with his lantern-slide shows. (Courtesy of Medford Historical Society and Museum.)

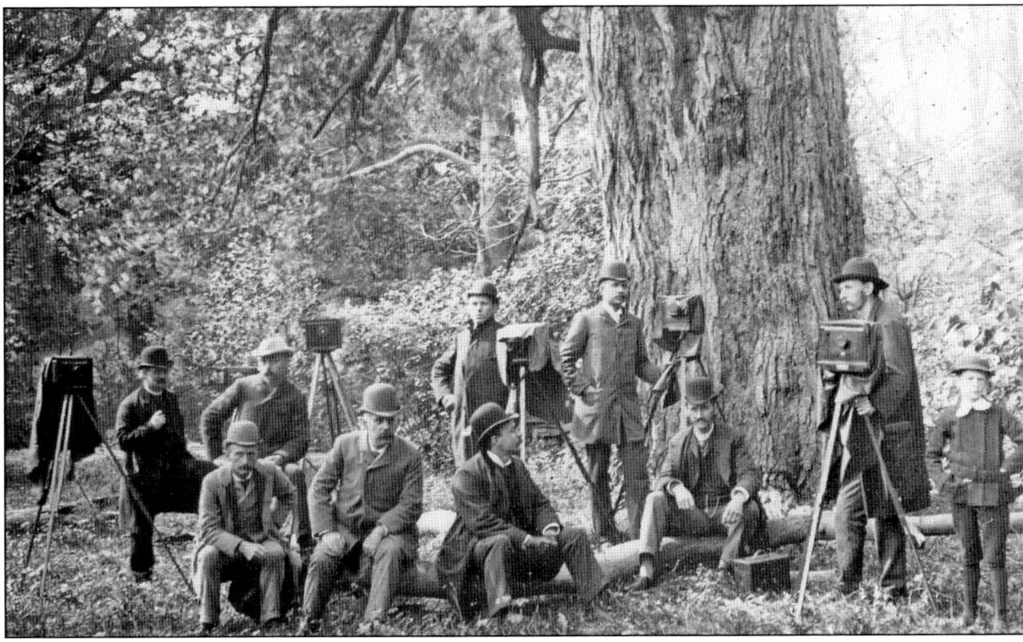

These c. 1891 photographs show the Mystic Camera Club in the Fells. The club was founded on June 4, 1889, in Medford. At first, club members met in private homes, but later they met in the Legion of Honor Hall, the Odd Fellows Hall, and the Riverside block on Main Street in Medford. They took field trips to scenic locations in and near the Fells, such as the Cascade. They also sponsored slide shows with themes such as the midnight ride of Paul Revere, New England poets, and Middlesex Fells. Margaret J. Bishop, a photographic printer in Boston, was the club's only female member and may be the woman in the photograph below. (Both, courtesy of the Medford Historical Society and Museum.)

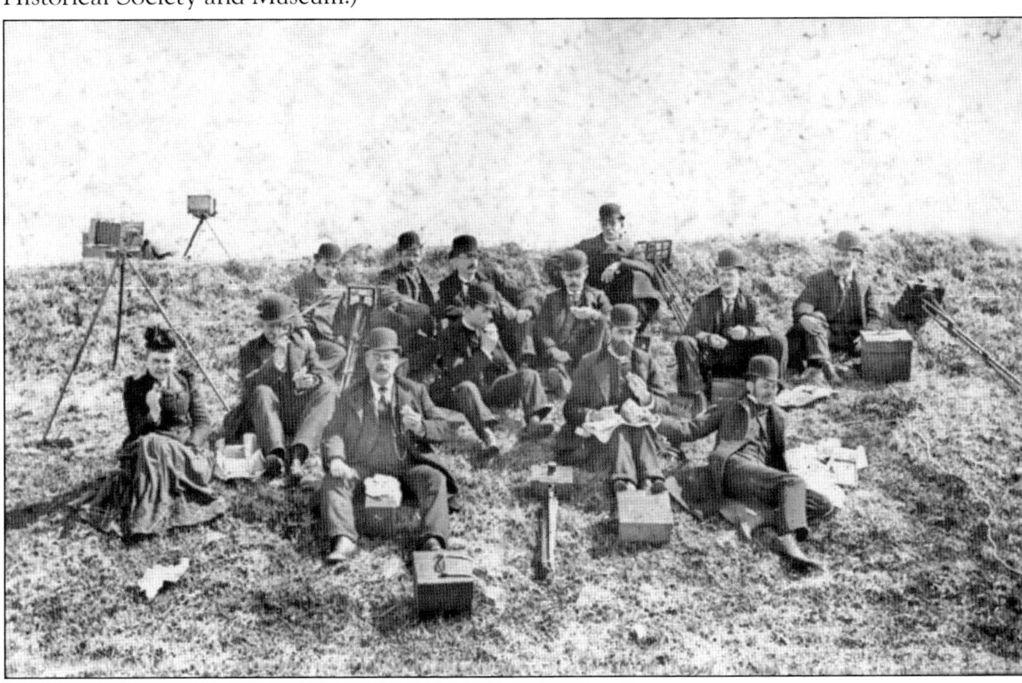

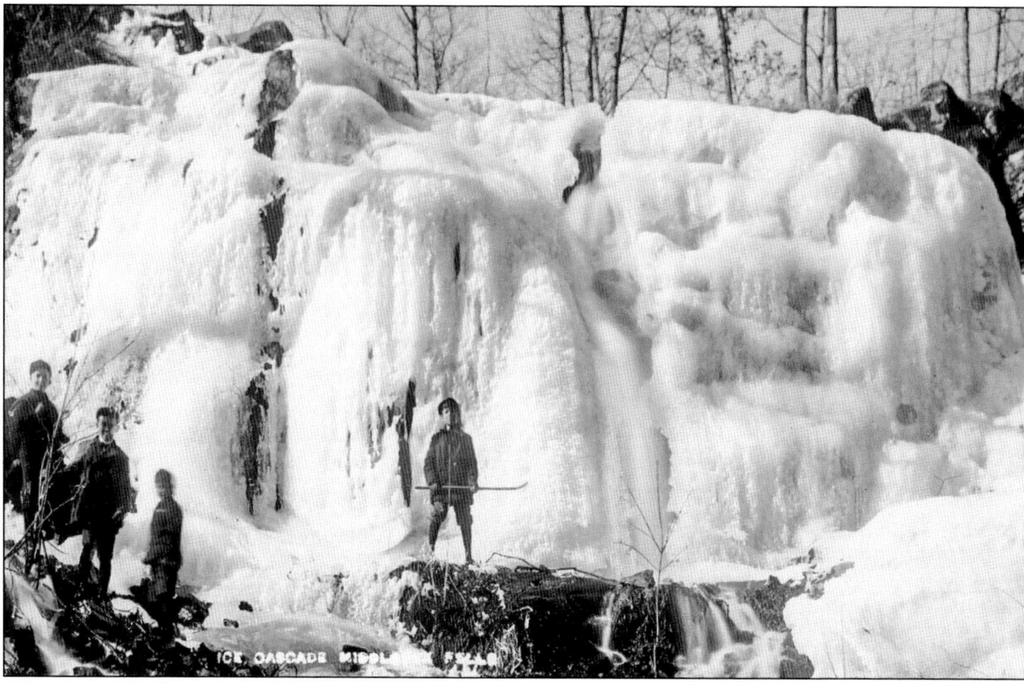

The Cascade forms as Shilly Shally Brook spills over bluffs in the southeastern Fells west of Washington Street in Melrose. This photograph was taken about 1890, but scenes like this occur every winter. The brook originates in a swampy area south of the Fells Reservoir and falls 40 feet over volcanic rocks. (Courtesy of Medford Historical Society and Museum.)

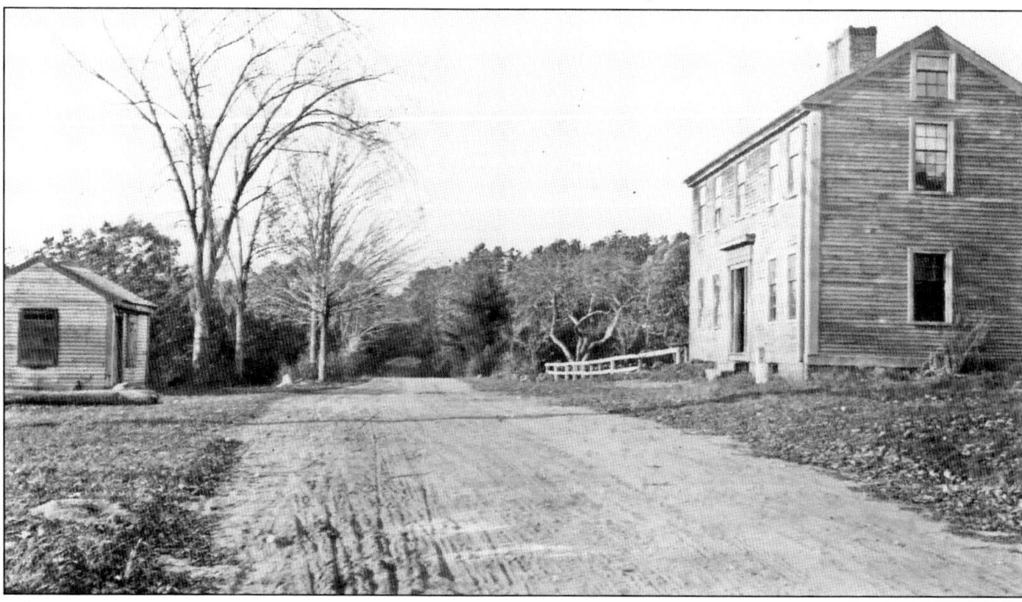

This 1890s photograph shows the tollhouse on the Andover and Medford Turnpike (Forest Street, now Route 28), about one and a half miles north of Medford center. The house was built in 1804 by carpenters Buckman and Wait for $300, near a location known as General Derby's Farm. The turnpike opened in 1806 with James Kidder as the first toll collector. Tolls ended in 1831 when the turnpike became a public road. (Courtesy of Ryan Hayward.)

Following the time-honored practice of artists making self-portraits, botanist and photographer George Davenport pulls a string to take this image of himself while sitting beside Shilly Shally Brook above the Cascade in Middlesex Fells about 1890. The string used to trip the camera shutter is visible in the foreground. (Courtesy of Medford Historical Society and Museum.)

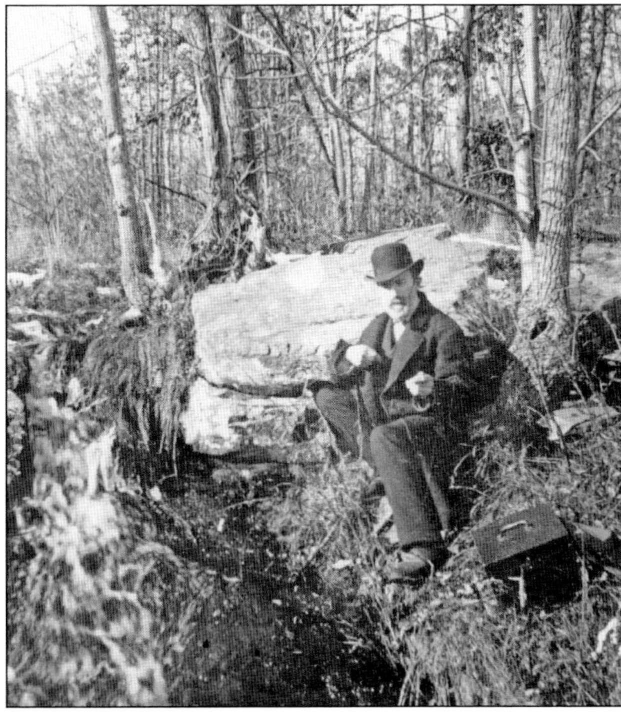

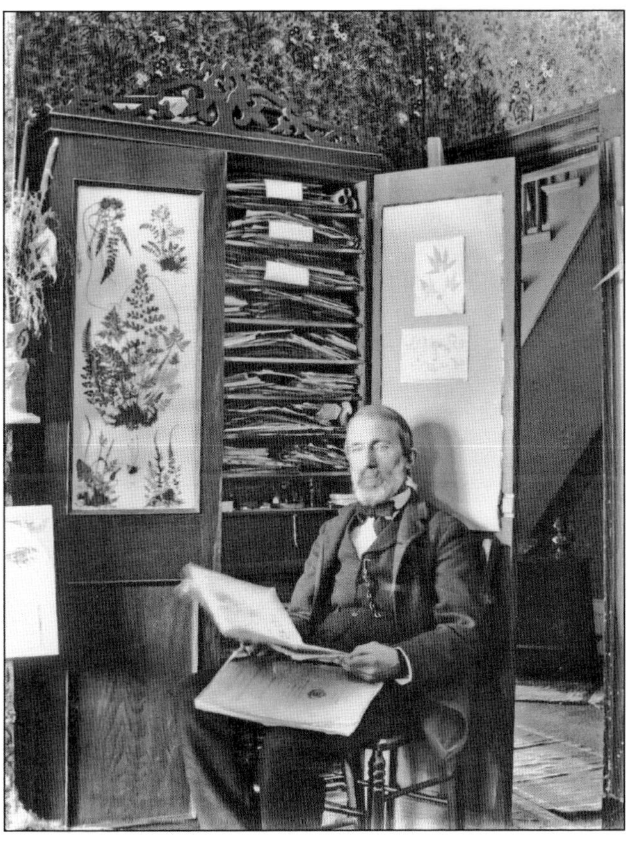

This 1890s image shows George Davenport in his house on Valley Street in Medford with his extensive fern collection. In 1872, Davenport joined the Massachusetts Horticultural Society (MHS) and, in 1879, it published his *Catalogue of the 'Davenport Herbarium' of North American Ferns*. He later donated the collection to the MHS and it awarded him its Appleton gold medal. (Courtesy of Tom McCarthy.)

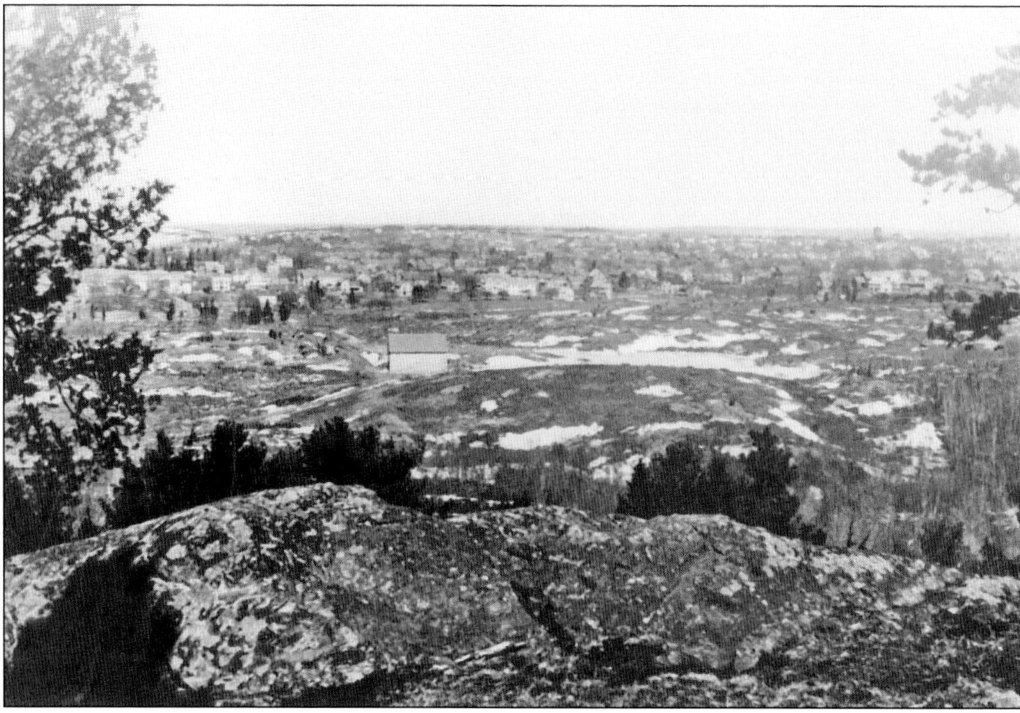

George Davenport captured this wintry image of Stoneham from the top of Bear Hill about 1890. The large building at left center is an icehouse for storing blocks of ice cut from Dike Pond to the northwest of Spot Pond. Dike Pond is now surrounded by apartments and houses. (Courtesy of Medford Historical Society and Museum.)

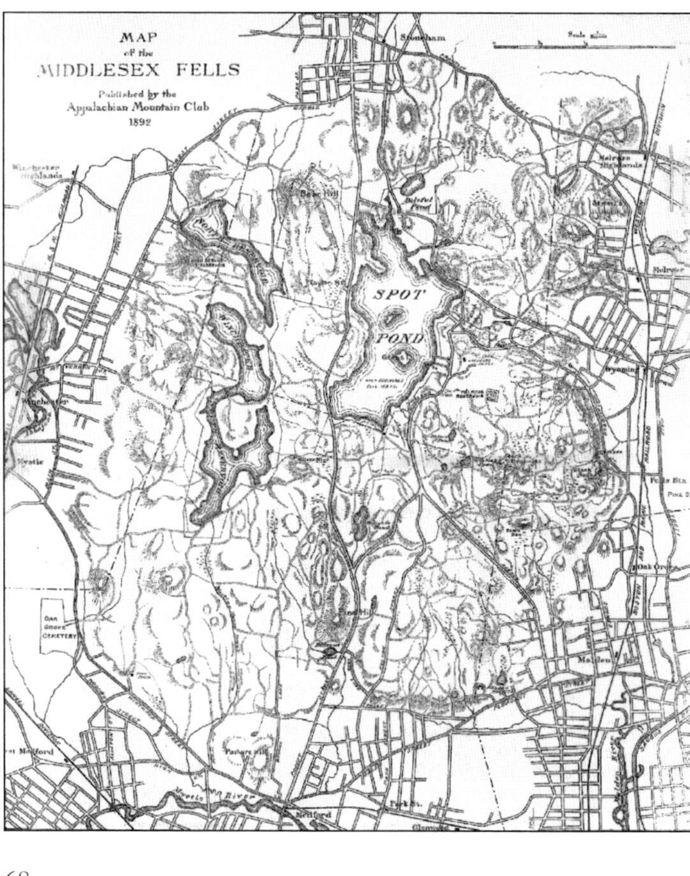

In January 1892, the AMC published this map of Middlesex Fells in its journal *Appalachia*, to update an 1886 version that had gone out of print. AMC secretary Rosewell B. Lawrence and I. Y. Chubbuck drafted the map after extensive fieldwork. (Courtesy of AMC Archives.)

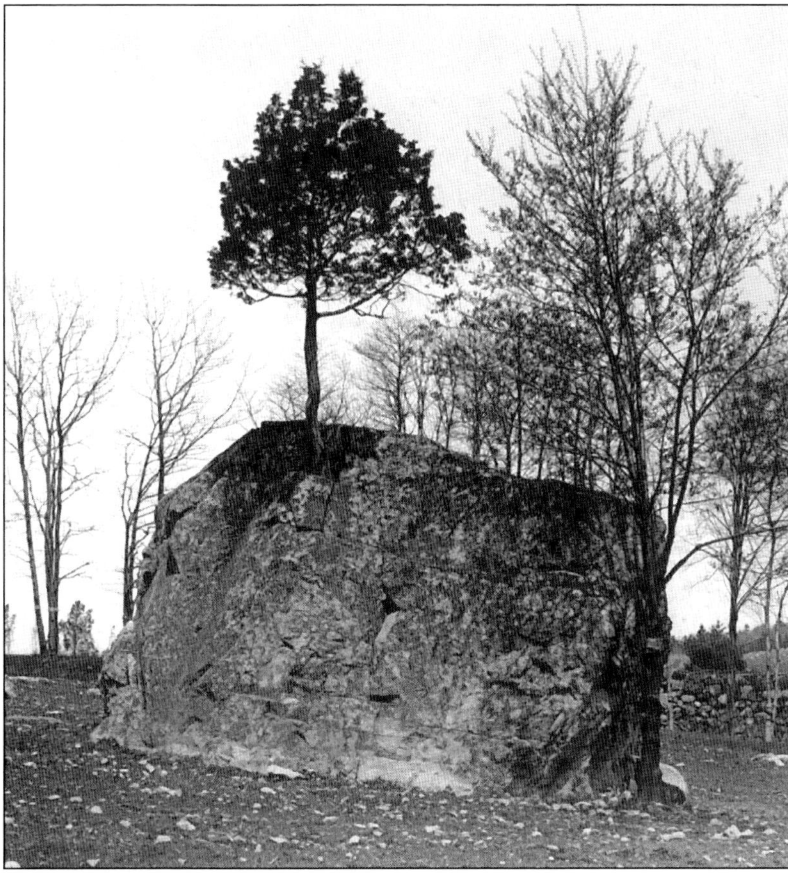

Cedar Rock was a 12-foot-high boulder near Whitmore Brook Road. In 1935, Ruth Dame Coolidge wrote in *Afoot in the Fells*, "It was a survival of the fittest and has attracted the attention . . . of scientific men, geologists and naturalists. They estimate the tree to be over 400 years old. Under favorable conditions the native red cedar . . . is of very slow growth, but here is one growing in no soil, but all rock." (Courtesy of Massachusetts State Archives.)

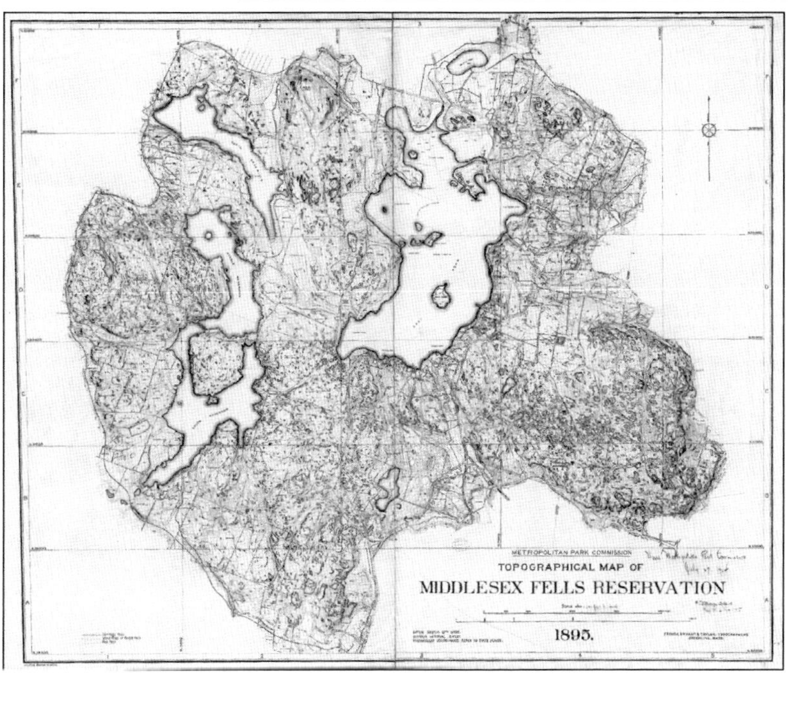

In 1895, the MPC published this topographic map of Middlesex Fells, surveyed by French, Bryant, and Taylor for Olmsted Brothers, landscape architects. It shows the reservation's boundaries and features as they existed in the late 19th century. (Courtesy of the National Park Service, ONHS.)

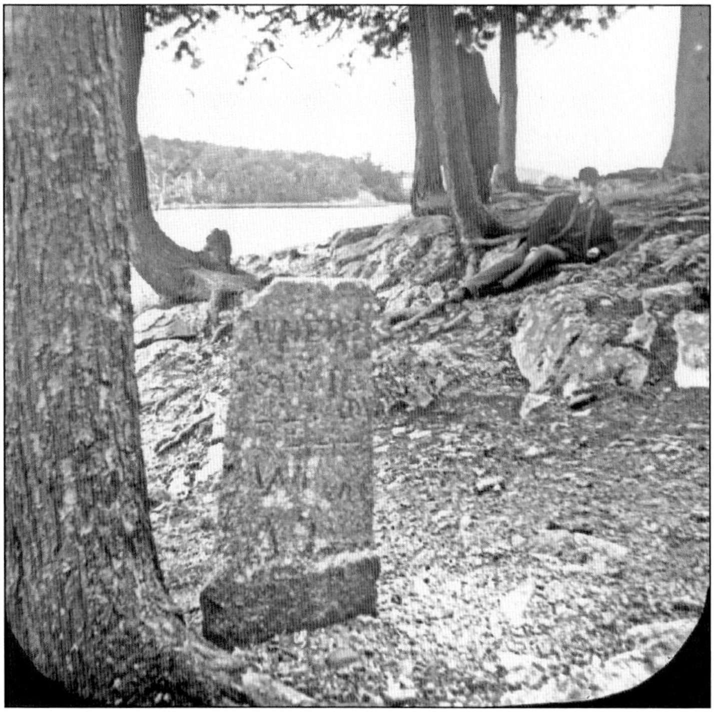

This slate monument on Great Island in Spot Pond reads simply "Where Shute Fell," in honor of a wrestler from Haywardville, known only by his last name. During the 19th century, this island was the site of many wrestling matches and prizefights. A legendary fight took place on May 1, 1856, between Edmund "Ned" Price of England and Joe Coburn of Ireland, which lasted 200 minutes and 160 rounds with no winner. The monument still exists. (Courtesy of Medford Historical Society and Museum.)

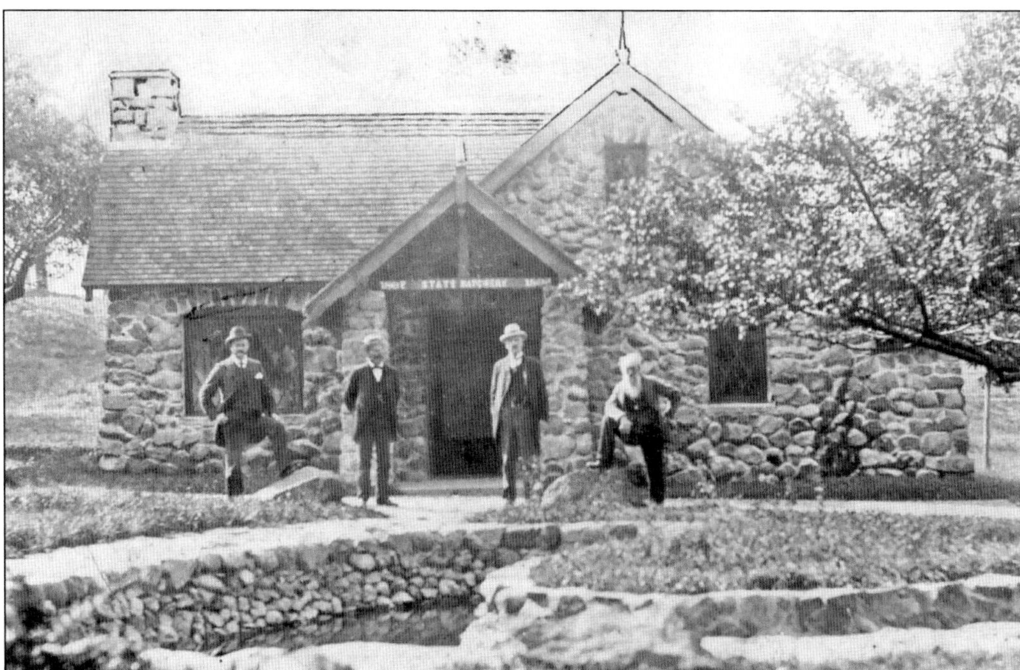

The Massachusetts Department of Fish and Game opened this fish hatchery on South Border Road in 1898. From left to right are commissioners J.W. Delano, E. Buffington, Isaiah Young, and Edward Brackett. In 1912, the MPC began using the hatchery as a maintenance building and allowed the Boy Scouts to use it for meetings from 1926 to 1964. The building still exists, but is privately owned and greatly modified. (Courtesy of Winchester Massachusetts Archival Center.)

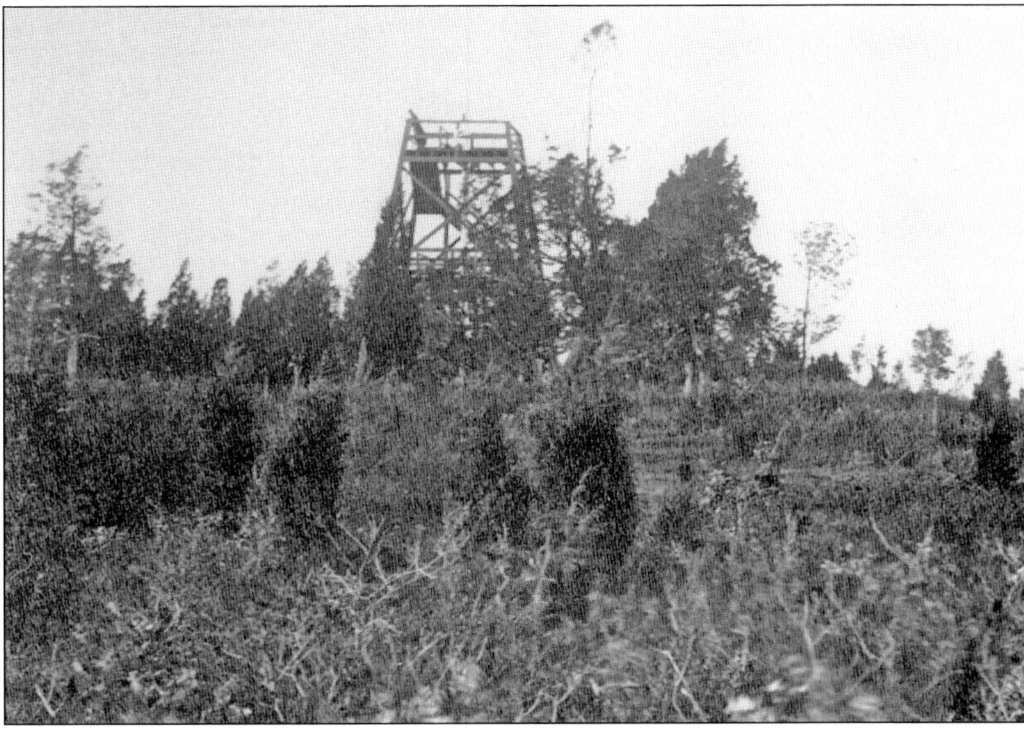

To encourage people to visit the Fells, the AMC built the wooden tower pictured above on Bear Hill in 1893. This photograph by Nathaniel Stebbins shows the tower on October 1, 1895. The MPC closed the tower in 1908, deeming it "no longer safe for public use." Two years later, the commission built a new tower of reinforced concrete (see page 78). (Courtesy of Massachusetts State Archives.)

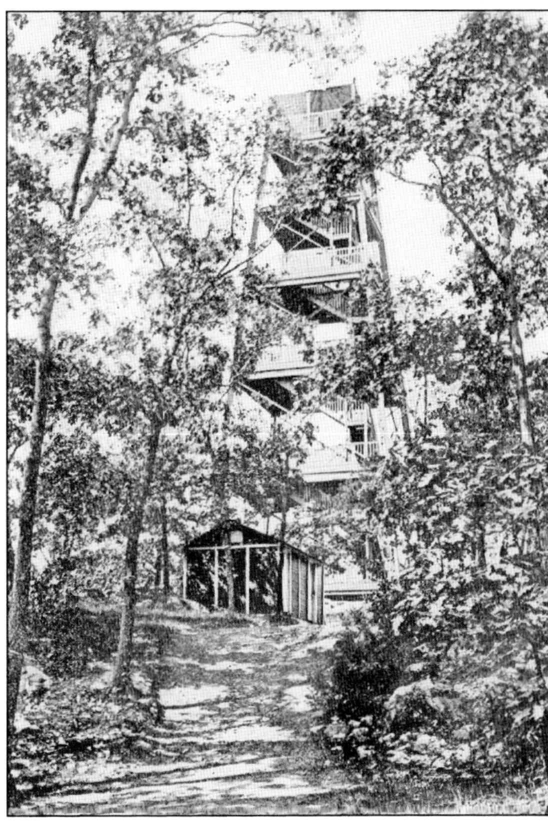

The 1899 Lawrence Tower on Rams Head Hill (or Rams Horn Hill) was designed by architect Lyman Sise and owned by Gen. Samuel C. Lawrence. On Sundays, the public could climb the 81-foot tower, which was almost as high as Bear Hill. In 1925, the Metropolitan Park Commission acquired about 285 acres of Lawrence's estate and incorporated it into an area of the Fells known as Lawrence Woods. Today, only foundations remain. (Courtesy of DCR.)

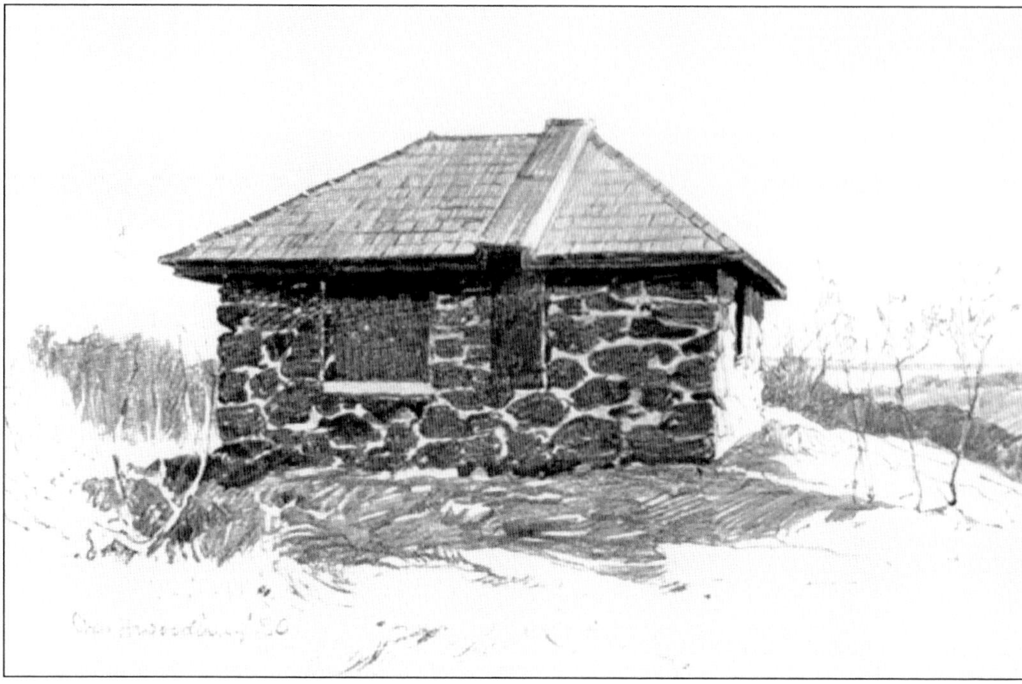

The Massachusetts Institute of Technology (MIT) built this geodetic observatory northwest of the Bears Den about 1898 to measure latitude and longitude. It was used for training civil engineering and astronomy students. Similar observatories were at Harvard University and Blue Hills Reservation. MIT chose this remote location to avoid vibrations from railroad and road traffic. The building contained magnetic, seismic, and gravity sensors and an astronomical transit. The transit was used in 1869 to survey the site of the Hoosac Tunnel in western Massachusetts and for navigation surveys during a MIT expedition to Sumatra in 1901. The above sketch was drawn by Charles H. Woodbury, an 1886 MIT graduate. The recent image below shows the remains of the observatory on the Rock Circuit Trail. (Above, authors' collection; below, courtesy of Mike Ryan.)

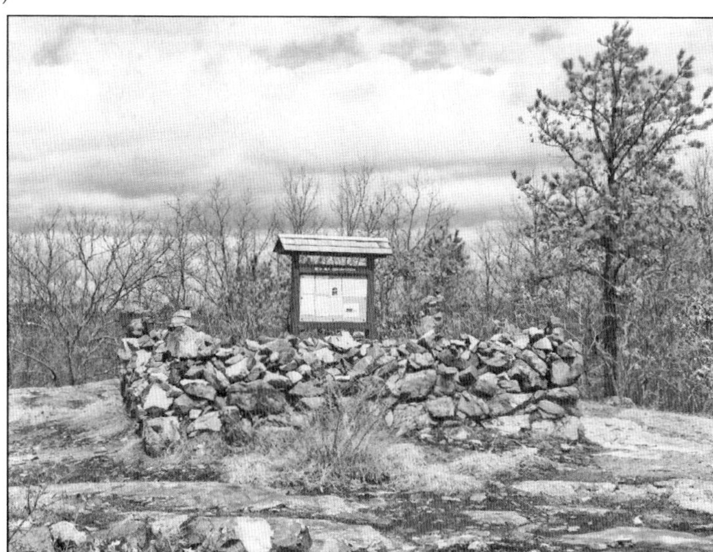

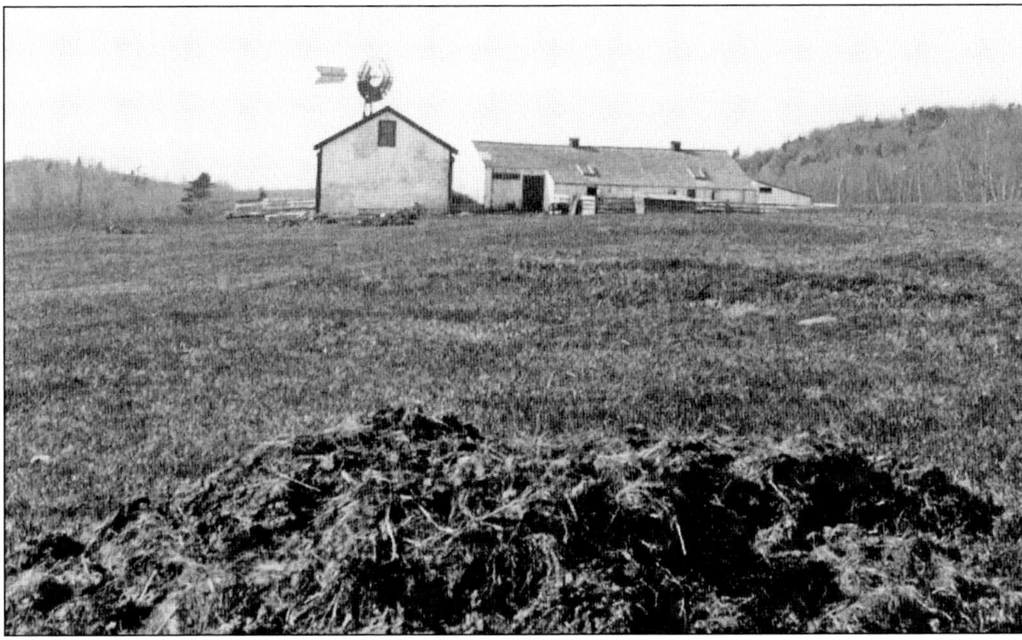

On April 30, 1894, Nathaniel Stebbins photographed Chandler's Piggery in the Sheepfold, west of Spot Pond. Frank E. Chandler (1852–1913), a Medford businessman and town official, bought the farm in 1884 and sold it 11 years later to the MPC for $35,000. During a 1901 visit, Frederick Law Olmsted Jr. noted the "barrenness and untidiness of the grounds" and "the presence of disorderly and detached outbuildings." The MPC kept the sheepfold in operation from 1902 to 1910. It is now a cleared field popular for exercising dogs. (Courtesy of Massachusetts State Archives.)

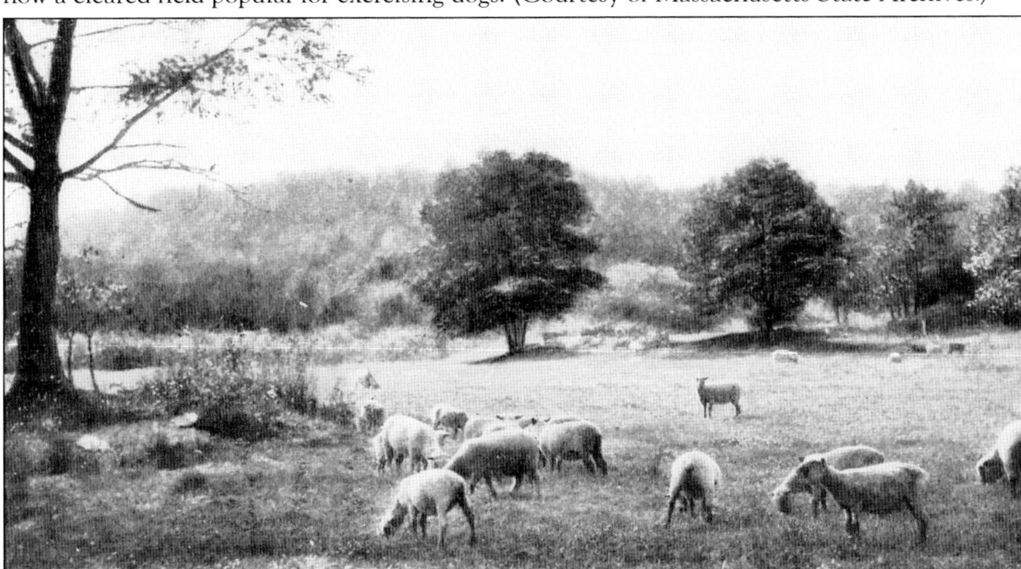

This 1905 postcard shows sheep grazing in the Sheepfold. The MPC introduced sheep to Middlesex Fells in 1902 as an inexpensive way to keep the field open for visitors. By 1909, the flock had increased to 26 ewes and rams. But this pastoral scene did not last long. In 1910, the MPC sold most of the sheep to local farmers and moved others to the Middlesex Fells Zoo. (Courtesy of DCR Archives.)

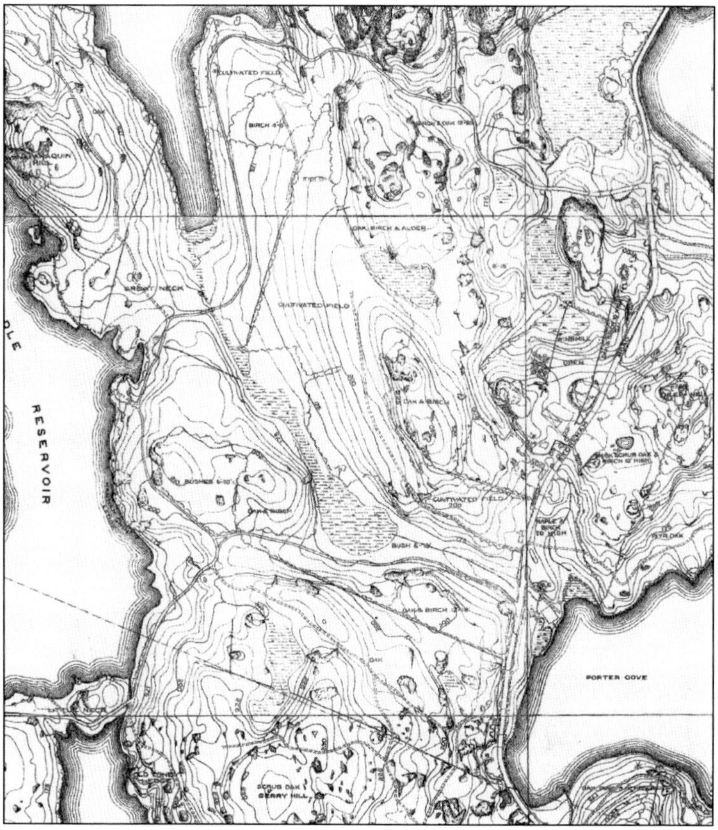

This section of the MPC's 1895 topographic map shows the Sheepfold. Winchester's reservoirs are at left and Spot Pond is at right. The road beside Spot Pond is the Andover and Medford Turnpike (Route 28). (Courtesy of DCR Archives.)

The MPC hired a shepherd and had a dog to keep track of the sheep. In 1907, the commission exhibited five sheep from the Sheepfold at the annual Brockton Fair and won awards. Despite their popularity, the sheep were removed from the Sheepfold in 1910. (Courtesy of Massachusetts State Archives.)

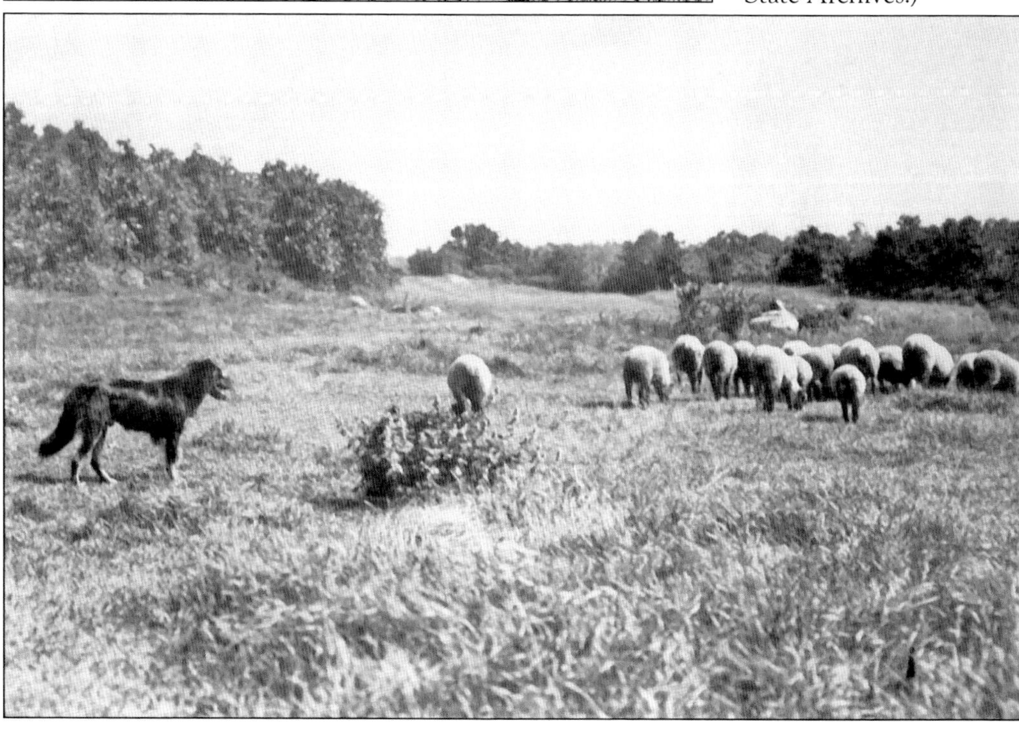

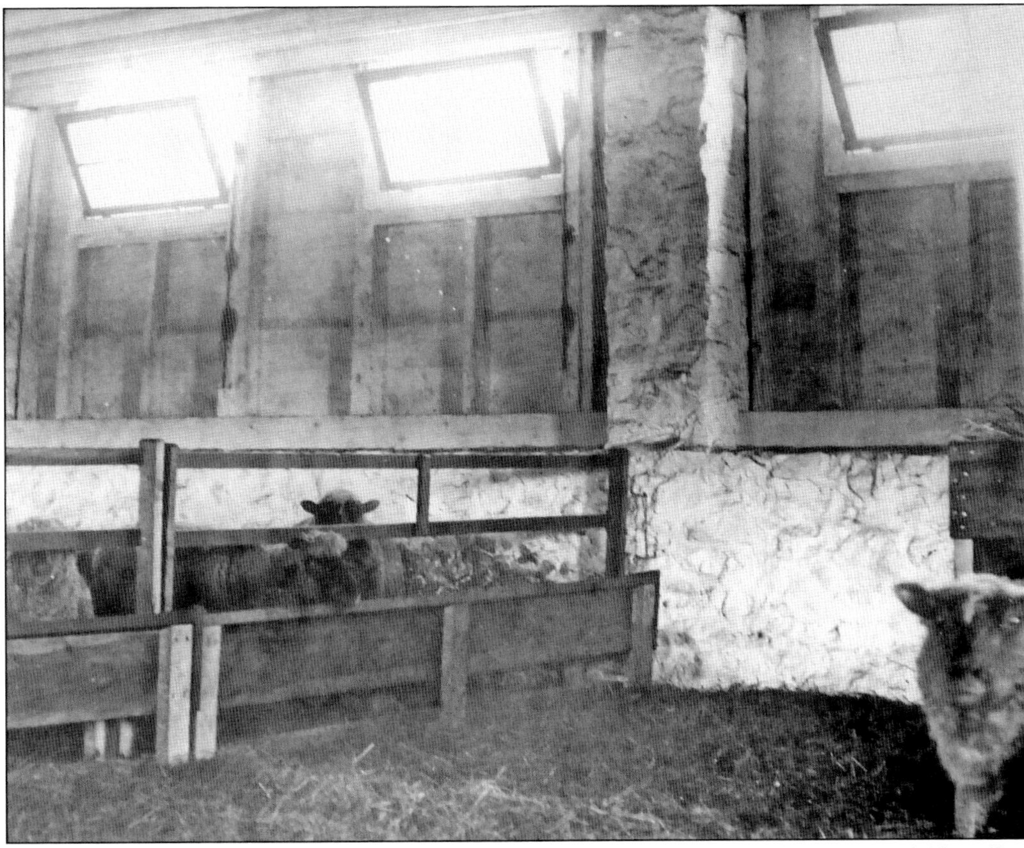

This 1905 image was taken inside the Sheepfold barn, which may have been part of Chandler's Piggery before it was taken by the MPC in 1895. In a 1908 report, the MPC notes that "the flock of sheep has steadily improved in quality, and sales therefrom have materially contributed to the cost of its (the sheepfold's) support." In 1910, when a trolley line ran through the Fells with a stop at the Sheepfold (see chapter 7), the barn was converted to Mary's Refreshment Stand, shown below in October 1937. Note signs on the roof for Moxie, an early mass-produced soft drink. According to the August 26, 1946, *Stoneham Independent*, the building was razed in 1942 due to the lack of business. (Both, courtesy of DCR Archives.)

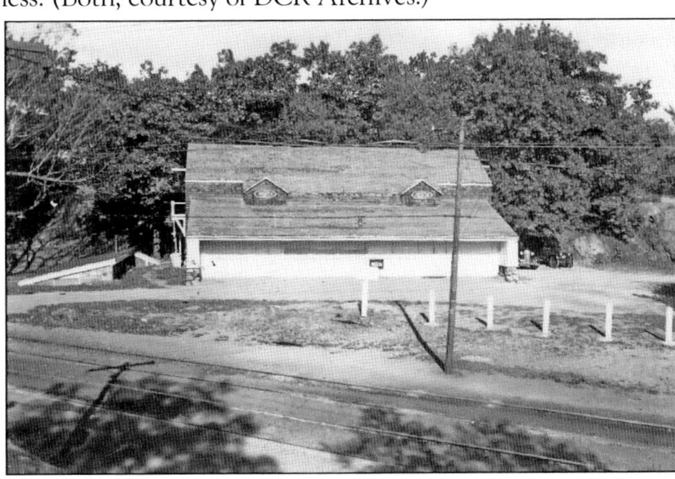

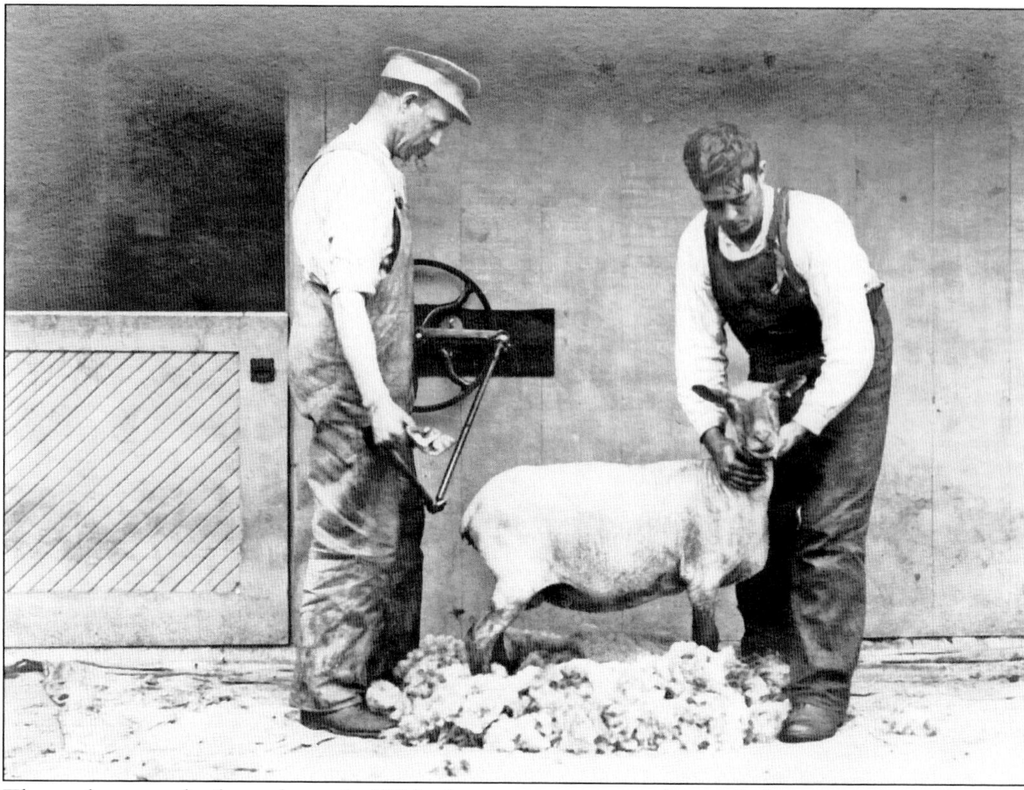

These photographs from the early 1900s show men using mechanical clippers to shear sheep. In 1888, the Wolseley Sheep Shearing Machine Company of London was the first to manufacture clippers like these. They were powered by a fixed hand crank linked to a shaft with two universal joints but had a limited range of motion. Mechanical clippers increased the number of sheep that could be sheared in a day, were less tiring to use than hand clippers, and caused the sheep less distress. (Both, courtesy of Massachusetts State Archives.)

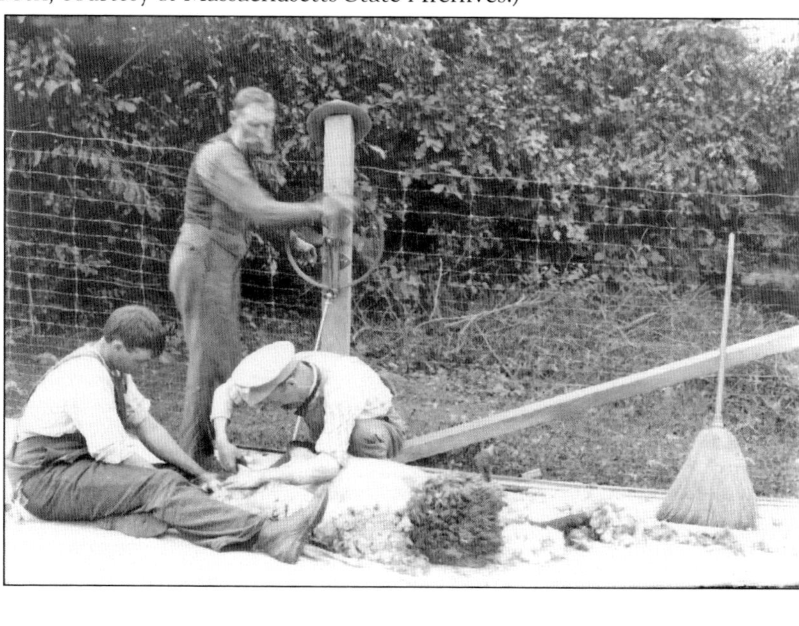

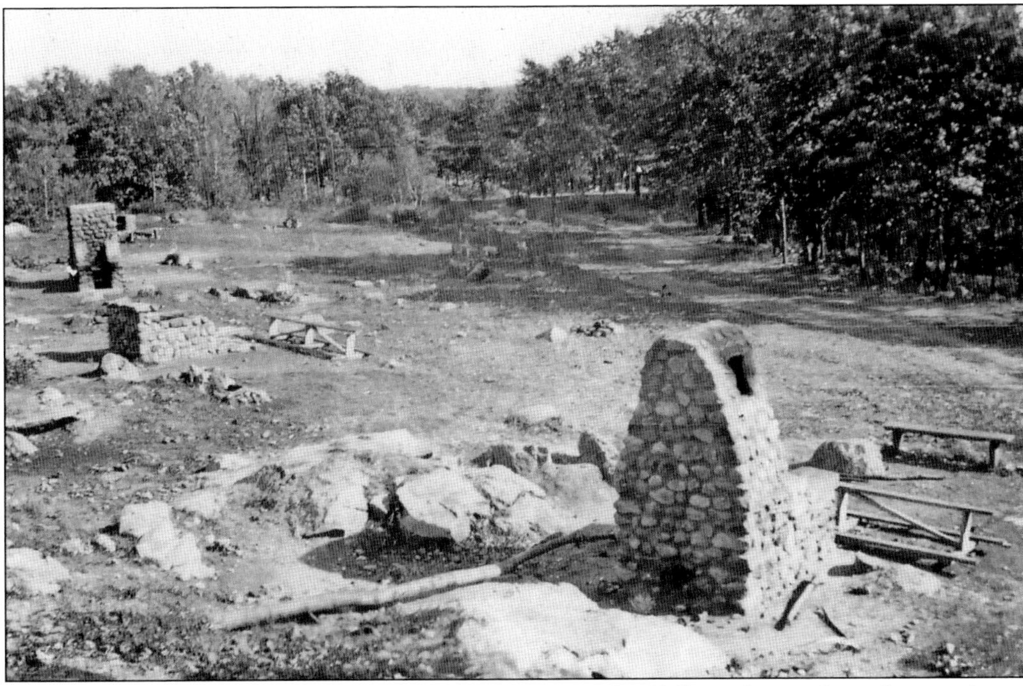

In the 1930s, in an effort to attract more visitors to the Fells and to reduce the number of unauthorized fires, the Metropolitan District Commission built this rustic camping and picnic area near the entrance to the Sheepfold. An MDC photographer captured this image in October 1937. (Courtesy of DCR Archives.)

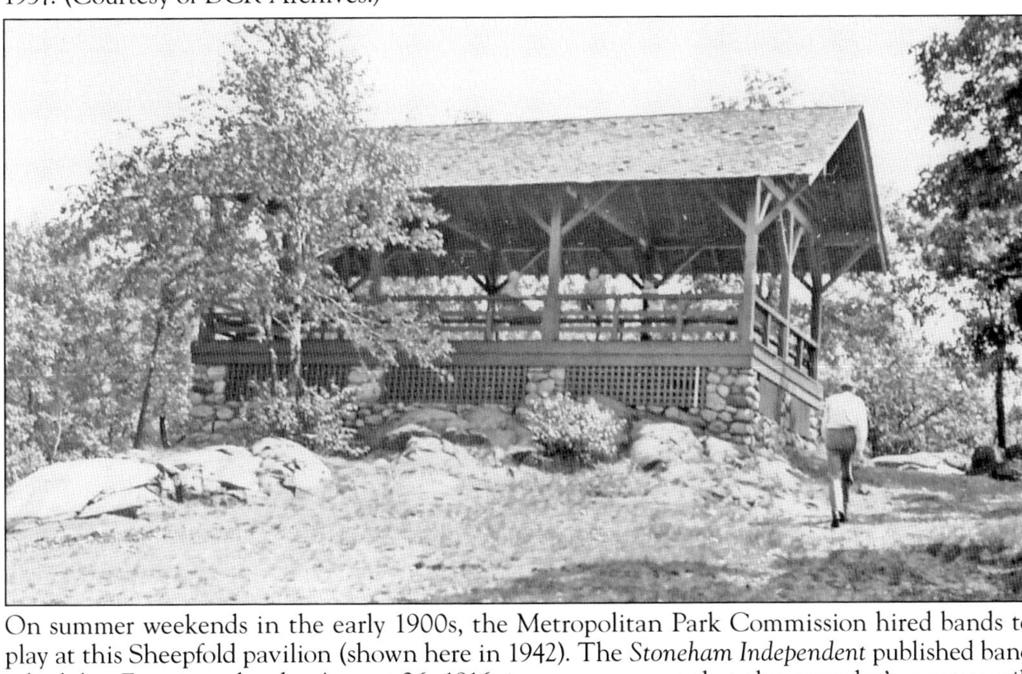

On summer weekends in the early 1900s, the Metropolitan Park Commission hired bands to play at this Sheepfold pavilion (shown here in 1942). The *Stoneham Independent* published band schedules. For example, the August 26, 1916, issue announces that the next day's concert will feature Sargent's Band, followed by Strachan's Band on September 3, and Germania Band on September 10. (Courtesy of DCR Archives.)

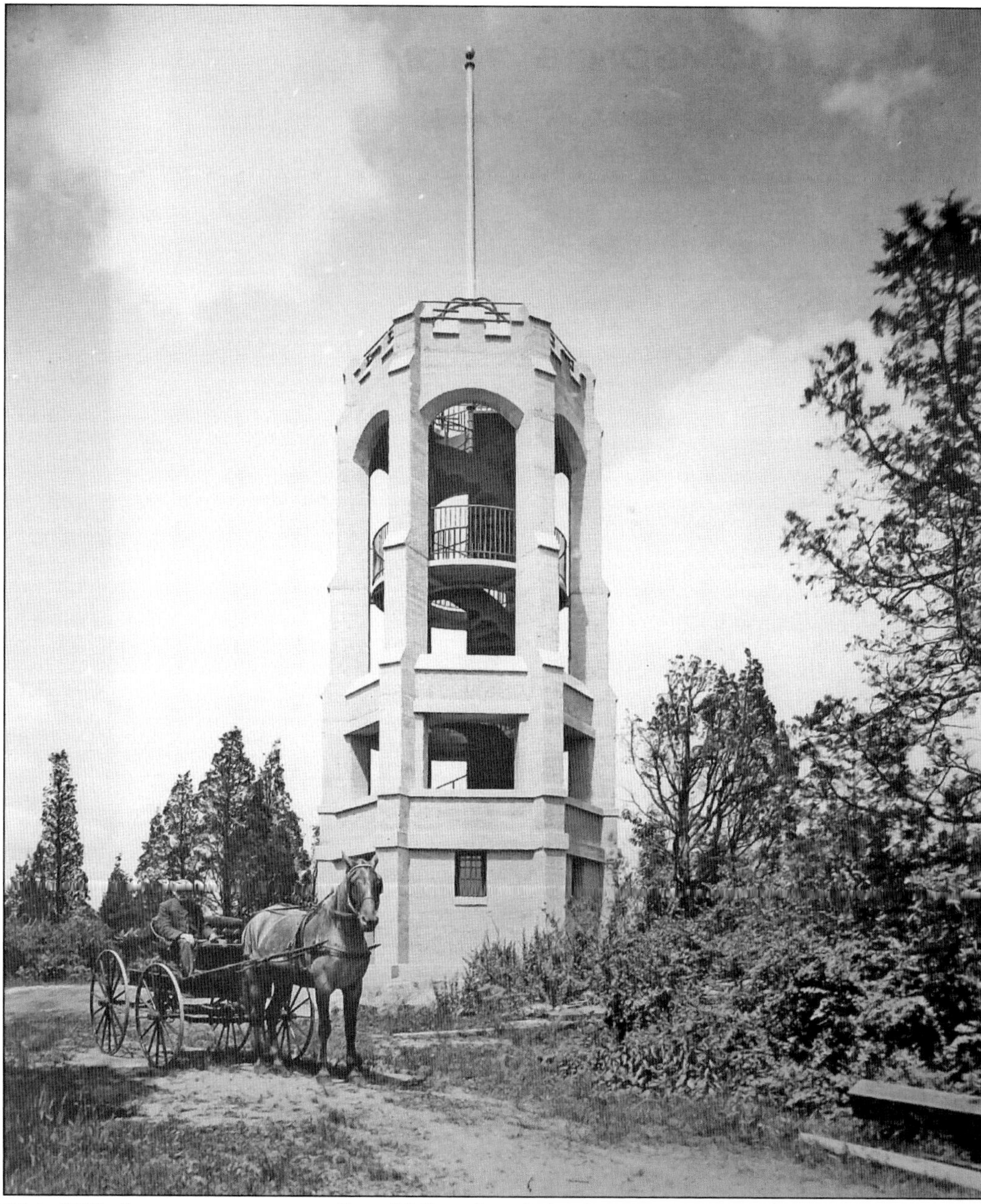

This 1910 observation tower on Bear Hill replaced the AMC's 1893 wooden tower. The MPC reported, "A new observation tower of unique and pleasing architectural form has been built of reinforced concrete." In 1632, John Winthrop viewed Spot Pond from this summit. Almost 250 years later in 1880, Elizur Wright met here with 200 friends to plan ways to protect the Fells. The tower still exists. (Photograph by Thomson and Thomson, courtesy of Historic New England.)

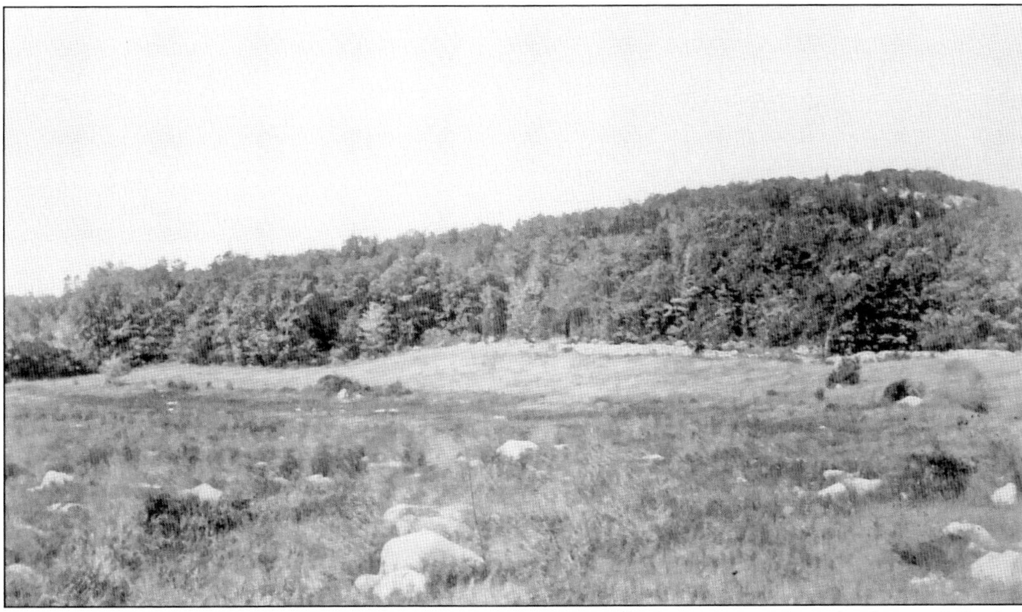

The 1895 view looking northeast (above) shows Pine Hill. Quarry Road at the base of the hill is lined with rock walls. South Border Road now crosses the foreground. The 1894 view looking north (below) shows Pine Hill. Elizur Wright's house is visible at far right. After Wright died in 1885, his children, Ellen and Walter, donated more than 20 acres, including Pine Hill, to the MPC. Wright's house was razed before 1924 and, in 1959, Interstate 93 was built across this area. (Both, photograph by Nathaniel Stebbins, courtesy of Massachusetts State Archives.)

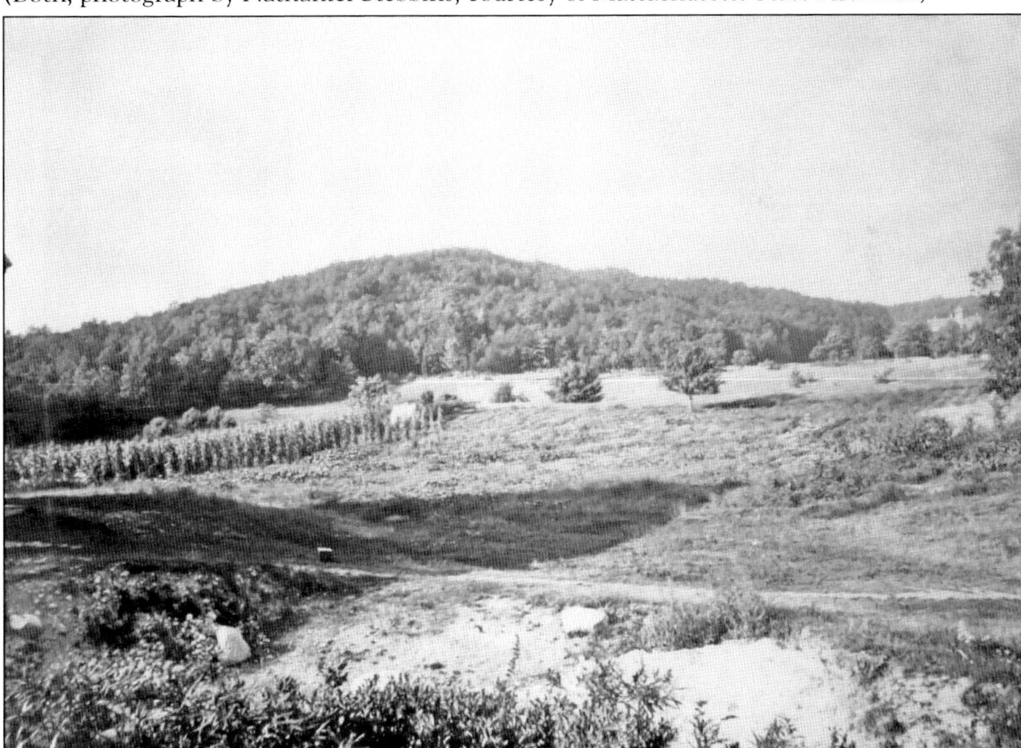

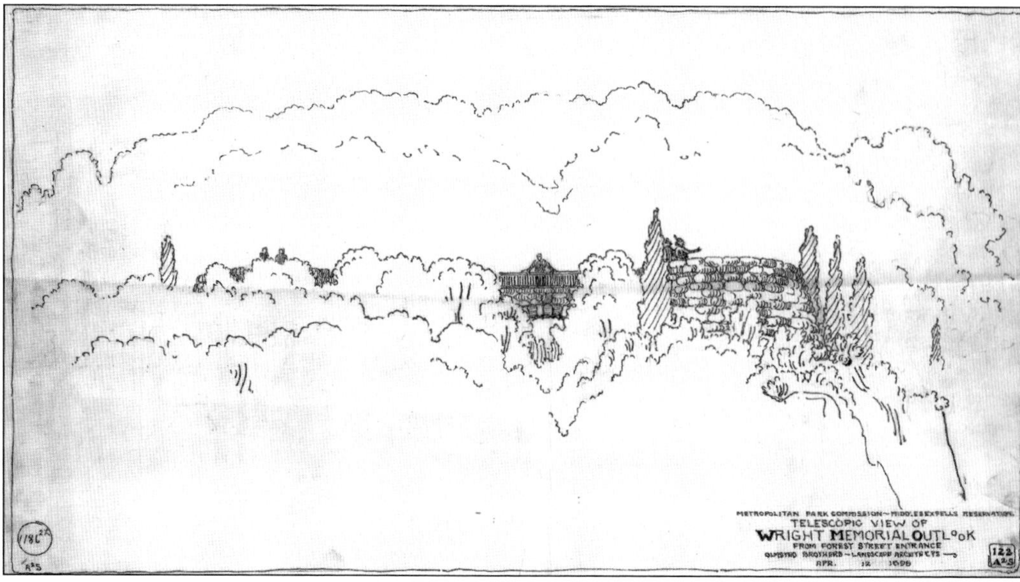

The MPC hired Olmsted Brothers, landscape architects, and Arthur Shurtleff to design a bastion or terrace monument at the summit of Pine Hill to honor Elizur Wright for his role in creating Middlesex Fells. In April 1898, Shurtleff produced these designs. Wright's daughter Ellen and others had raised over $3,000 to build the tower, but the project was put on hold because of disagreements over design and cost. In October 1937, Shurcliff (who had changed the spelling of his name in 1930) provided the MDC with a new design for a square tower using local granite. Shurcliff modeled this tower after the Great Blue Hill Observation Tower (known locally as Eliot Tower), which he had designed a few years earlier. Wright's tower remains a popular hiking destination and the top of the tower provides a spectacular view of Boston and the Blue Hills beyond. (Both, courtesy of DCR Archives.)

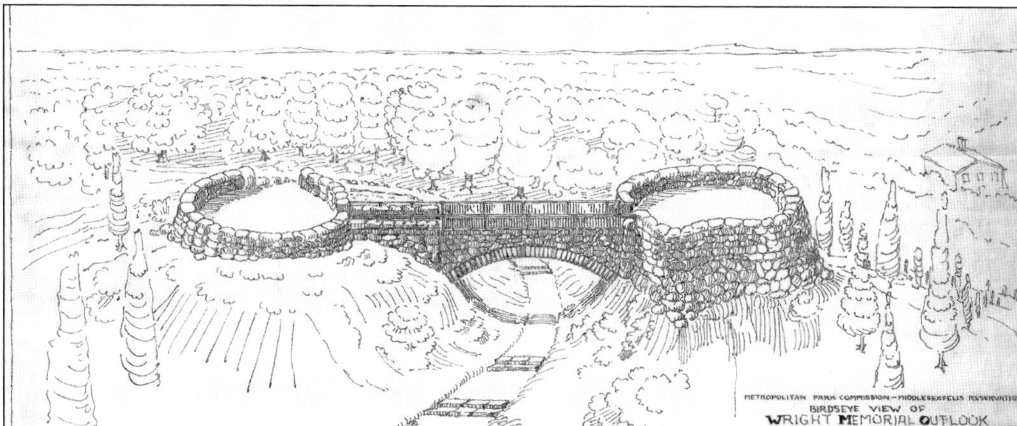

In 1937, the WPA built Wright's Tower according to Arthur Shurcliff's design shown here. He specified that "the size of the stones should conform as closely as possible to the stones used in the tower on the summit of Great Blue Hill . . . the tower is to stand as shown by the white paint marks I placed on the ledge . . . the door is to be placed on the east side." (Courtesy of DCR Archives.)

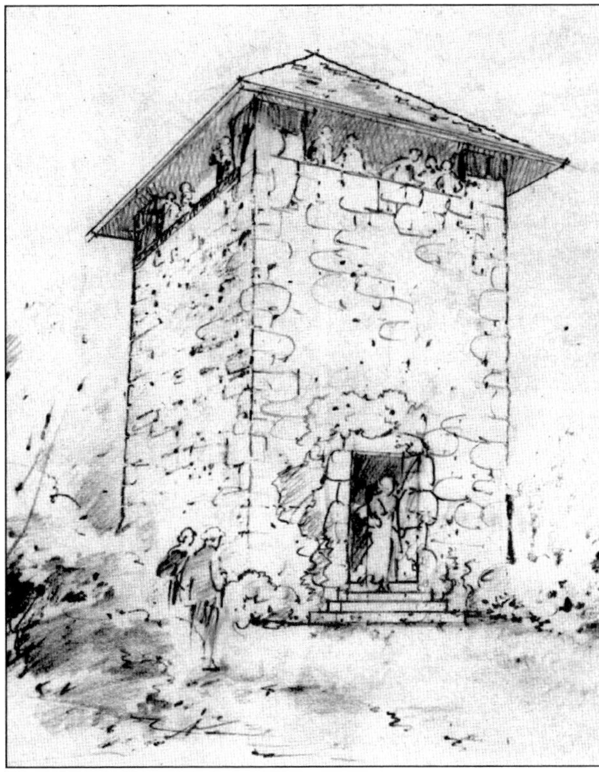

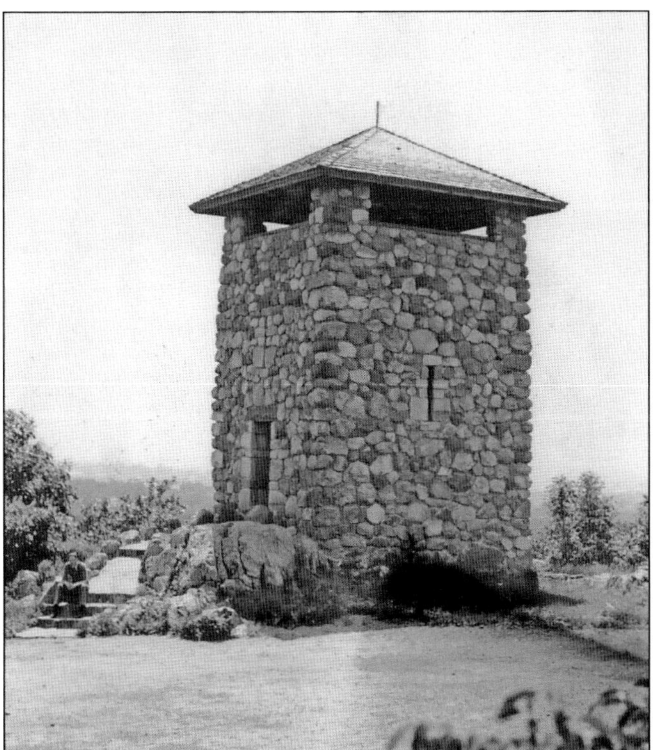

This 1942 image shows the completed tower. In 2005, Friends of the Middlesex Fells became concerned about vandalism and contacted State Rep. Paul Donato of Medford and State Sen. Patricia Jehlen, who jointly sponsored a bill that provided the DCR with $100,000 for repairs. (Courtesy of DCR Archives.)

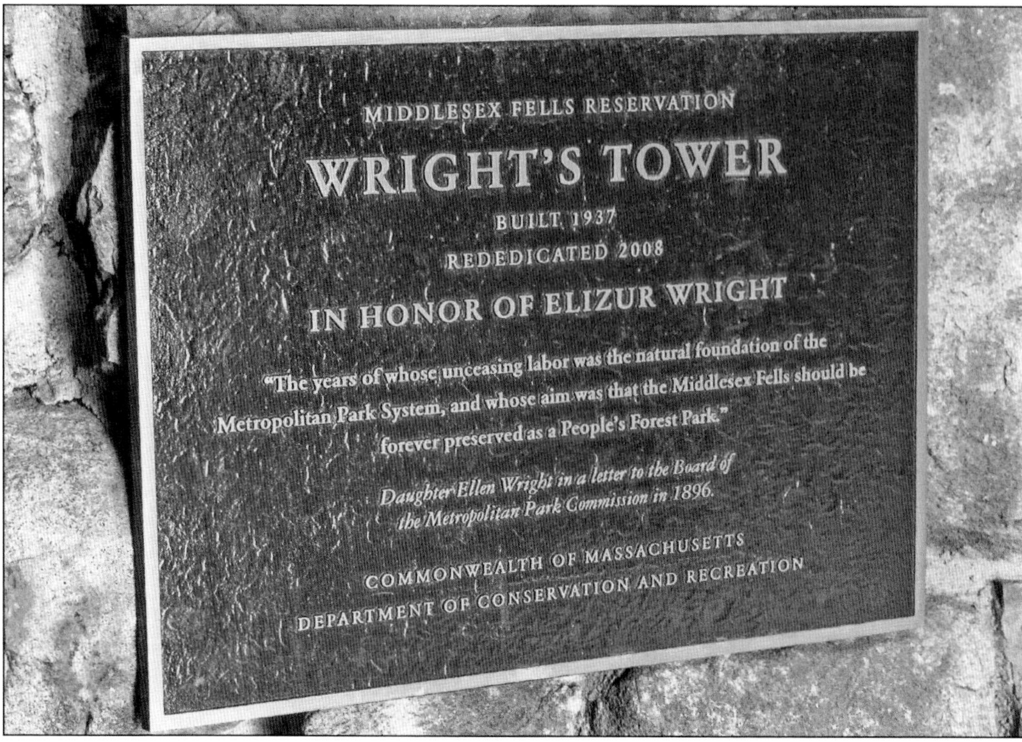

Wright's Tower was rededicated in a ceremony on Pine Hill on May 24, 2008. The DCR set a plaque inside the tower with an inscription somewhat changed from one suggested by Ellen Wright (Elizur Wright's daughter) in an August 1896 letter to the MPC. Her original wording was, "(In honor of Elizur Wright) The years of whose unceasing labor was the natural foundation of the Metropolitan Park System, and whose aim was that the 'Middlesex Fells'—known first as the 'Five Mile Woods'— and, in his time, still a more than five mile wilderness, should be wholly and at once secured, and as a People's Forest Park, its woods be forever preserved." Below, Ted Wright, Elizur's great-great-grandson, addresses the crowd. (Both, courtesy of Mike Ryan.)

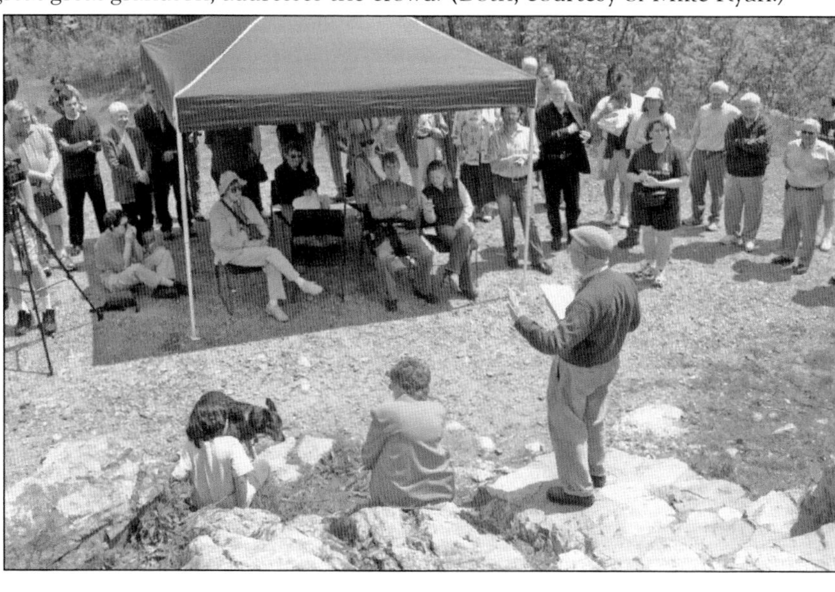

Five

Gypsy Moth Wars

É. Léopold Trouvelot (1827–1895), a French artist, astronomer, and amateur entomologist, is best known for accidentally releasing gypsy moth larvae from his house in Medford. In 1867, he returned from a trip to France with gypsy moth egg masses hoping that they might be used for silk production. About two years later, larvae escaped from Trouvelot's backyard, probably through holes in nets made by birds. About 10 years later, the first outbreaks began in his neighborhood. According to Robert J. Spear in his 2005 book on the first gypsy moth war:

> Many residents kept large metal cans, pails, or coal scuttles in their yards to receive the thousands of caterpillars they swept off their houses, brushed from trees, or picked each evening from porches, railings, and board walks. Scores of citizens brought pots of boiling water from their houses to scald the hairy crawlers on their fences, and soon the paint was blistered off of most of the pickets in Medford. Others either doused the insects with kerosene and set them ablaze or dug pits, raked the larvae in, and buried them alive.

By 1890, the moth had spread into Middlesex Fells. Under pressure to move quickly, the state passed an "Act to Provide against Depredations by the Insect known as Ocnaria Dispar or Gypsy Moth." The act established a commission to fight the moth. In 1891, Charles Riley, entomological adviser to the Gypsy Moth Committee, proposed to clear-cut the Fells. In 1893, the committee proposed to clear trees after egg-laying time, followed by complete burning of the land in winter and a second burning in the spring. When word of this plan got out, there was an uproar from the public, including Ellen Wright (Elizur's Wright's daughter), and from the Metropolitan Park Commission (MPC). The plan was shelved, and the legislature reduced and delayed funding for the Gypsy Moth Committee. After this, the committee reassessed its strategy of drastic tree cutting and focused on spraying and tree wrapping.

The moth wars continued through the 1930s. CCC men from nearby Breakheart Reservation traveled to Middlesex Fells on work details. As well as building trails and fire roads, they sprayed trees for gypsy moths. WPA workers joined them in the effort. But they failed to eradicate the pest, and the gypsy moth is now one of the most destructive insects in the eastern United States.

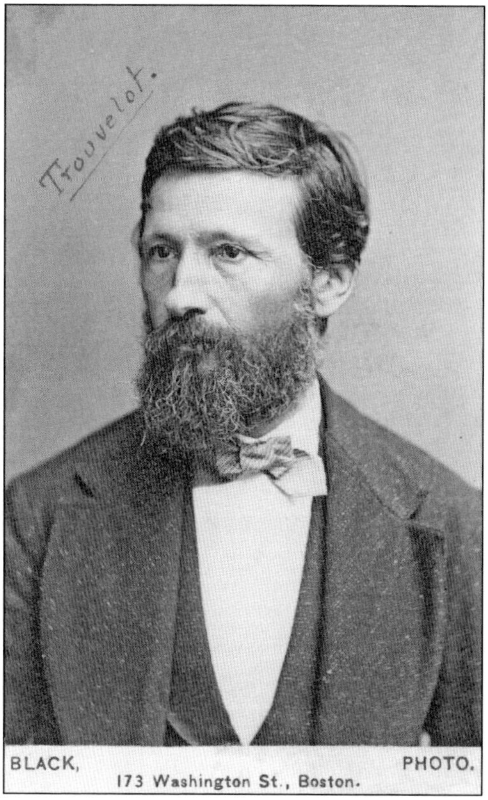

Étienne Léopold Trouvelot is best known for introducing the gypsy moth to North America. An amateur entomologist, he cultivated moth larvae on five acres behind his house. After larvae escaped their nets, he notified local entomologists, but they took no action. He went on to become an astronomical illustrator and obtained a position at the Harvard College Observatory in 1872. Working with Harvard's 15-inch refractor, Trouvelot prepared hundreds of sketches for *Astronomical Engravings from the Observatory of Harvard College* (1876). This portrait was taken by photographer James Wallace Black, famous for taking the first aerial photograph in the United States, in 1860, from a balloon above Boston. Trouvelot returned to France in 1882 to continue his work in astronomy. Below is his house on Myrtle Street in Medford in 1895. The house still exists. (Left, courtesy of the University of California Santa Cruz Special Collections; below, courtesy of DCR Archives.)

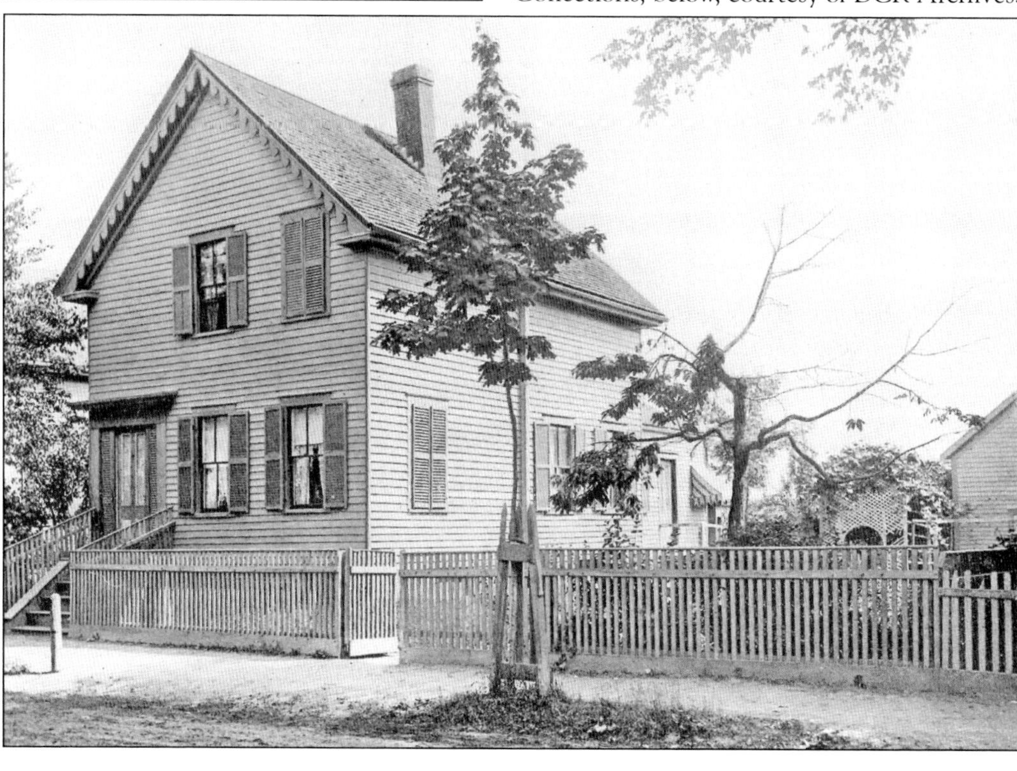

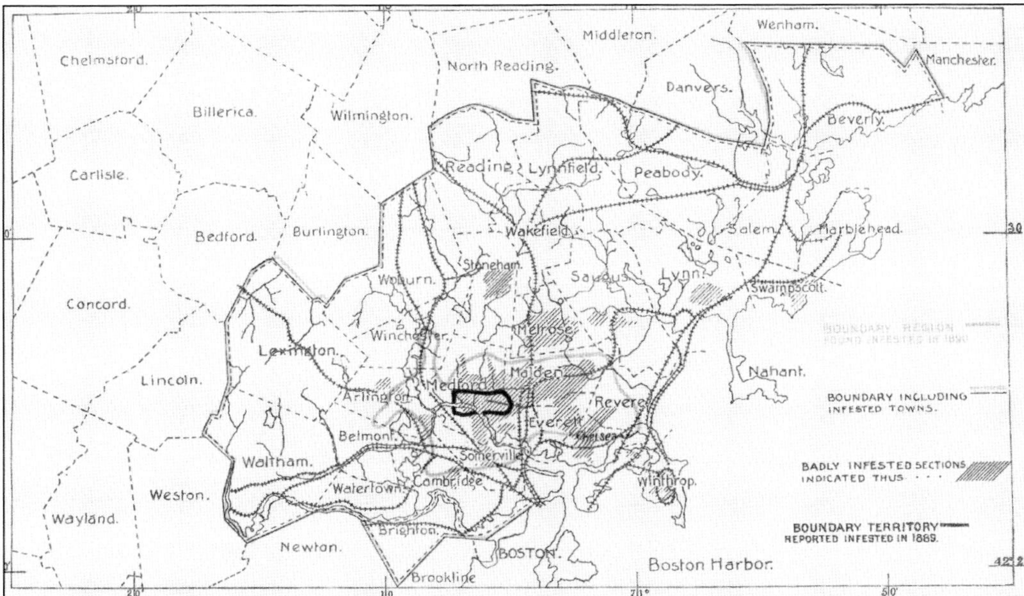

MAP II. Map showing the territory actually infested by the gypsy moth as determined in 1891 by the State Board of Agriculture, and the total areas which, in 1889 and 1890, respectively, were supposed to be infested.

This map is included in the 1896 book *The Gypsy Moth* by Edward H. Forbush and Charles H. Fernald. It shows the rapid spread and extent of gypsy moth infestation by 1891 according to the Massachusetts State Board of Agriculture. (Courtesy of DCR Archives.)

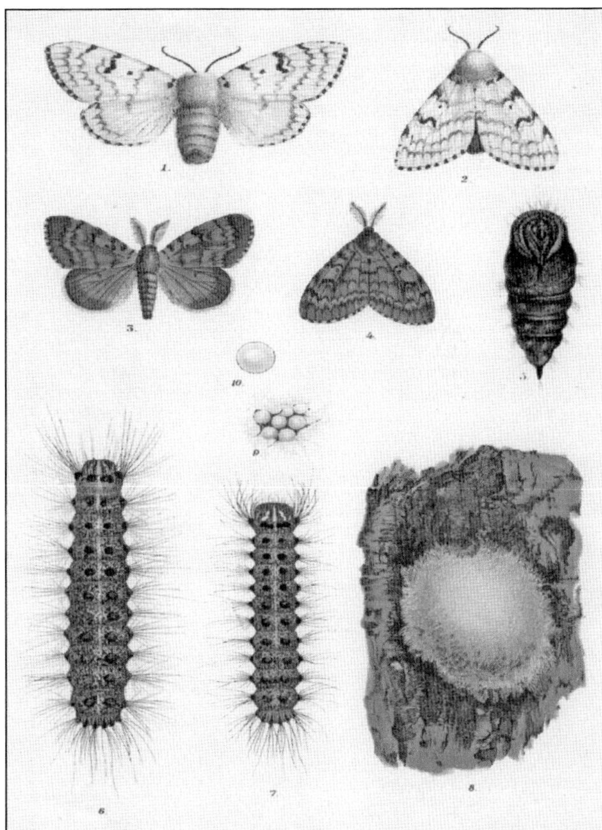

This illustration by Joseph Bridgham was published in *The Gypsy Moth*. It identifies the life stages of *Porthetria dispar*, including (from top to bottom) female with wings spread, female with wings folded, male with wings spread, male with wings folded, pupa, one greatly enlarged egg, several enlarged eggs, female caterpillar, male caterpillar, and egg cluster on bark. Each female moth can lay from 400 to 600 eggs. (Courtesy of DCR Archives.)

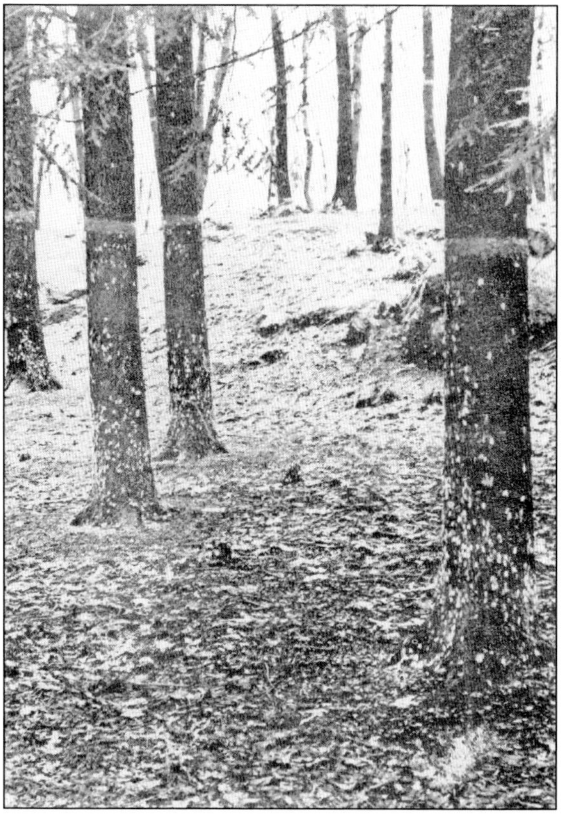

By 1889, egg clusters were on trees throughout the Medford area. According to Forbush and Fernald, egg masses winter over on trees, stones, and walls, and eggs hatch from late April through early May. Larvae reach maturity from mid-June to early July, and the pupal stage lasts from late June to early July. Adult moths emerge by mid-July. (Courtesy of DCR Archives.)

A gypsy moth crew employed by the Metropolitan Water and Sewerage Board sprays trees in July 1911 with lead arsenate. The toxic poison, also known as Disparene, was mixed with 10 parts of water. Workers are at the corner of Main and South Streets in Stoneham, north of Spot Pond, now the site of a gas station. (Photograph by Oliver Tryon, courtesy of Massachusetts State Archives.)

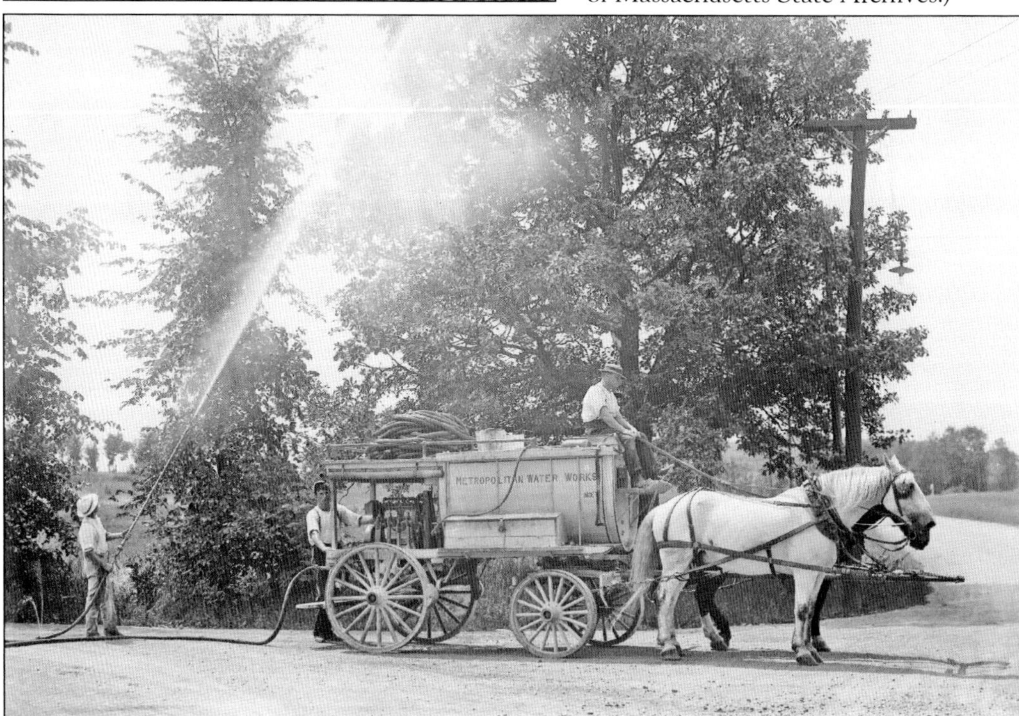

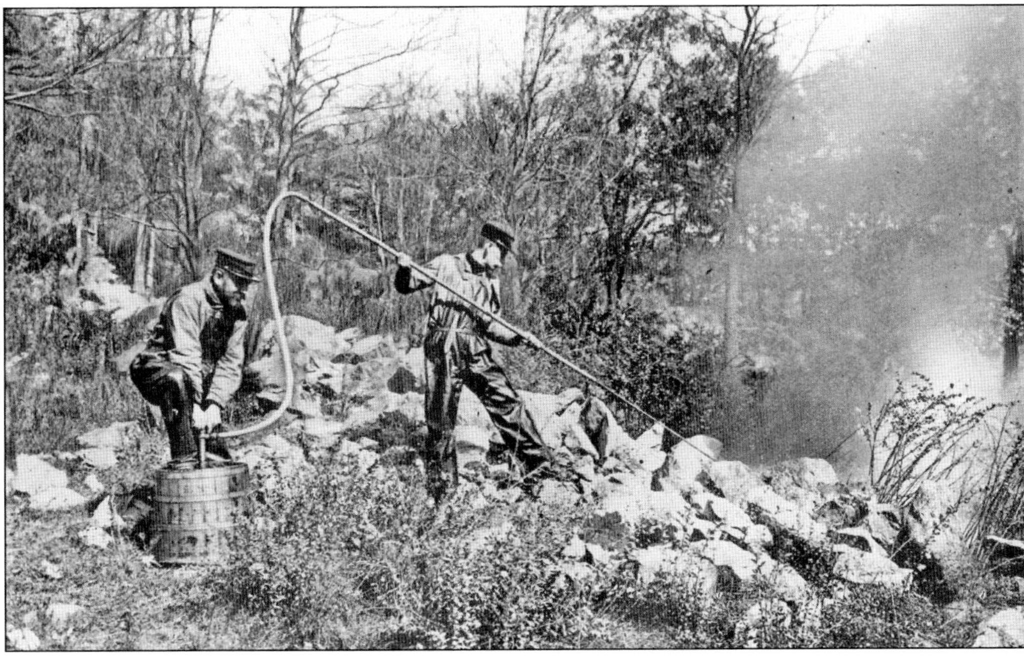

Men use a cyclone burner to kill eggs on a stone wall in Medford about 1892. Fire was one of the tools commonly used to combat the moth. After several trials, paraffin gas oil became the preferred fuel. Men worked nine hours a day, beginning at $1.50 a day. Superintendents were paid $3.00 to $3.50 a day. (Courtesy of DCR Archives.)

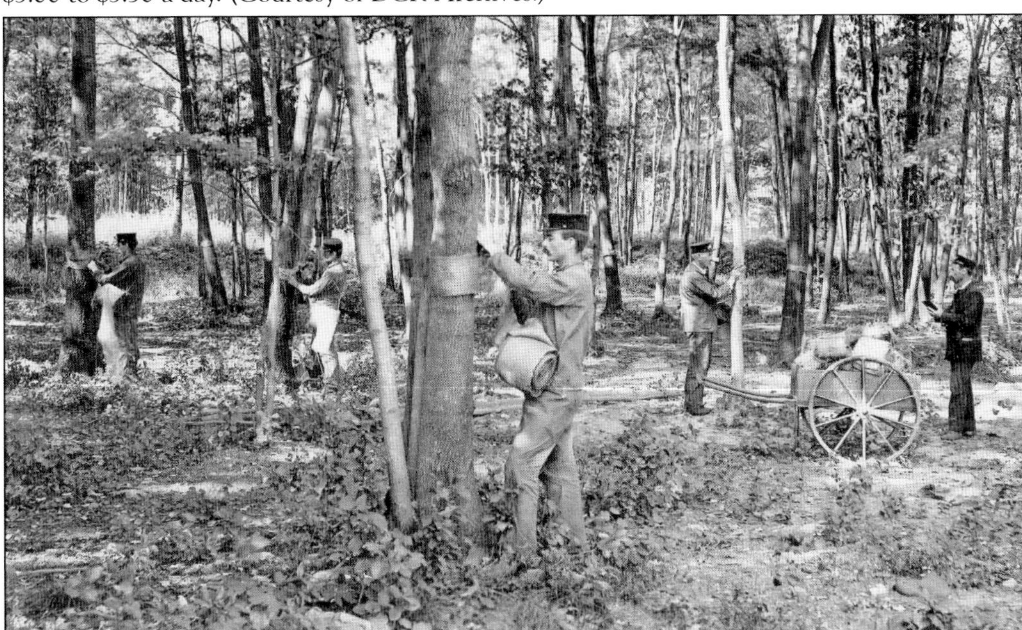

Gypsy moth inspectors apply burlap bands around tree trunks around 1893. In 1891, state researchers discovered that gypsy moth caterpillars would hide under burlap and not climb any farther. A sticky substance known as Tanglefoot, made of castor oil and vegetable gum, was also applied to tree trunks to impede the caterpillars. (Courtesy of DCR Archives.)

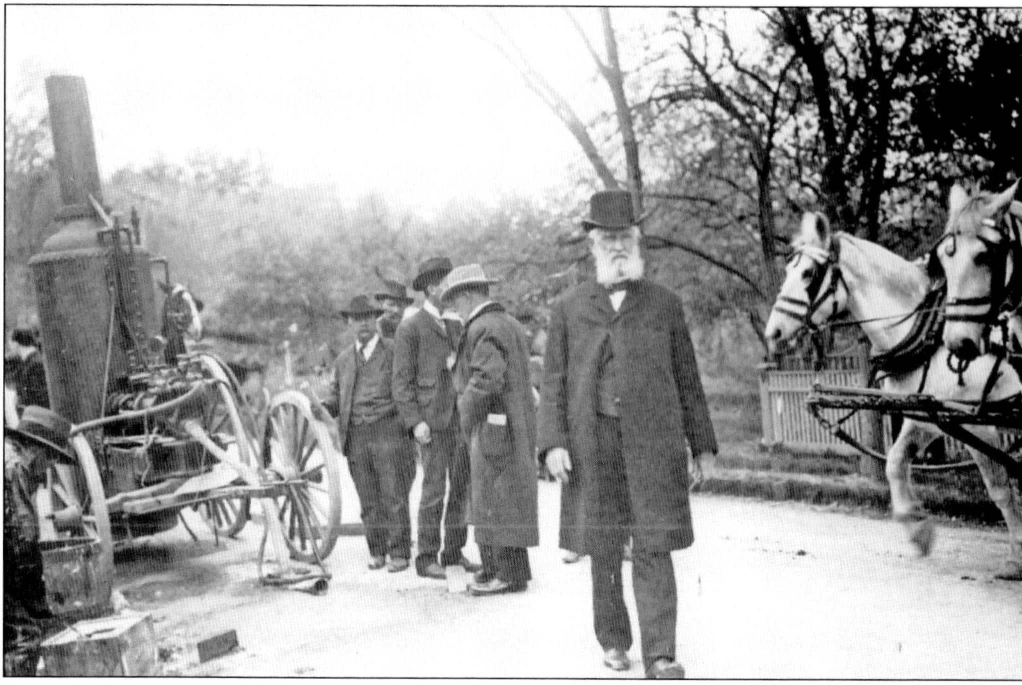

Samuel C. Lawrence (1832–1911), Medford's first mayor, was promoted to brigadier general in 1862 after injuries sustained at the First Battle of Bull Run. He inherited a large property and rum distillery business in Medford. When gypsy moths invaded his property, Lawrence reportedly spent half a million dollars of his own money to combat the pests. The image above shows an imposing Lawrence walking past a steam-powered pump used to spray lead arsenate into trees. Below, gypsy moth field inspectors pose for a photograph in the 1890s. Their dark clothing identifies them as Lawrence's employees (state employees had white uniforms.) In 1925, the Metropolitan District Commission acquired about 285 acres from Lawrence's estate and incorporated it into an area of the Fells known as Lawrence Woods. (Above, courtesy of Medford Historical Society and Museum; below, courtesy of DCR Archives.)

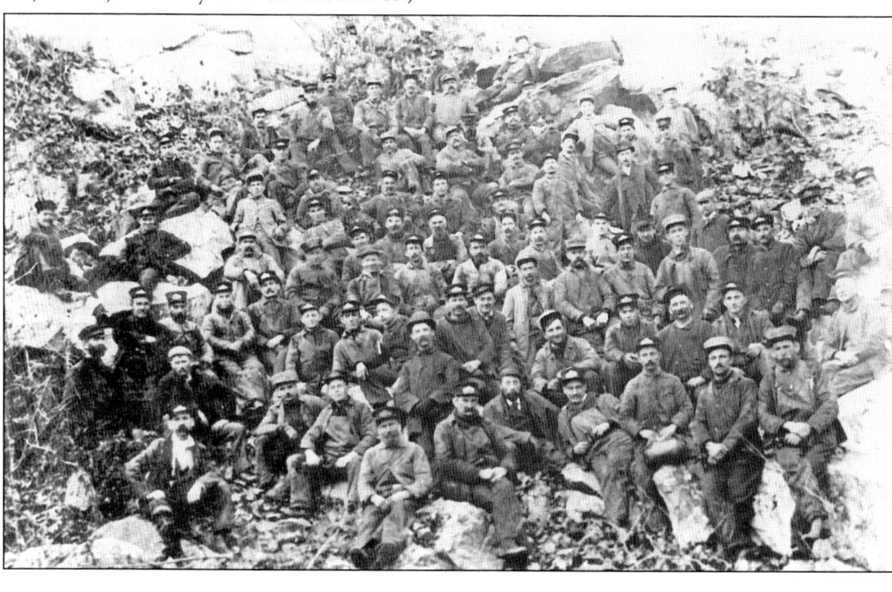

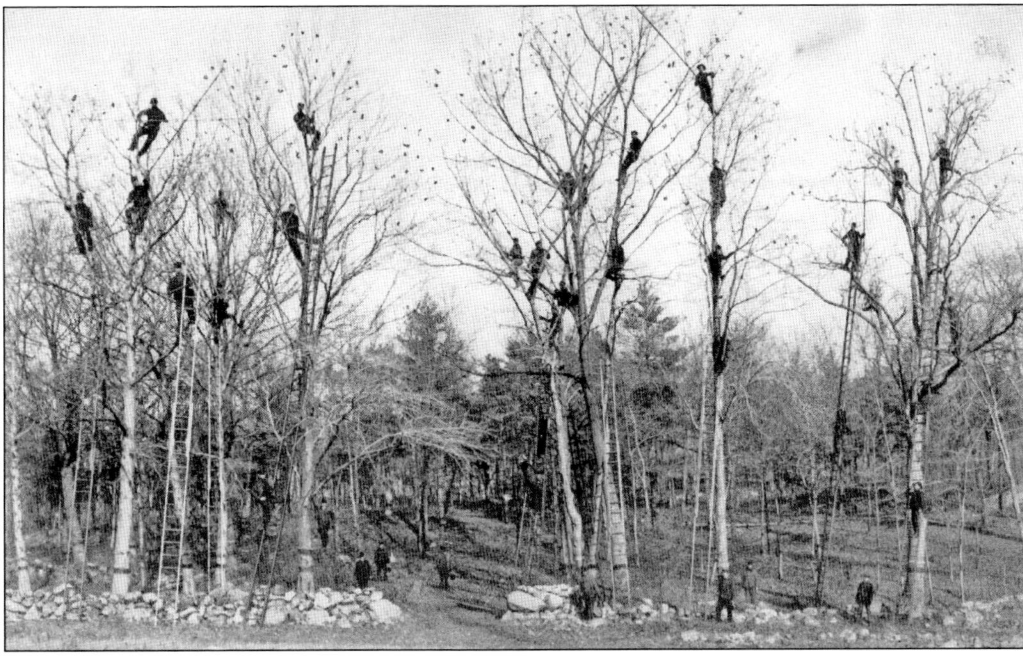

Perched high in the treetops in November 1905, workers hired by Gen. Samuel Lawrence remove gypsy moth egg masses and nests of brown-tail moths in the southwestern Fells. Foreman Thomas F. Doyle led five gangs, each with seven men. (Courtesy of DCR Archives.)

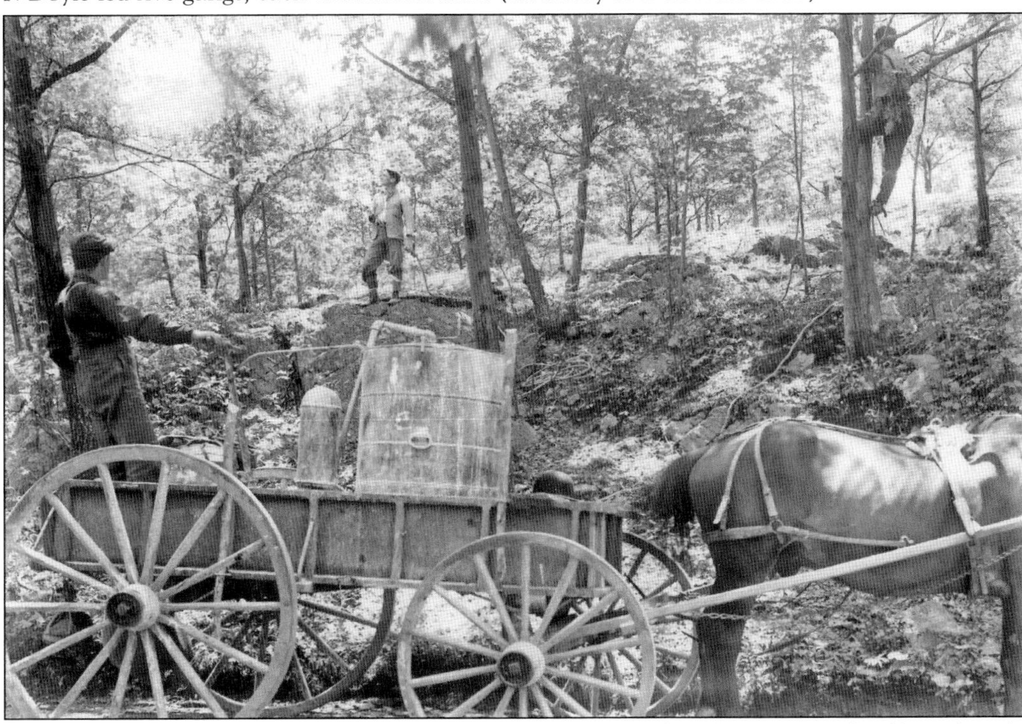

Workmen remove egg masses and spray lead arsenate from a hand pump on a buckboard in the Fells on June 14, 1906. Larger pumps powered by steam and gasoline engines sprayed up to 150 feet into roadside trees and shrubs. (Courtesy of DCR Archives.)

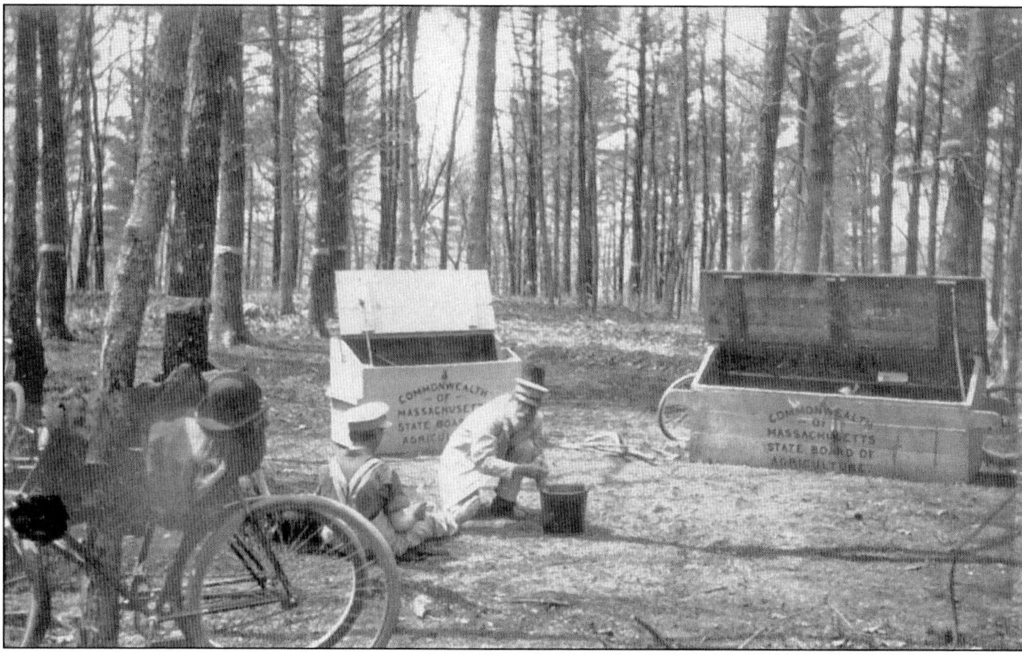

On May 9, 1898, Arthur Shurtleff of Olmsted Brothers, landscape architects, took this photograph of men from the State Board of Agriculture as they prepared to thin trees and destroy egg masses in a grove north of Wright's Pond. Below, inspectors pose for a group portrait. (Above, courtesy of the National Park Service, ONHS; below, courtesy of DCR Archives.)

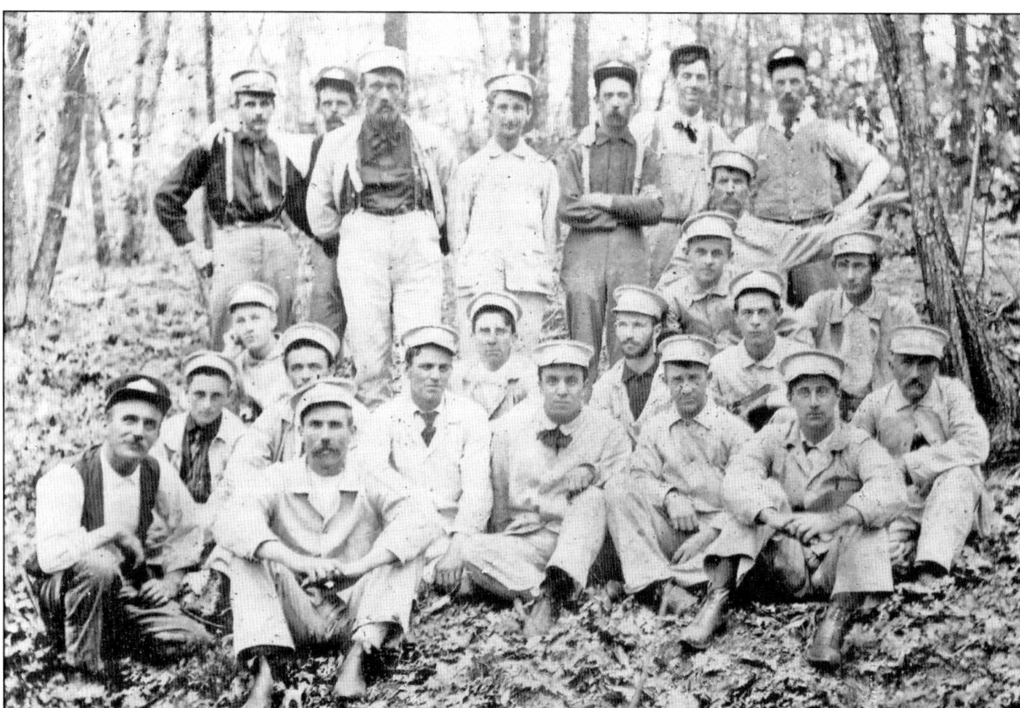

Six

Stone Zoo

From the late 1600s, a farm existed near the northeastern shore of Spot Pond. It was owned, in turn, by Joseph Browne, Daniel Gould, Pamelia Gould, Philander Ames, Rebekah Ames, and Charles Frost before it was taken in July 1891 by the Spot Pond Water Company. In 1898, it was transferred to the Metropolitan Water Board. Charles P. Price, first superintendent of Middlesex Fells Reservation, lived at the farm from 1896 to 1908. While there, he began keeping wildlife caught on the reservation. The collection eventually attracted public interest. In 1905, the state gave it a budget and called it the Middlesex Fells Zoo. By 1930, the zoo had 458 animals, mostly local species, and attracted 5,000 to 10,000 visitors on Sundays. However, typical of early 20th-century zoos, most animals were kept in small concrete enclosures.

In the 1950s, thousands flocked to an attraction called the Kiddy Zoo, based on Mother Goose stories. But more ambitious plans were soon in the works. In 1959, Walter Stone became director of the Middlesex Fells and Franklin Park Zoos and brought in large, exotic animals, such as elephants, giraffes, zebras, and a pygmy hippopotamus, and oversaw construction of an aviary. However, Stone's tenure was cut short in 1968 by his death in a head-on car crash in New Hampshire. In 1969, the zoo was renamed the Walter D. Stone Memorial Zoo.

Stone Zoo was popular during the 1970s and 1980s, but closed for two years after the state cut its funding in 1990. Debate ensued about the fate of the animals. Over 450 were moved to Franklin Park and other zoos, but several remained at the Stoneham site, including Major, the legendary polar bear, and some colobus monkeys. After the zoo closed in November 1990, Richard R. Tisei, the area's state senator, sponsored legislation creating Zoo New England (ZNE), a nonprofit corporation, to run both Franklin Park and Stone Zoos. ZNE redid the zoo layout, emphasizing smaller animals such as cranes, snow leopards, gray wolves, gibbons, river otters, and black bears, and reopened Stone Zoo on June 6, 1992. In July 2009, ZNE threatened to close if Gov. Deval Patrick carried out a proposal to cut $4 million from the zoo's budget. Most funding was restored, and the zoo remains open.

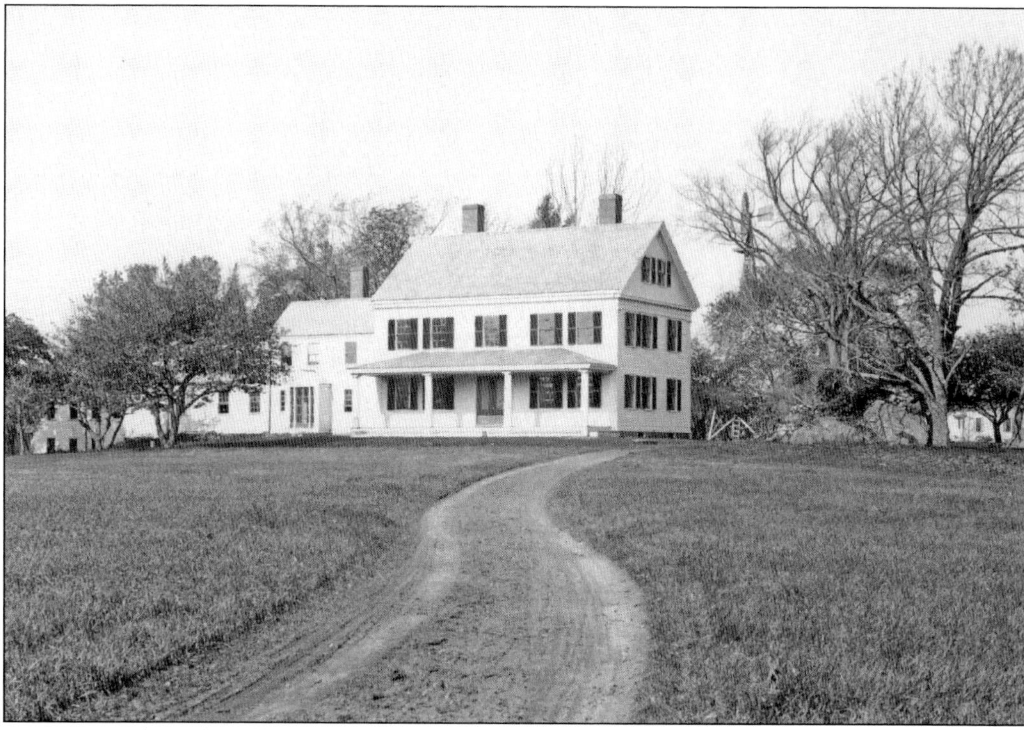

In 1896, Nathaniel Stebbins captured this view of the Gould-Frost farmhouse. Daniel Gould, grandson of Stoneham settler John Gould, bought the property from Joseph Browne in 1712. On the evening of November 25, 1819, three thieves entered the house and stabbed Jacob Gould, Daniel's descendant. They made off with over 1,000 silver dollars. Gould died the next day. The farm eventually became part of Middlesex Fells Zoo, but was razed in the 1960s. (Courtesy of Massachusetts State Archives.)

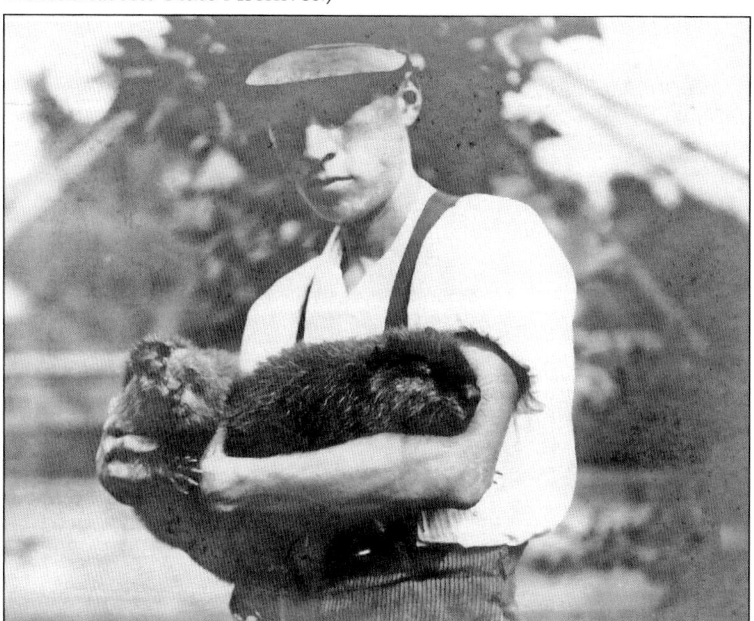

A Middlesex Fells Zoo worker holds two animals from the local woods. By 1900, the zoo had, among other animals, porcupines, Canada geese, foxes, partridges, hawks, owls, and pintail ducks. Edward A. Brackett, a Massachusetts fish and game commissioner (see page 70), raised ring-necked pheasants behind his house in Winchester and donated several to the zoo. (Courtesy of DCR Archives.)

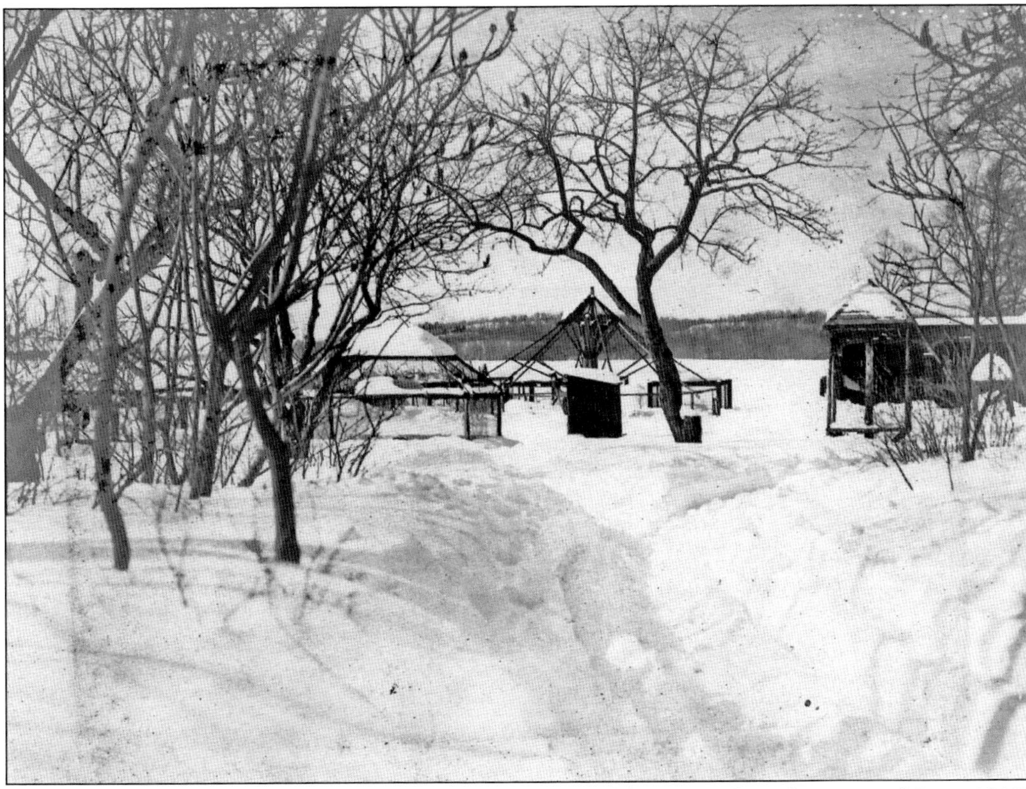

These images show the Middlesex Fells Zoo in winter (about 1905) and summer (about 1912). Many zoo animals were kept in crude indoor shelters. By 1912, the zoo had added nonnative animals, such as a wildcat and a bear from Maine. (Above, courtesy of DCR Archives; below: courtesy of Historic New England.)

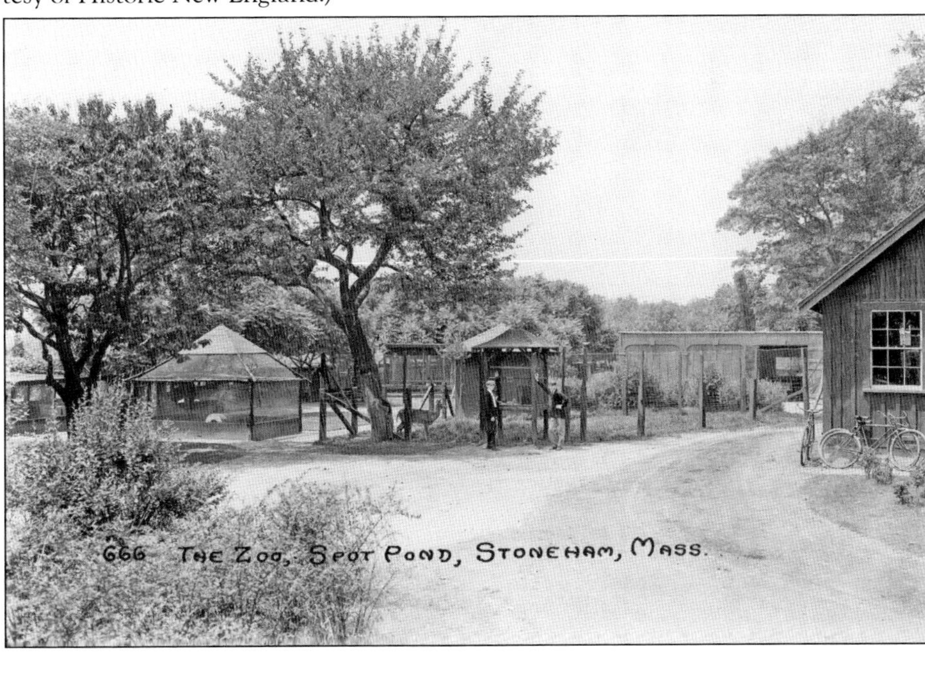

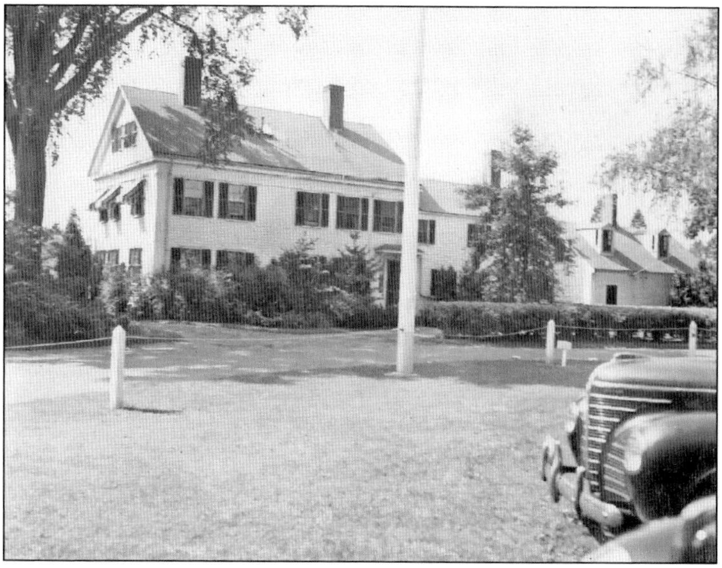

This view shows the Gould-Frost Farm at the Middlesex Fells Zoo in 1942. The farm, like many in New England, had outbuildings connecting the farmhouse and barn to reduce the need to go outside during winter. From 1896 to 1908, Charles P. Price, first superintendent of Middlesex Fells, lived in the farmhouse, as did Walter D. Stone and his family five decades later. (Courtesy of DCR Archives.)

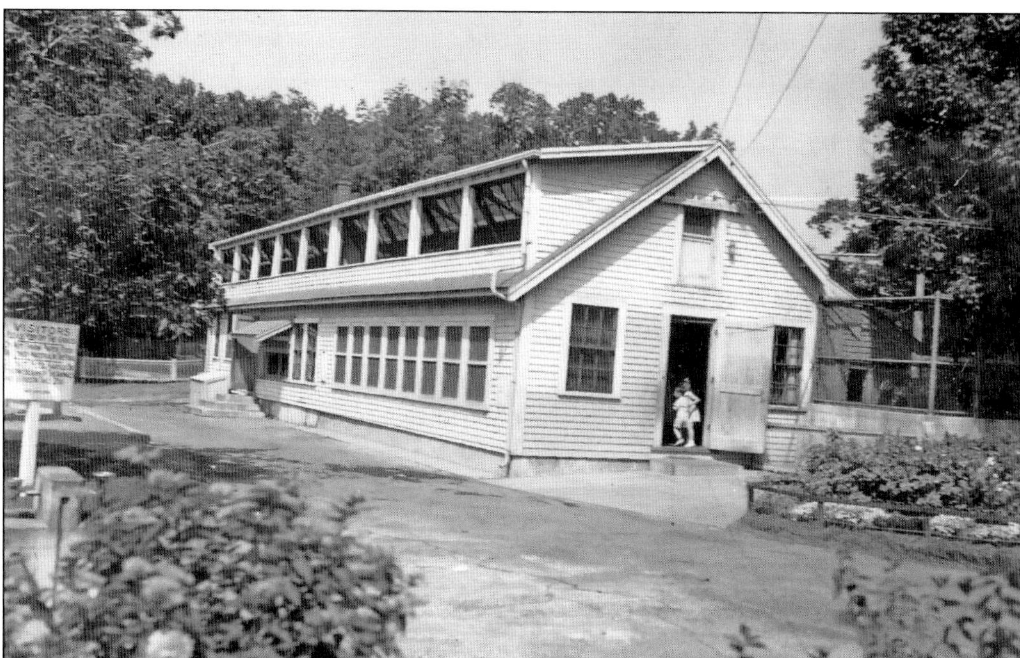

The monkey house, shown here in 1942, also contained lions, tigers, and venomous snakes. After injuring its keeper in November 1948, a tiger escaped from its cage. About 35 people quickly fled through both doors. After three hours, MDC police shot and killed the tiger when they could not lure it back to its cage. Outside, more than 500 people were held back by mounted police and traffic was tied up by curious motorists. (Courtesy of DCR Archives.)

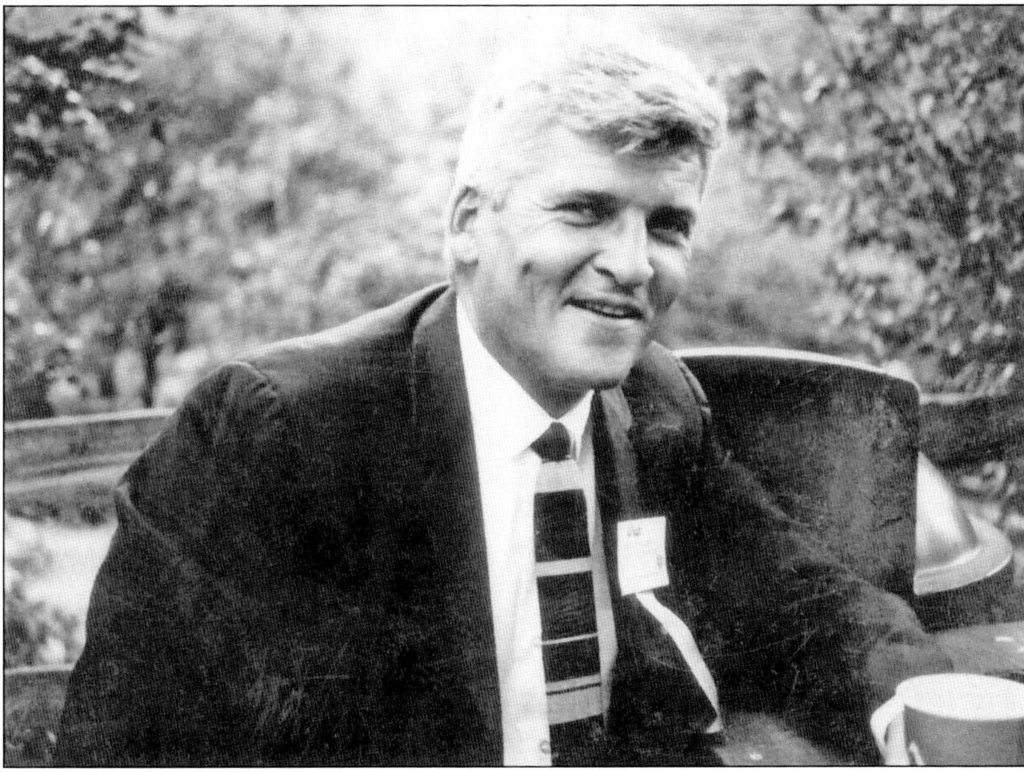

Walter D. Stone (1925–1968), a native of Worcester, Massachusetts, was curator and director of the Middlesex Fells and Franklin Park Zoos from 1959 to 1968 and president of the American Association of Zoological Parks and Aquariums. On September 23, 1968, he was killed in a head-on car collision in Londonderry, New Hampshire, leaving behind his wife, Betty, and nine children. (Courtesy of DCR Archives.)

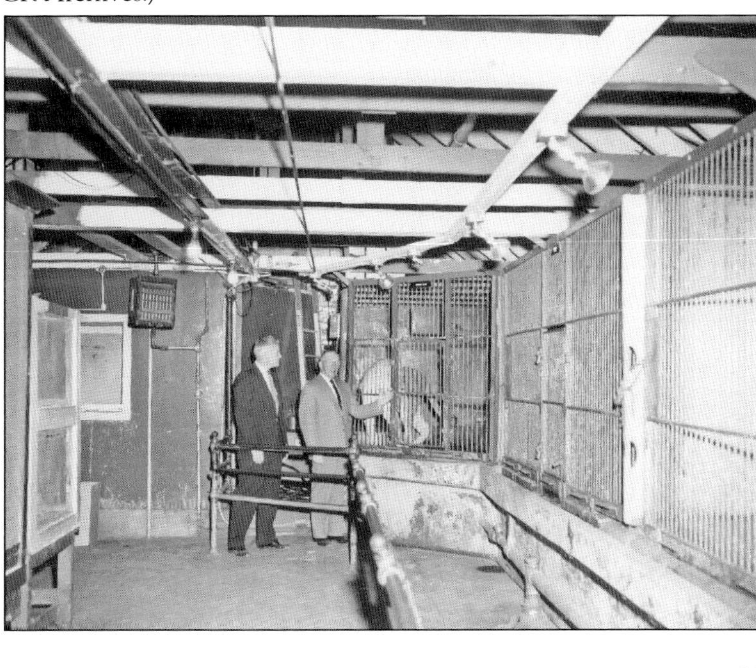

Walter Stone (left) and a colleague inspect the lion, tiger, and leopard cages located on the north side of the monkey house. During his tenure, Stone greatly improved zoo facilities, increased public attendance, and updated animal habitats at both Franklin Park and Middlesex Fells Zoos. (Courtesy of DCR Archives.)

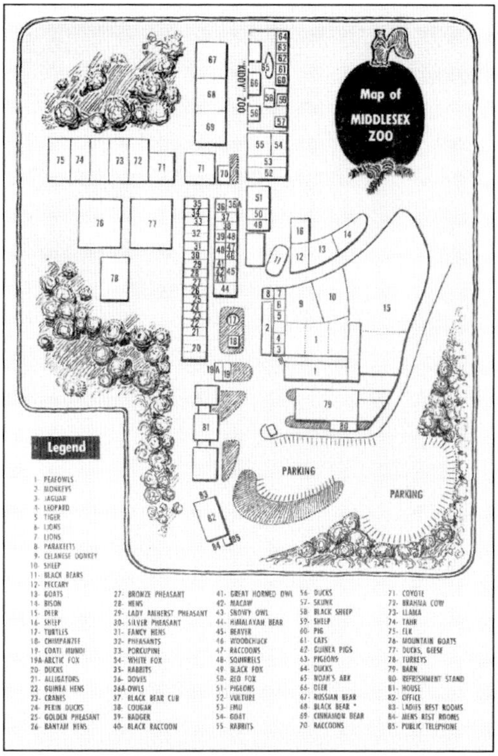

The Middlesex Fells Zoo published the map at left in 1956. At this time, the zoo had over 60 animal species, including lions from Africa, bears from Russia, and macaws from South America. Walter Stone made many changes after he became zoo director in 1959. The 1971 aerial photograph below is strikingly different from the 1956 map. Among additions were otter and seal exhibits (round tank at lower center) and a large aviary (right center). Elephants were in the square building (upper center), and other large animals roamed in an open area (upper left). From 1971 to 2000, the popular polar bear, Major, lived in the semicircular enclosure (left side of large exhibit building), now the home of black bears from Georgia. Except for the aviary, many buildings and exhibit areas still remain, although some are greatly modified. (Both, courtesy of DCR Archives.)

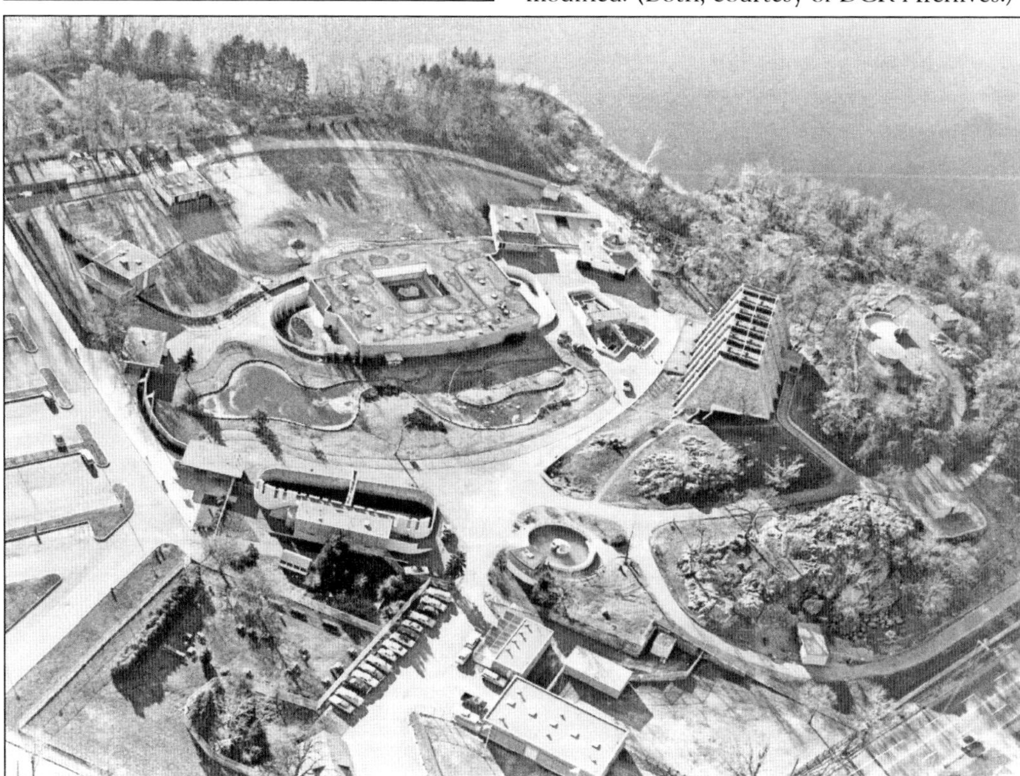

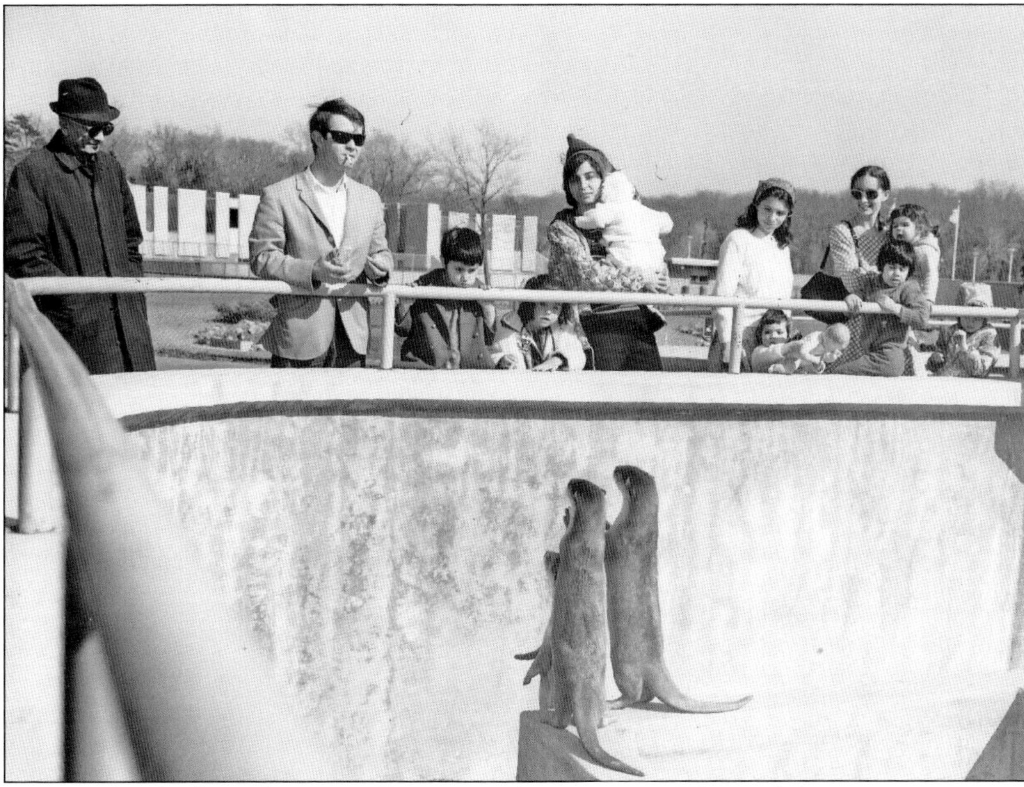

Otters and seals, shown here in 1967, were popular attractions. These exhibits were among many that were added while Walter Stone was curator at both the Middlesex Fells and Franklin Park Zoos. (Both, courtesy of DCR Archives.)

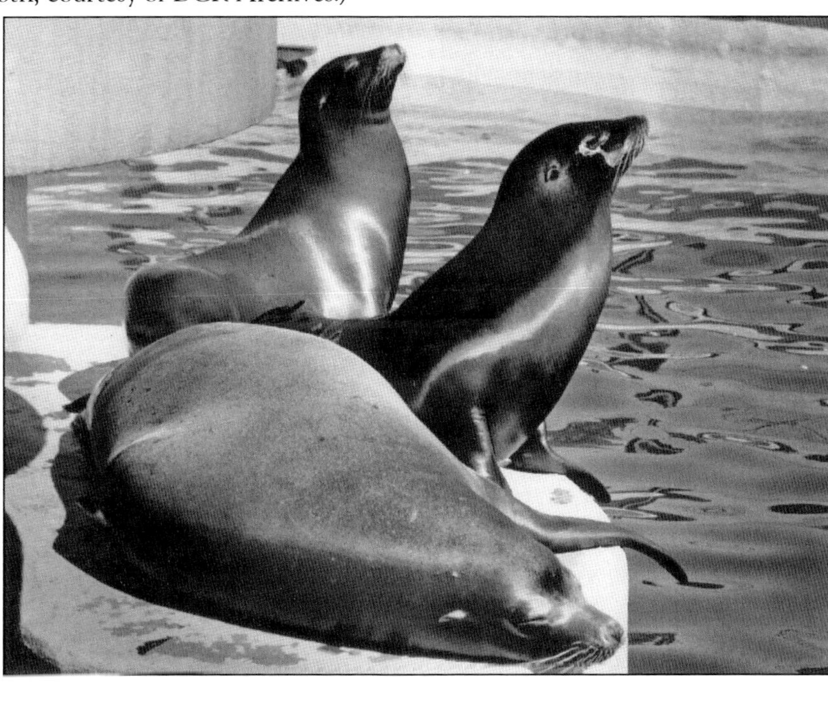

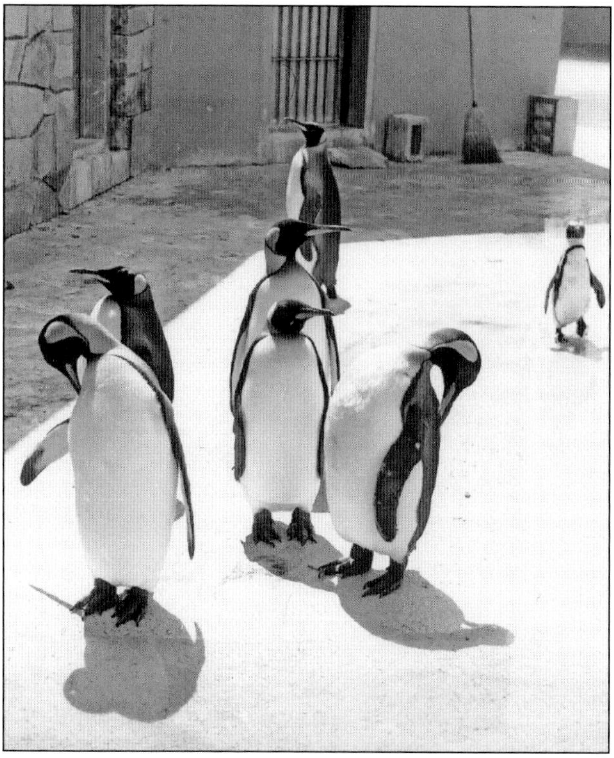

Penguins, shown here on a sunny day in May 1967, were highly popular. The zoo, now managed by the nonprofit corporation Zoo New England, no longer has penguins, but has other birds that live in or near water, including flamingos, black-necked cranes, hooded mergansers, and whooping cranes. (Courtesy of DCR Archives.)

The Middlesex Fells Zoo published a guidebook in 1956, featuring short descriptions of its expanding collection of native and exotic animals. (Courtesy of DCR Archives.)

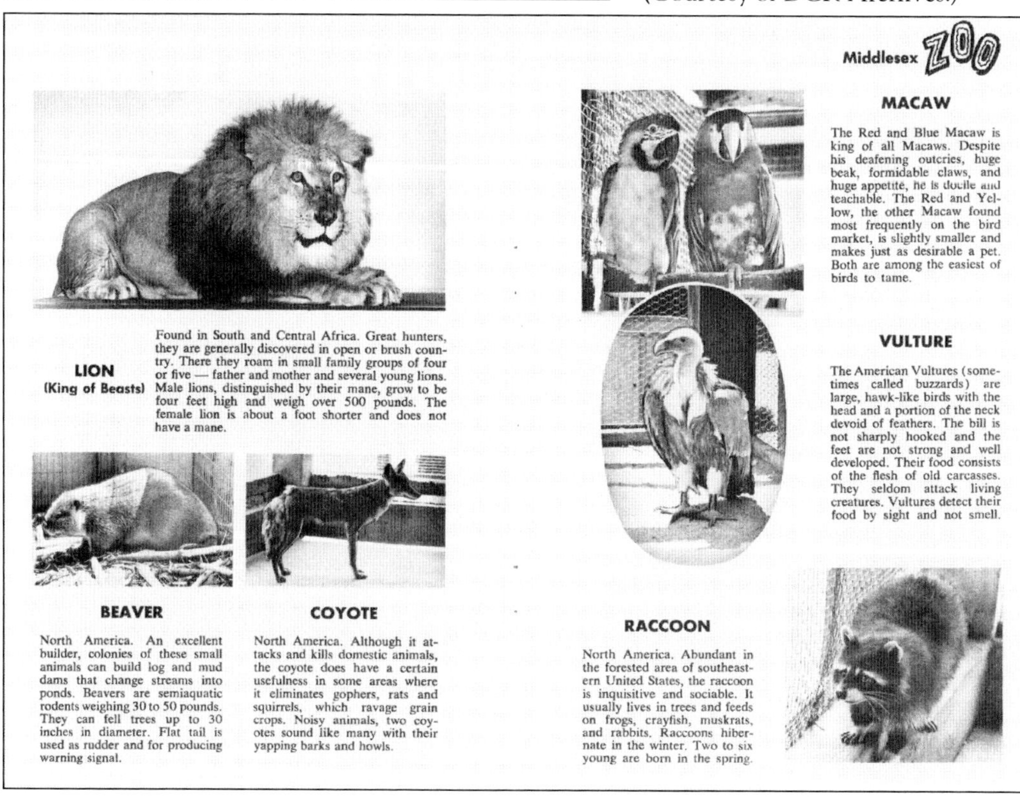

Middlesex ZOO

LION (King of Beasts)

Found in South and Central Africa. Great hunters, they are generally discovered in open or brush country. There they roam in small family groups of four or five — father and mother and several young lions. Male lions, distinguished by their mane, grow to be four feet high and weigh over 500 pounds. The female lion is about a foot shorter and does not have a mane.

BEAVER

North America. An excellent builder, colonies of these small animals can build log and mud dams that change streams into ponds. Beavers are semiaquatic rodents weighing 30 to 50 pounds. They can fell trees up to 30 inches in diameter. Flat tail is used as rudder and for producing warning signal.

COYOTE

North America. Although it attacks and kills domestic animals, the coyote does have a certain usefulness in some areas where it eliminates gophers, rats and squirrels, which ravage grain crops. Noisy animals, two coyotes sound like many with their yapping barks and howls.

MACAW

The Red and Blue Macaw is king of all Macaws. Despite his deafening outcries, huge beak, formidable claws, and huge appetite, he is docile and teachable. The Red and Yellow, the other Macaw found most frequently on the bird market, is slightly smaller and makes just as desirable a pet. Both are among the easiest of birds to tame.

VULTURE

The American Vultures (sometimes called buzzards) are large, hawk-like birds with the head and a portion of the neck devoid of feathers. The bill is not sharply hooked and the feet are not strong and well developed. Their food consists of the flesh of old carcasses. They seldom attack living creatures. Vultures detect their food by sight and not smell.

RACCOON

North America. Abundant in the forested area of southeastern United States, the raccoon is inquisitive and sociable. It usually lives in trees and feeds on frogs, crayfish, muskrats, and rabbits. Raccoons hibernate in the winter. Two to six young are born in the spring.

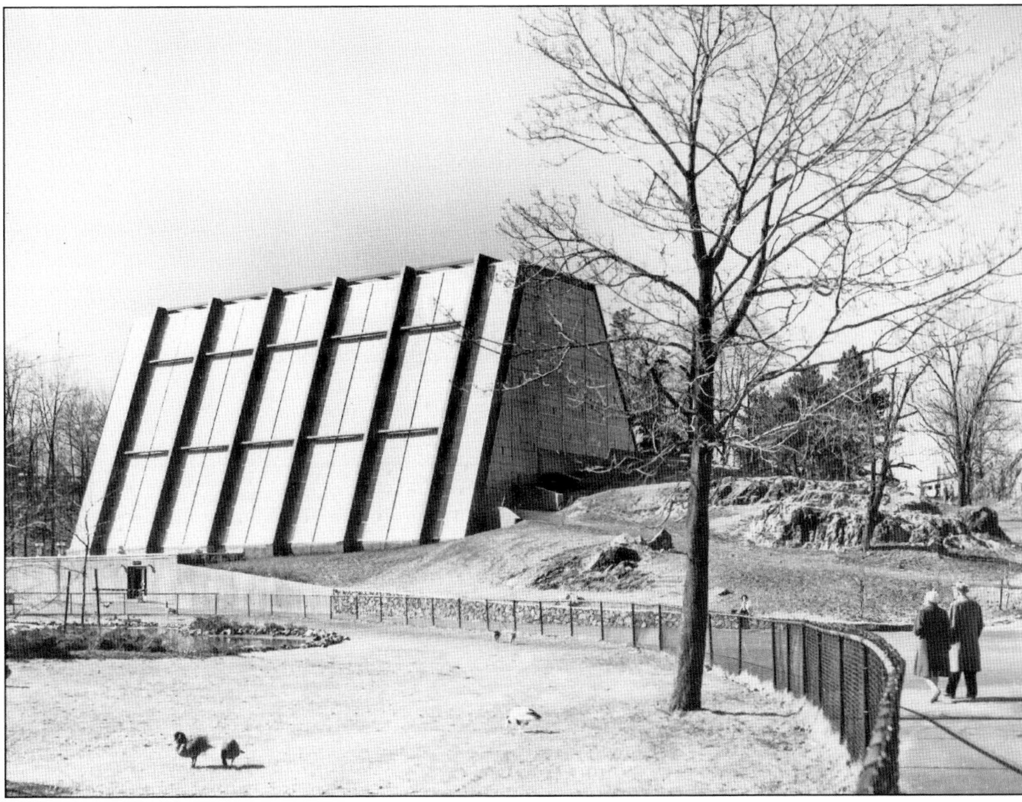

These photographs show the large indoor aviary, which was built about 1968, near the end of Walter Stone's tenure as zoo director. When Stone Zoo reopened in 1992 after a two-year closure, the aviary was renovated, but it was razed a short time later. The site of the aviary is now fenced off and overgrown. (Both, courtesy of DCR Archives.)

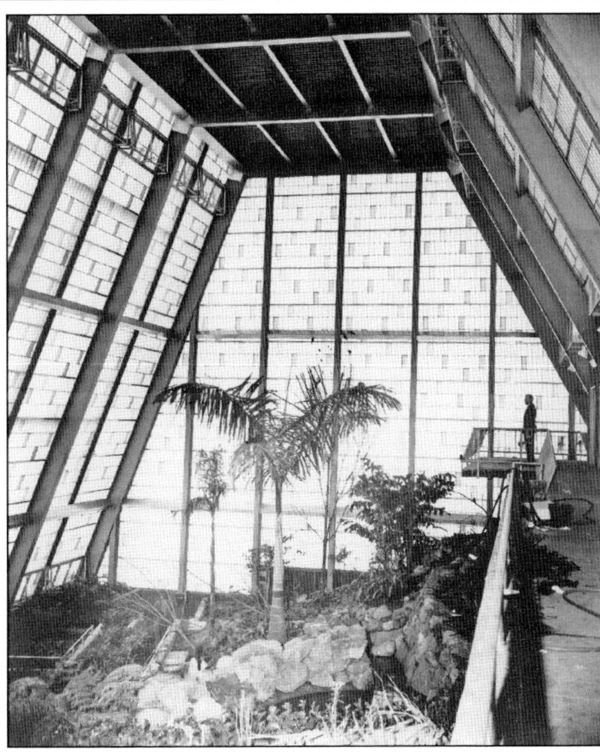

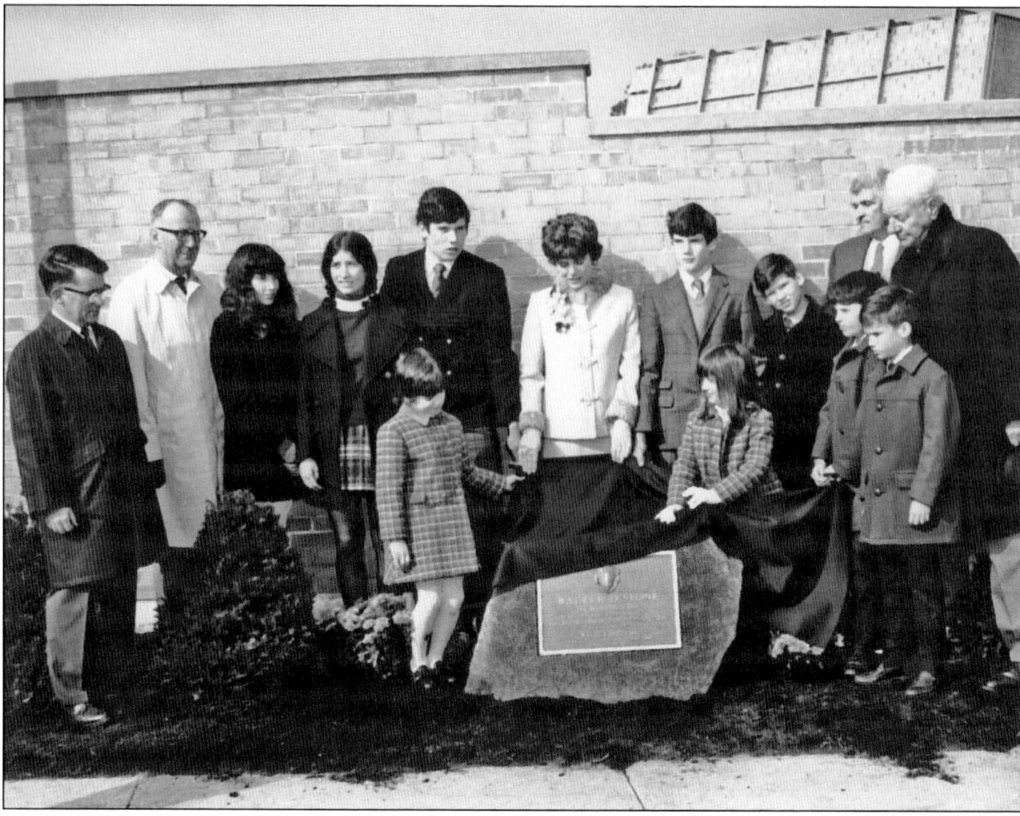

On November 1, 1969, a ceremony was held to unveil a bronze plaque honoring Walter D. Stone. The photograph shows Elizabeth "Betty" Stone and her nine children at the ceremony. Also present are (at far left, from left to right) Rep. Daniel C. Towse and state senate president Maurice A. Donahue and (at far right, from left to right) Walter Stone's brother William and Richard I. Furbush of the Metropolitan District Commission. (Courtesy of DCR Archives.)

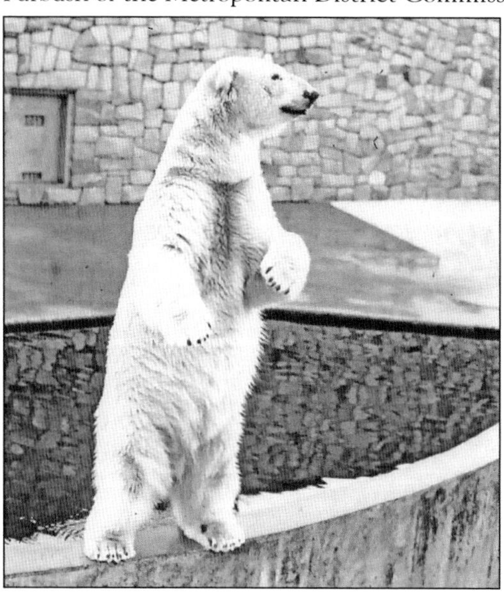

A polar bear captured in Siberia in 1966 was brought to Stone Zoo on July 1, 1979, from the Worcester Science Center. Standing eight feet tall and weighing 900 pounds, Major was one of Stone Zoo's key attractions. Every January, crowds attended his birthday party. Major was the oldest polar bear in captivity until his death in June 2000. (Courtesy of Zoo New England.)

Seven

Early Years of the Reservation

Within a year of its creation in 1893, the Metropolitan Park Commission had acquired Blue Hills, Middlesex Fells, Stony Brook, and Beaver Brook (Waverly Oaks), and parks began to surround Boston, just as Charles Eliot had envisioned. Under the Boulevard Act of 1894, the MPC began building parkways to connect reservations. The Fells and Blue Hills Parkways were among the earliest, providing the public with scenic routes for early automobiles, horse-drawn carriages, and saddled horses.

In 1900, the state legislature passed a bill allowing the MPC to grant trolley lines to street railway companies within the metropolitan parks, opening the way for cheap, convenient transportation. As reported in the *Boston Evening Transcript* on May 16, 1900, "It is the only way the great majority can ever enjoy great tracts of surpassing natural beauty now practically inaccessible, which have been purchased with public funds." The article notes that "a line running along Forest Street from Medford Square, the meeting point of four existing lines, to Stoneham, on the north, would run through the center of the Middlesex Fells . . . It would pass the beautiful Spot Pond woods, run along the shore to the pond itself, and pass under great Bear Hill." The article concludes that trolleys would make the parks what they ought to be—the pleasure grounds of the people.

In 1905, the Boston Elevated Railway Company and the Boston & Northern Street Railway proposed this line to Stoneham and, in 1910, the first trolleys ran through the Fells, with popular stops at the Sheepfold and Porter Cove. Early visitors to the park were enamored of its wildness, some finding and recording various species of birds, animals, and plants. Many strolled along pond shorelines and relaxed in picnic groves.

In the 1930s, the CCC had 32 camps in Massachusetts, one based in nearby Breakheart Reservation. CCC men traveled to Middlesex Fells on work details, where they sprayed trees for gypsy moths (see chapter 5) and built trails and fire roads. WPA workers also battled insects and built roads, and worked on larger projects, including building Wright's Tower and improving Bellevue Pond.

For 36 years, the trolley line was a great success, but eventually it could not compete with automobiles or buses. The last trolley through the Fells ran in July 1946, a month after two trolleys collided head-on on a trestle near the Sheepfold. Within a few years, the expanding federal highway system bisected the Fells with Interstate 93.

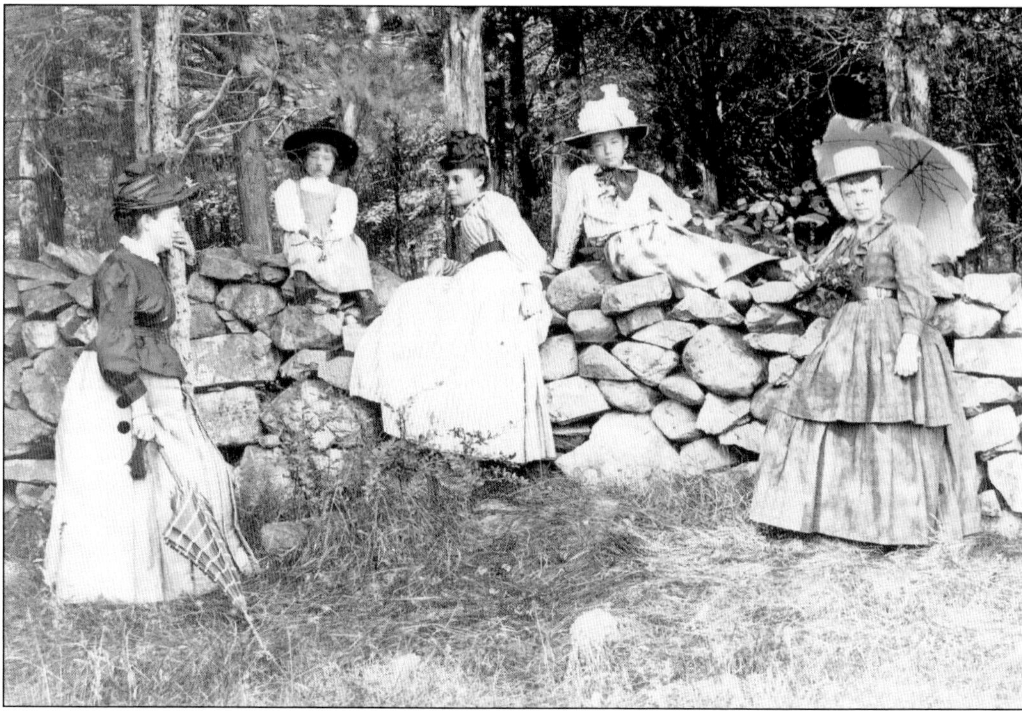

Women and girls pose for a photograph in the Fells about 1900. In the Victorian era, women visiting parks wore full skirts and hats, carried parasols, and were expected to engage in passive recreation. During this era, women could not vote, sue, or own property. By 1900, the women's suffrage movement was underway, but it was not until 1920 that American women gained the right to vote. (Courtesy of Historic New England.)

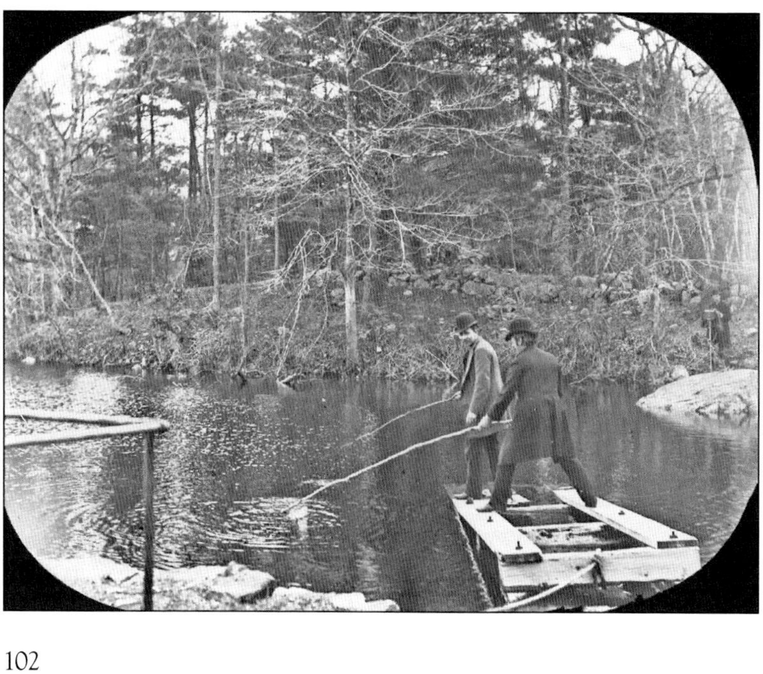

This is one of George Davenport's lantern slides, which he showed at public meetings in the 1880s to promote the idea of setting aside the Middlesex Fells. In this image, members of the Mystic Camera Club stand with sticks on a makeshift dock while a photographer at right watches. (Courtesy of the Medford Historical Society and Museum.)

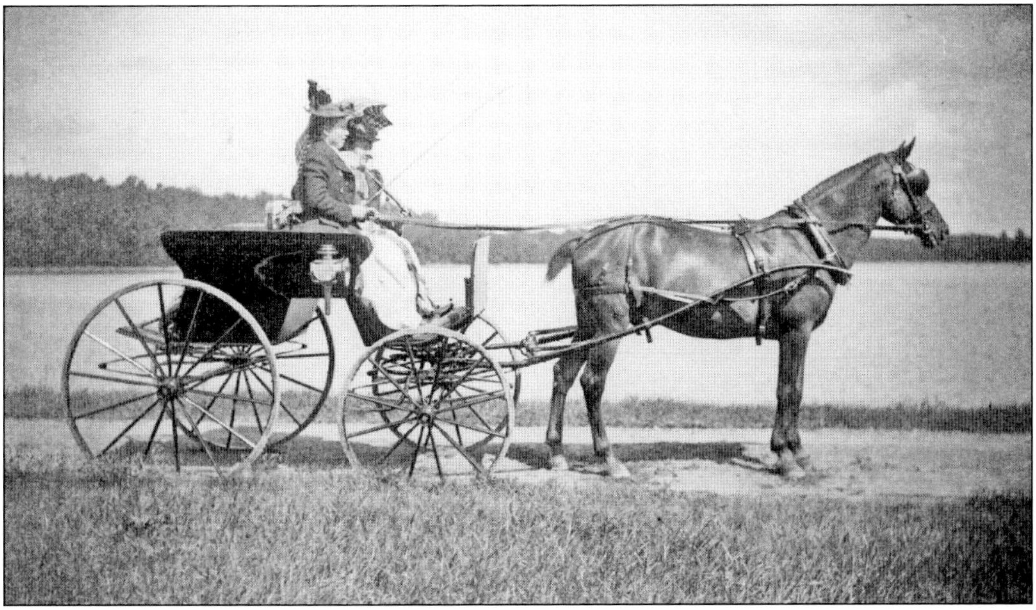

Leslie D. Bangs (1873–1919) and a friend take a ride along Winchester's North Reservoir about 1890. Bangs (holding the reins) was the daughter of Elisha Dillingham Bangs, a prominent banker in Winchester. (Courtesy of Winchester Archival Center.)

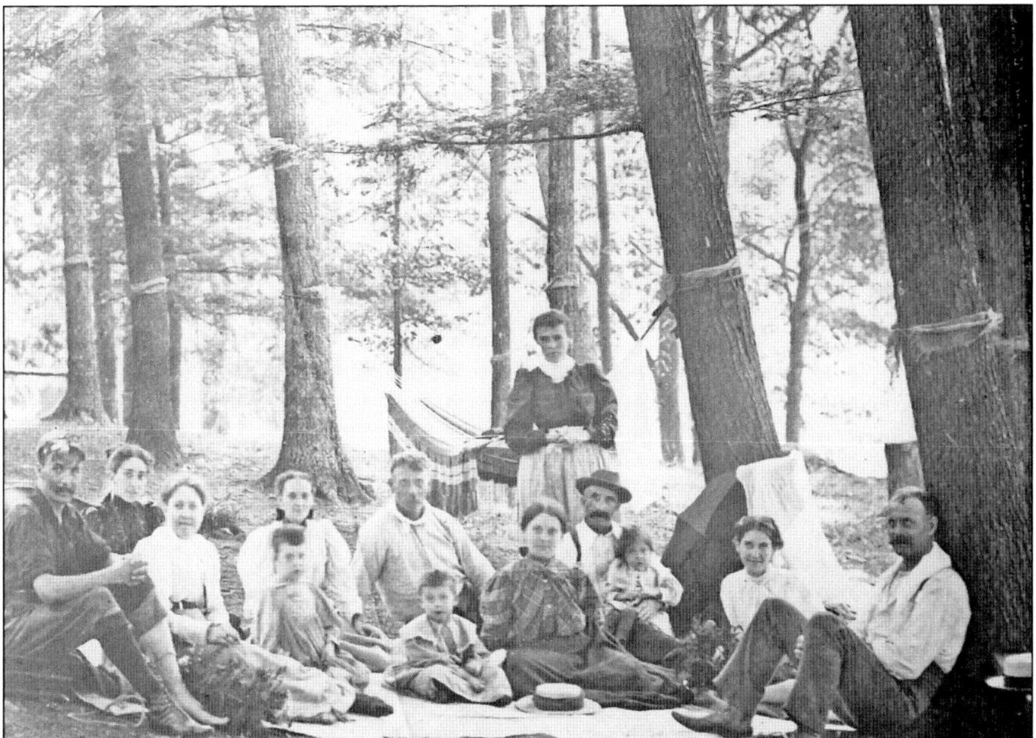

A large family poses for a photograph in the Fells about 1905. Thousands of people from cities and towns in the Boston area took day trips to the Fells to relax and enjoy the natural setting. (Courtesy of Massachusetts State Archives.)

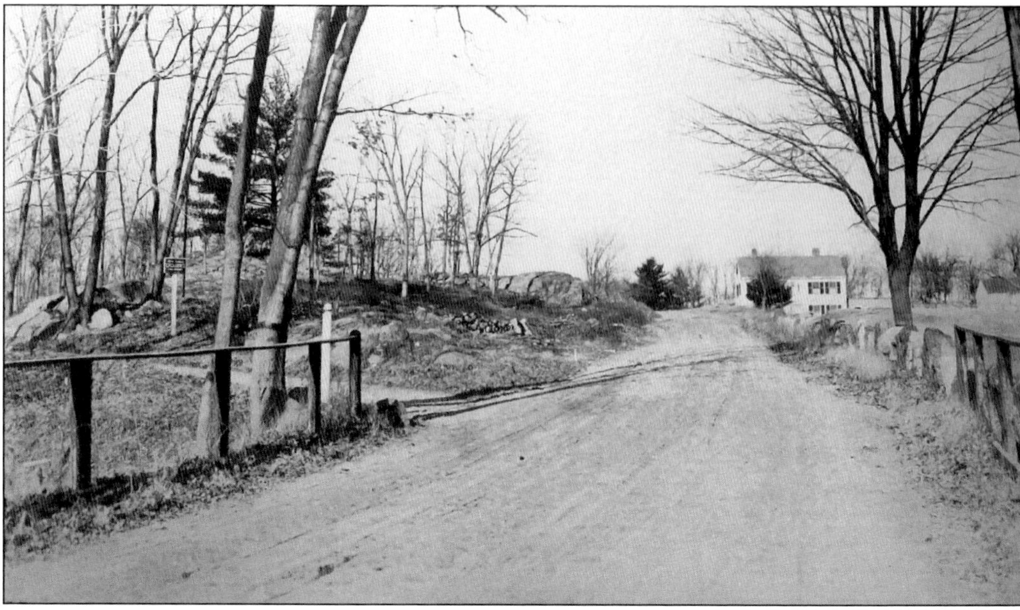

These images show the Andover and Medford Turnpike (also known as Forest Street, now Route 28) from two locations. On January 10, 1908, Nathaniel Stebbins took the photograph above, with a view looking north towards Samuel Tay's farmhouse in Medford (see page 18). He returned to the turnpike in October to take a photograph of Porter Cove on Spot Pond. These views illustrate how roads looked throughout New England at the dawn of the automobile era when most people still traveled by horse, wagon, or on foot. (Both, courtesy of Massachusetts State Archives.)

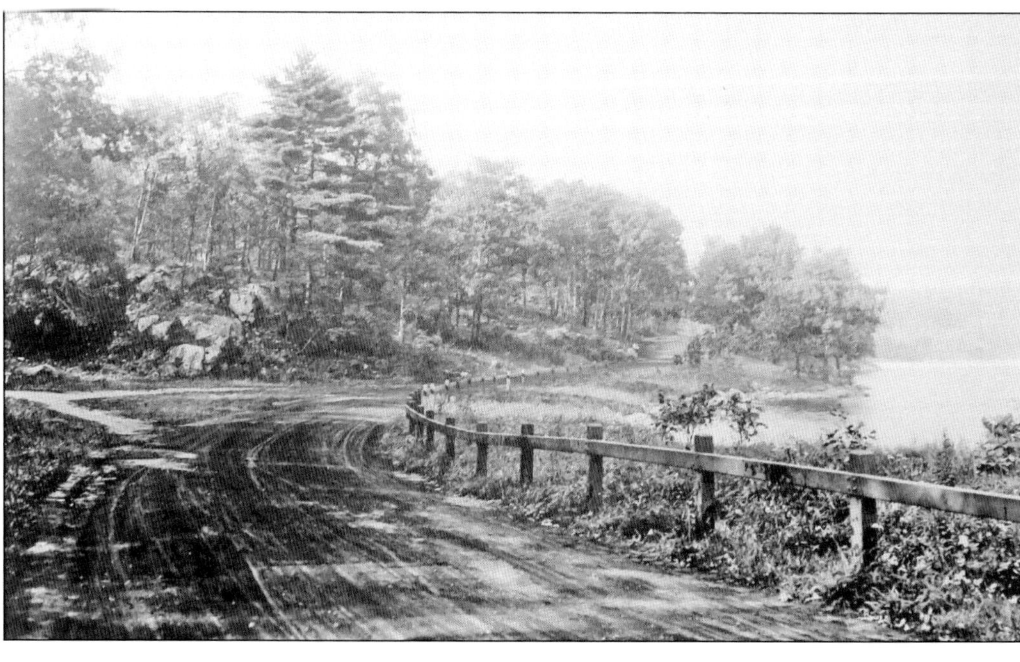

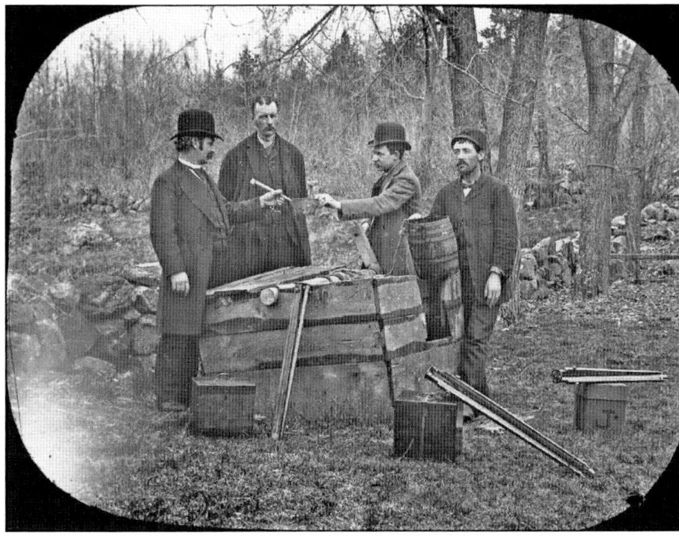

George Davenport took this photograph of members of the Mystic Camera Club at a well in Middlesex Fells about 1891. Until the advent of municipal water supplies, people relied on private wells, springs, and cisterns for drinking water. Malden, Melrose, Medford, and Winchester first laid pipes and water mains in the 1870s. In the 1880s, Stoneham began receiving water from Crystal Lake in Wakefield. (Courtesy of the Medford Historical Society and Museum.)

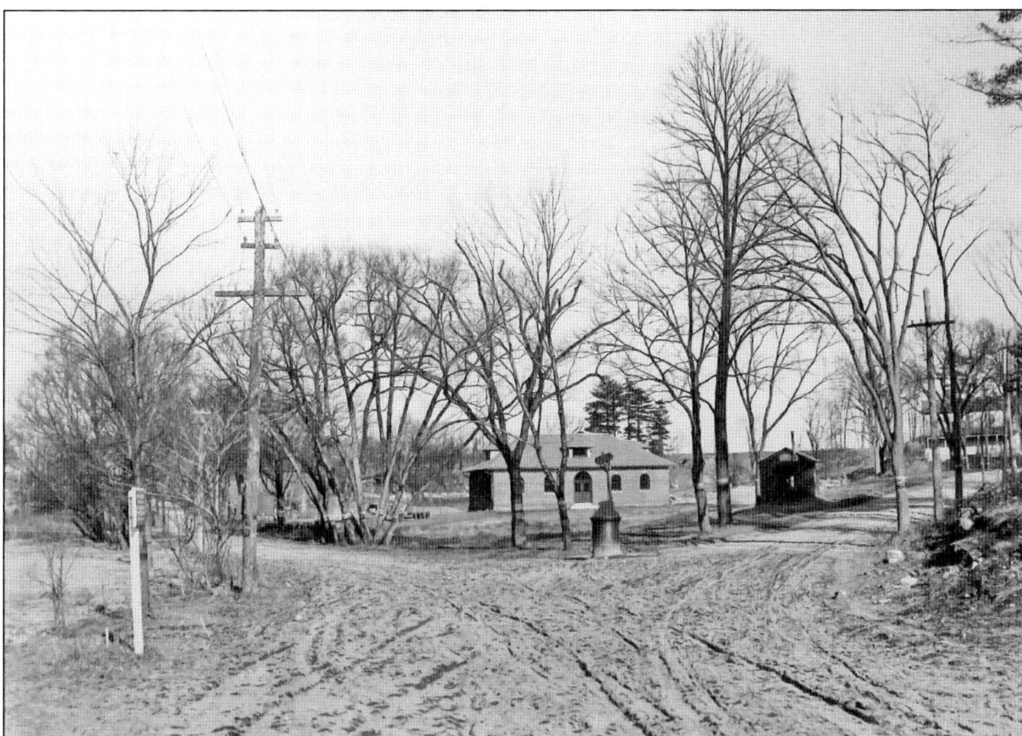

This image, taken by Nathaniel Stebbins on January 10, 1908, shows the intersection of Forest Street (left) and Elm Street in Medford. The pumping station at center regulated flow from Wright's Pond when it was used as a reservoir. Trees are wrapped with burlap to stop gypsy-moth caterpillars from climbing to feed on leaves (see chapter 5). Wright's Pond is owned by the City of Medford and is now part of Wright's Park south of Spot Pond. (Courtesy of Massachusetts State Archives.)

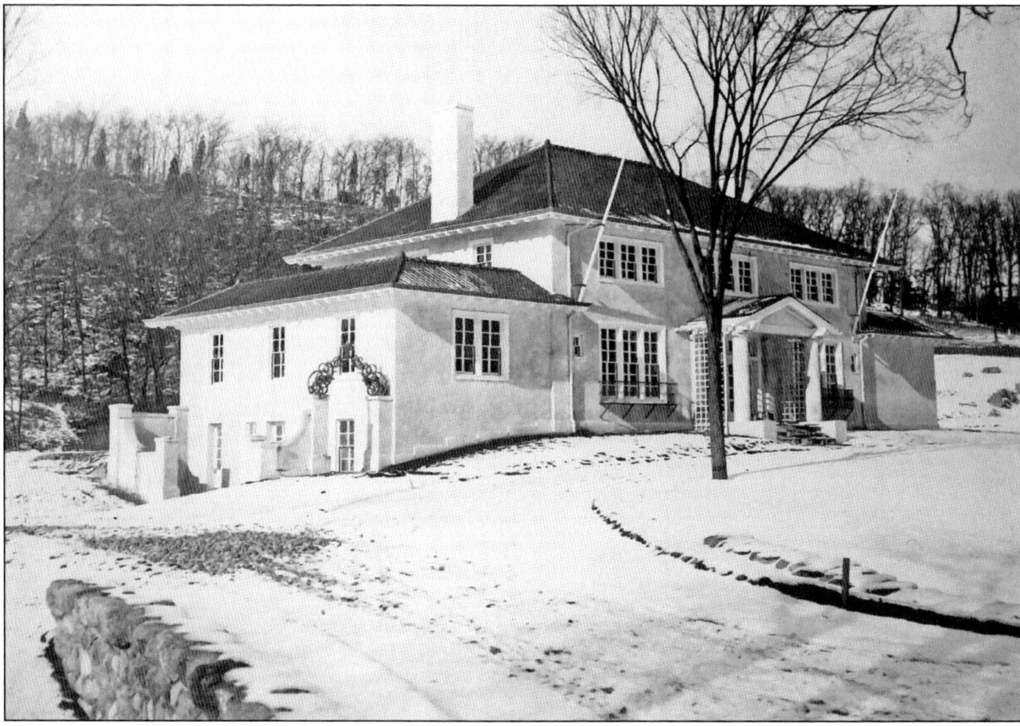

The MPC Police Headquarters, shown here soon after its construction in 1908, was located near Gravelly Brook and just south of the Elizur Wright House on Forest Street. It was designed by Stickney and Austin, built by Rowe Contracting Company, and landscaped by Olmsted Brothers. The headquarters building was razed in 1959 during construction of Interstate 93. (Courtesy of Massachusetts State Archives.)

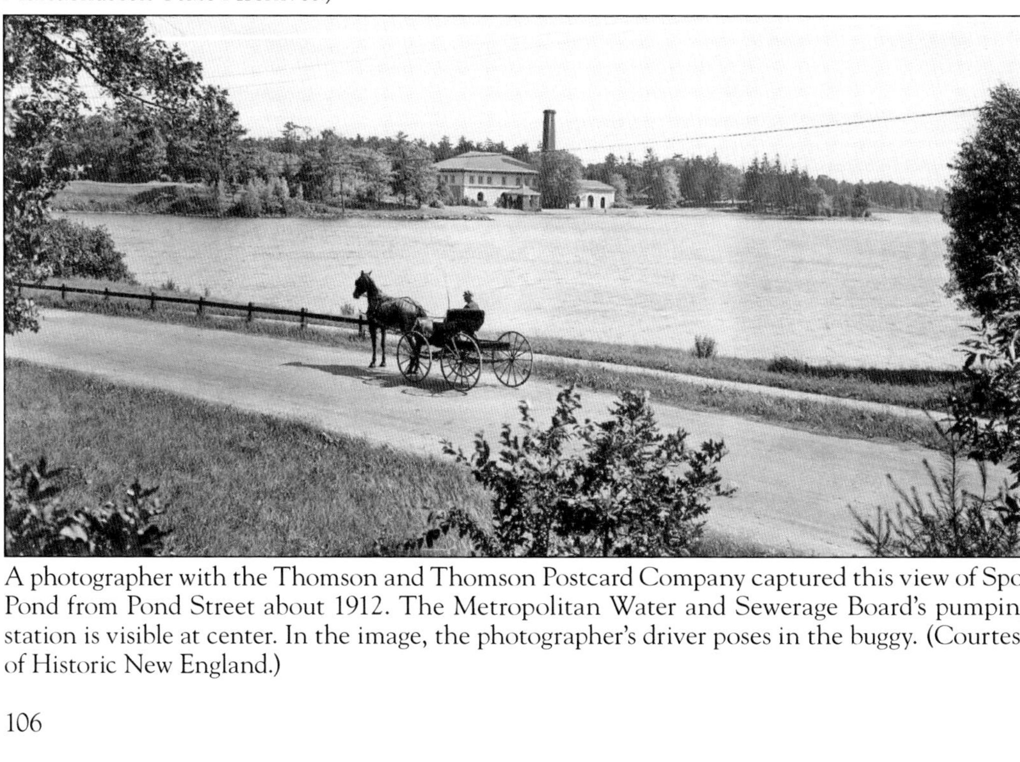

A photographer with the Thomson and Thomson Postcard Company captured this view of Spot Pond from Pond Street about 1912. The Metropolitan Water and Sewerage Board's pumping station is visible at center. In the image, the photographer's driver poses in the buggy. (Courtesy of Historic New England.)

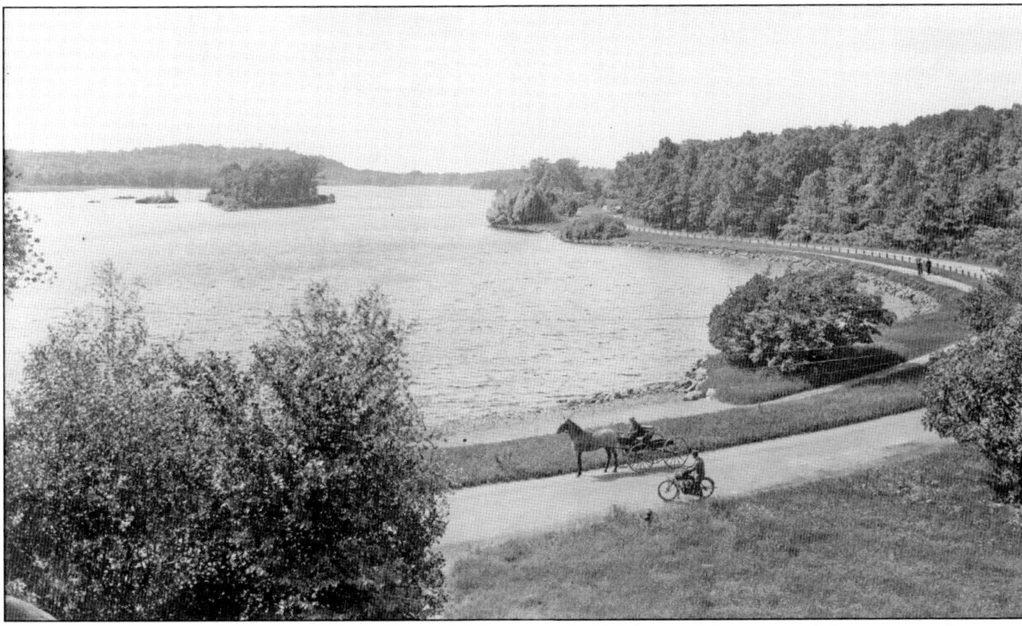

This photograph, taken about 1912 by the Thomson and Thomson Postcard Company, shows an MDC police officer on a motorcycle and a driver for the company chatting on Woodland Road. The view is from Old Pepe's Cove looking northwest towards Bold Point, which is now an island due to the raising of Spot Pond's water level in 1900. Bear Hill is visible in the distance at left. (Courtesy of Historic New England.)

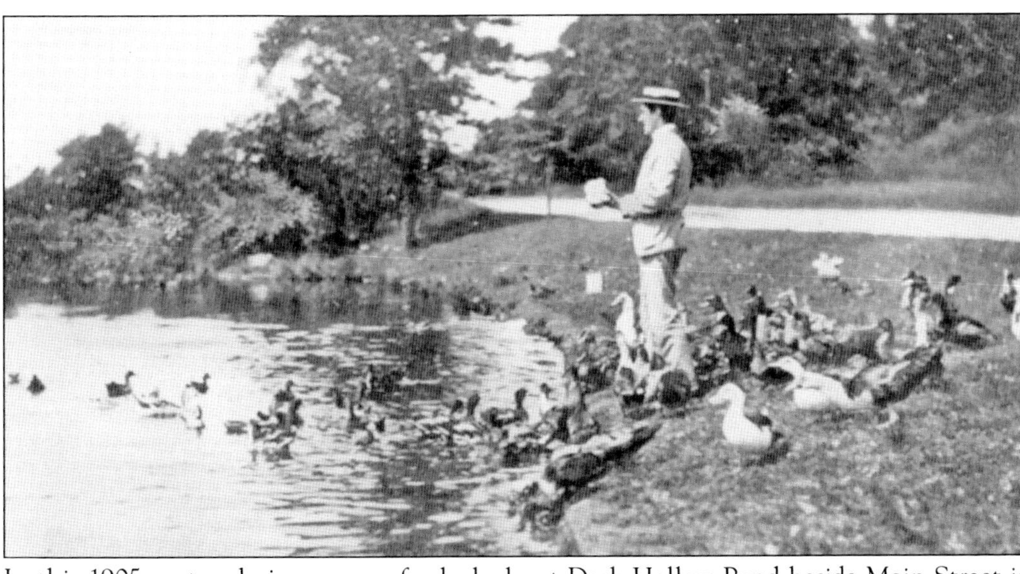

In this 1905 postcard view, a man feeds ducks at Dark Hollow Pond beside Main Street in Stoneham. Some ducks were kept at the Middlesex Fells Zoo over the winter. The pond was a marsh before it was dammed in 1899. In 1959, half of the pond was filled during construction of Interstate 93. (Courtesy of DCR Archives.)

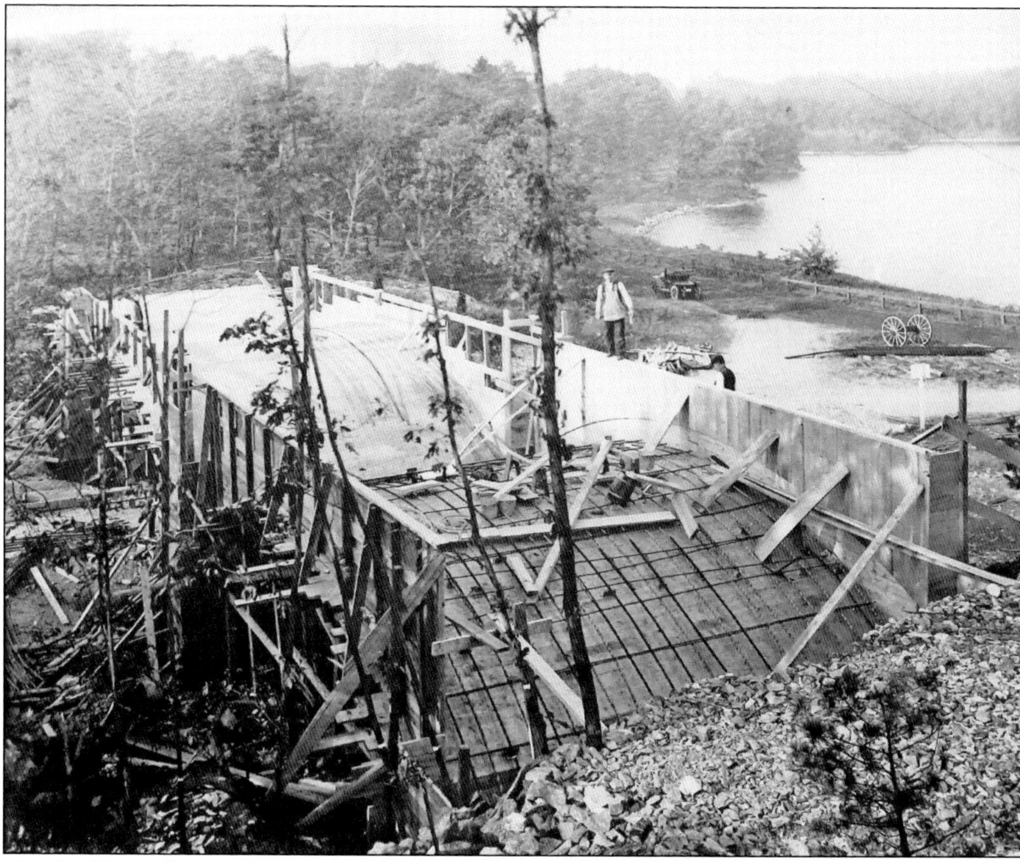

Men build a trolley trestle over Brooks Road at Porter Cove in October 1908. Brooks Road, which runs from Porter Cove southwest toward Winchester's South Reservoir, was built just four years earlier. Although this trestle was destroyed in 1959 during construction of Interstate 93, three other trolley trestles still remain in the Fells. (Both, photograph by Nathaniel Stebbins, courtesy of Massachusetts State Archives.)

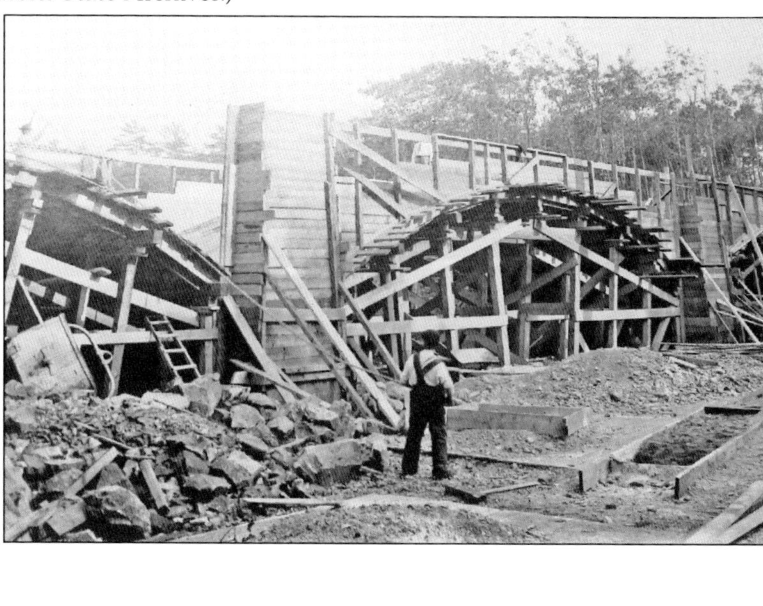

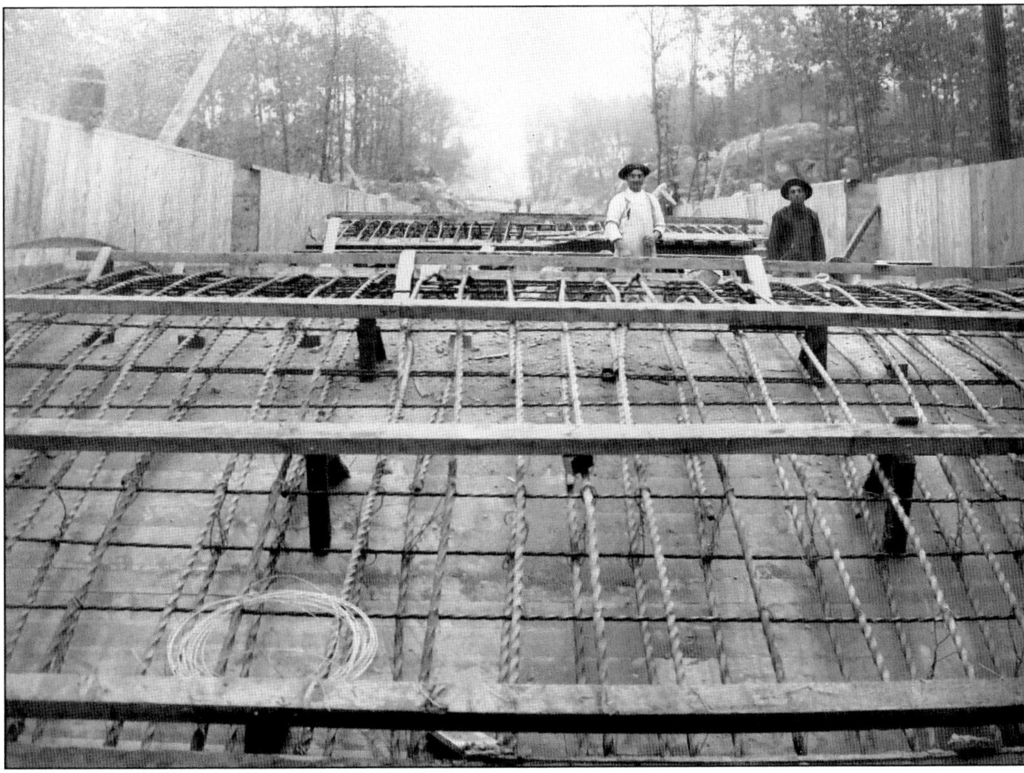

Men install steel supports on the three arches of Brooks Road streetcar trestle in October 1908. This steel framework was needed to support the heavy trolleys, which could weigh up to 23 tons. Below, men cover the supports with concrete. (Both, photograph by Nathaniel Stebbins, courtesy Massachusetts State Archives.)

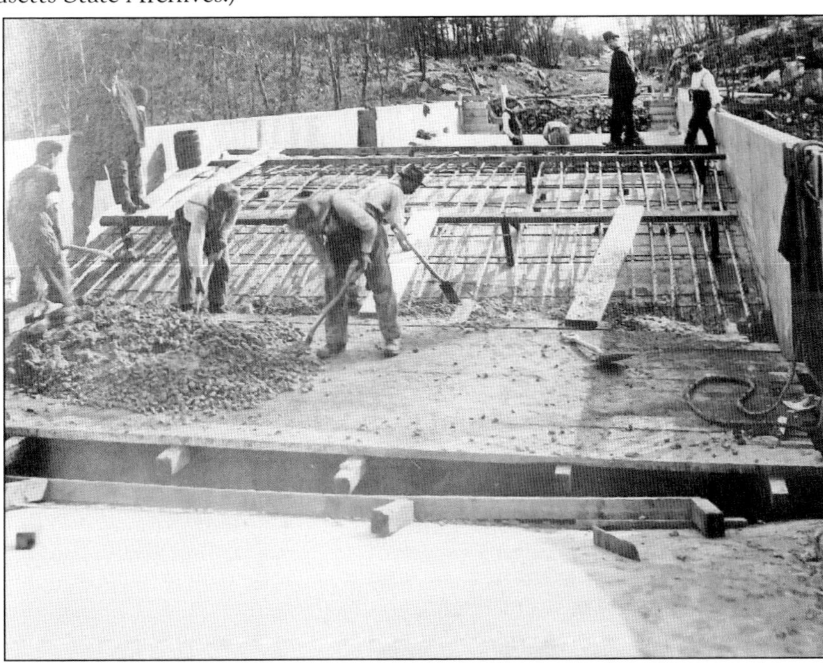

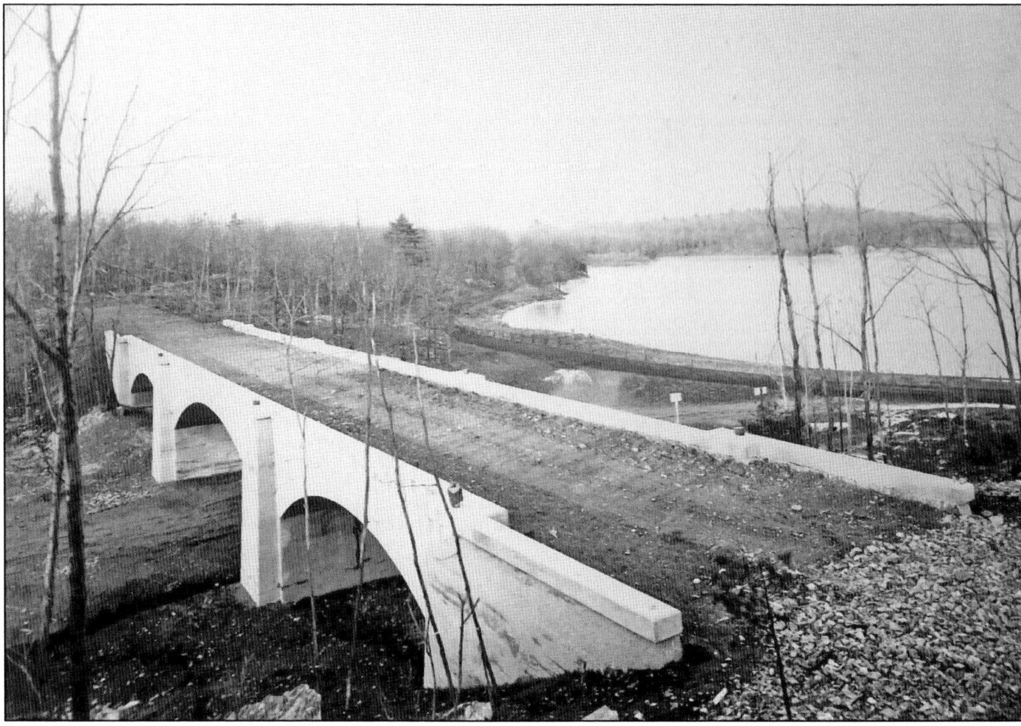

The photograph above, taken on January 6, 1909, shows the west side of the nearly completed Brooks Road trestle beside Spot Pond. On April 1910, trolleys began running through the Fells between Medford Square and Stoneham Center. To build this line, contractors used 5,800 wooden ties and 258 tons of rail, at a cost of $76,000. The image below shows the same scene after 1910. (Both, photograph by Nathaniel Stebbins, courtesy Massachusetts State Archives.)

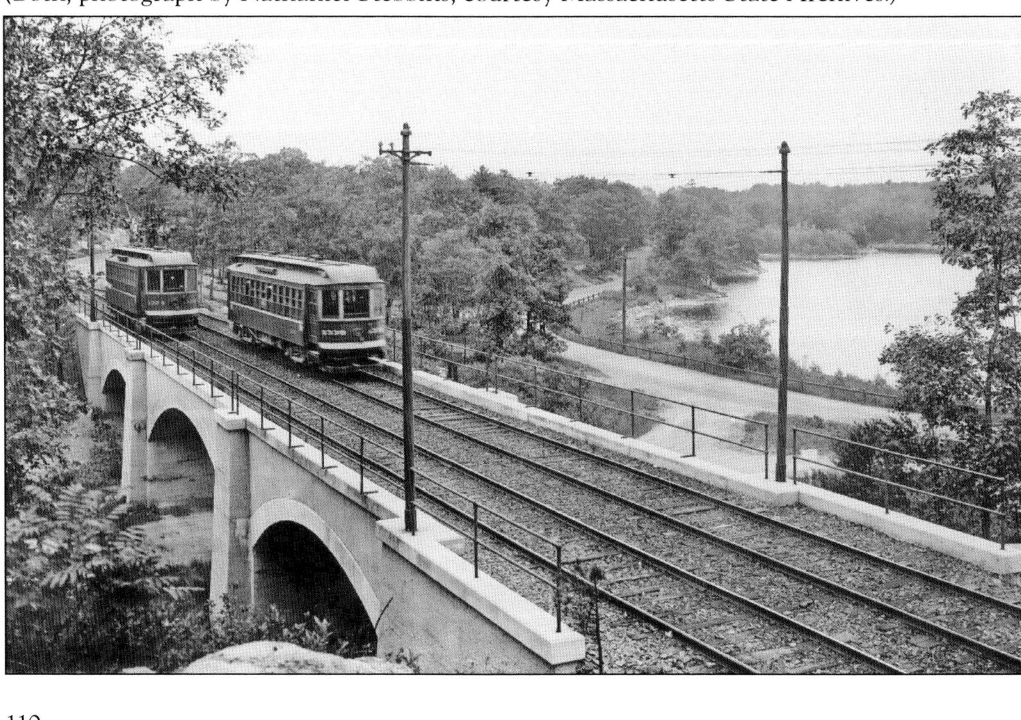

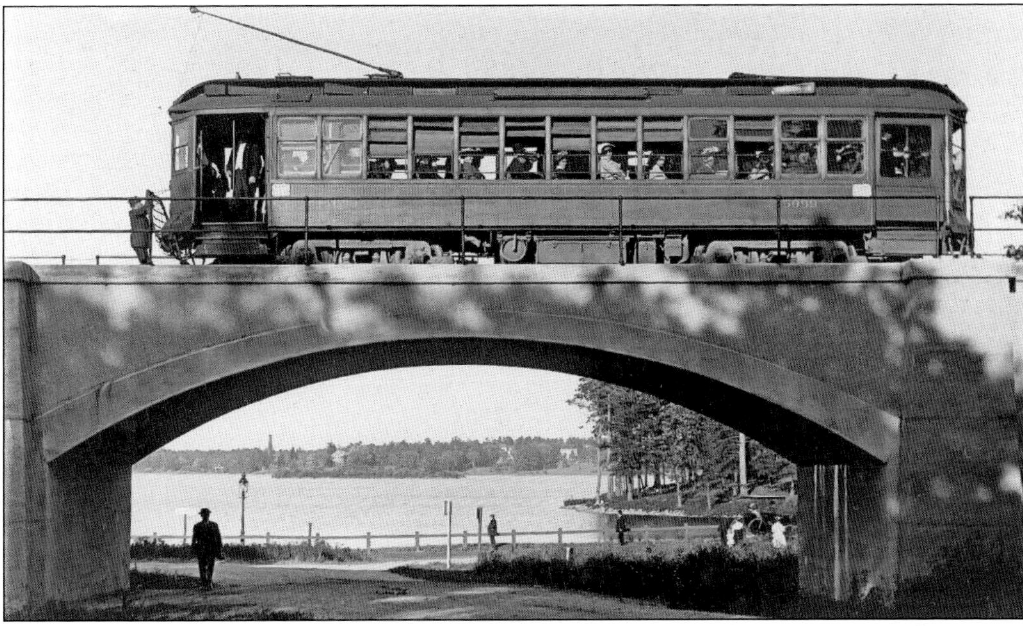

The April 16, 1910, edition of the *Stoneham Independent* reports that the Boston & Northern Street Railway Company "proposes to run the new type, big semi-convertible, easy access cars . . . fitted with four 50 horsepower motors . . . and equipped with exceptionally heavy and solid trucks." Each car could seat 52 passengers. In this 1912 photograph, one of these trolleys stops on the Brooks Road trestle as people walk under it to reach Spot Pond. (Courtesy of Historic New England.)

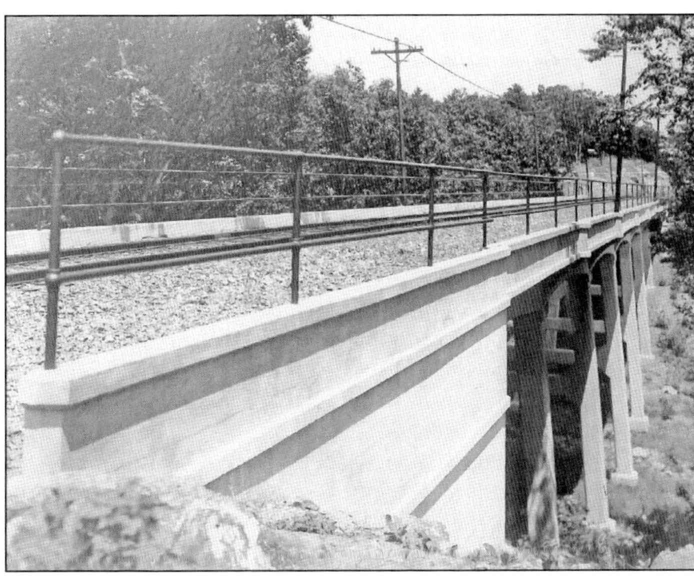

This image shows the new concrete trestle next to Dark Hollow Pond on July 20, 1910. Transit Commission engineer John E. Palmer supervised construction of the 275-foot-long bridge over a 40-foot ravine at a cost of $21,500. The *Stoneham Independent* reported "there are only one or two trestles in this country of similar size and construction." The trestle still exists, but is in disrepair. (Photograph by Nathaniel Stebbins, courtesy of Massachusetts State Archives.)

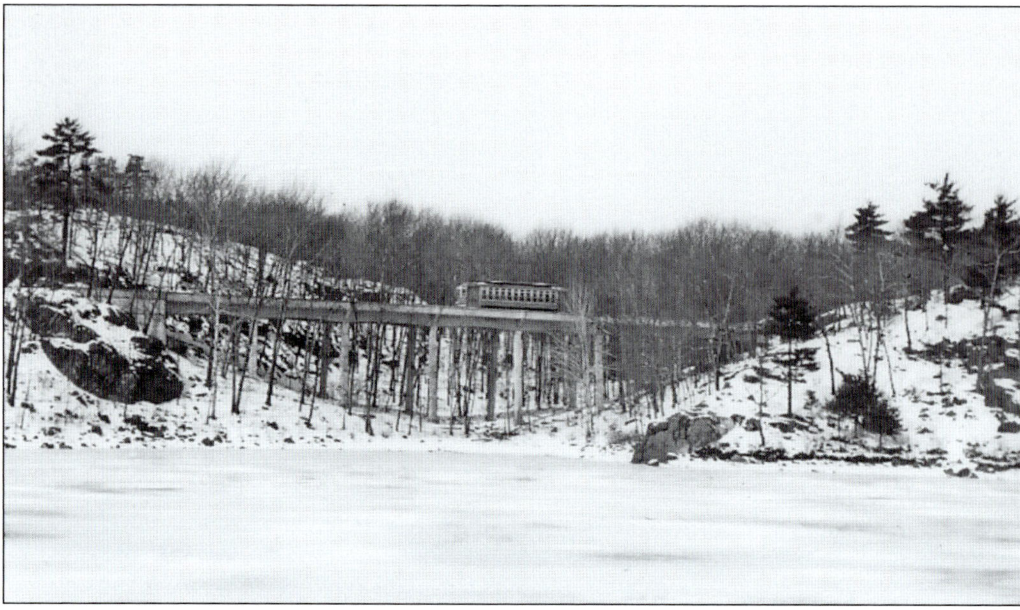

Charles Duncan took this photograph in the 1940s of a trolley heading north to Stoneham over the trestle next to a frozen Dark Hollow Pond. This trolley ran year-round and had electric heaters under the seats to keep passengers warm. (Courtesy of Lester H. Stephenson Jr.)

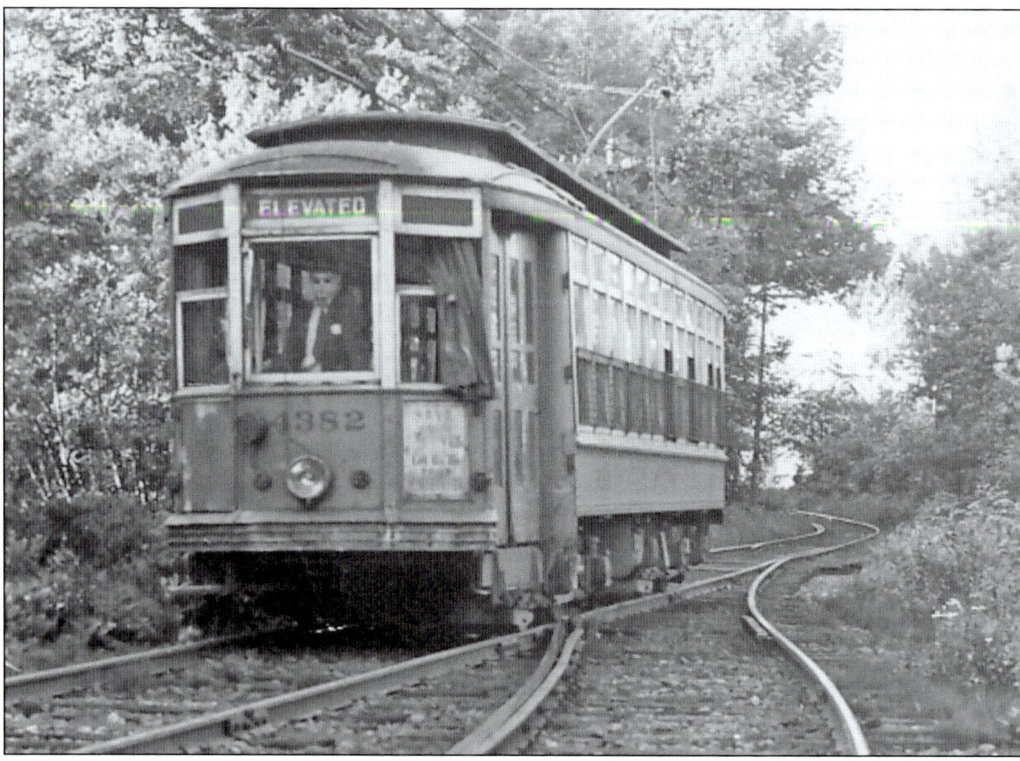

Trolley No. 4382 heads south through the Fells towards Medford on June 10, 1946. The trolley is at the "turnout" north of the Sheepfold where the single-track line changed to a double track. It remained double from here to Medford Square. (Courtesy of Lester H. Stephenson Jr.)

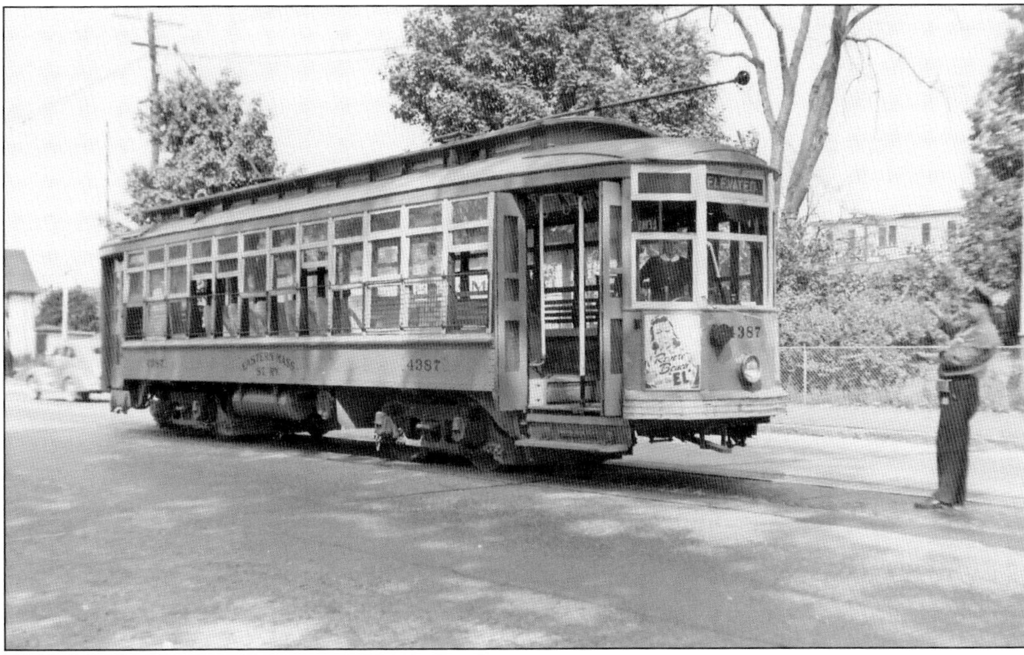

This 1940s image taken by Charles Duncan shows motorman Lester Stephenson adjusting a trolley pole near Stoneham Center. At this time, Stephenson had been a motorman for about two years, following in the steps of his father, who drove trolleys through the Fells until 1933. Below, Duncan took this photograph of his son Arthur and Stevenson before the trolley headed back to Medford Square. Riding the trolleys, popularly called "the Yellow Peril," took about a half hour to go from Stoneham to Medford. (Both, courtesy of Lester H. Stephenson Jr.)

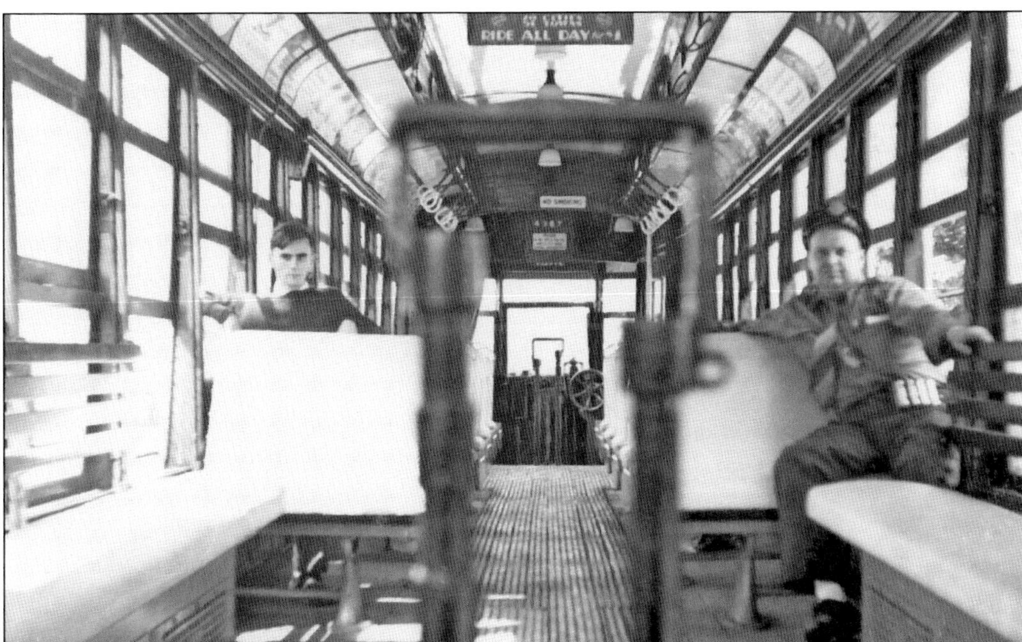

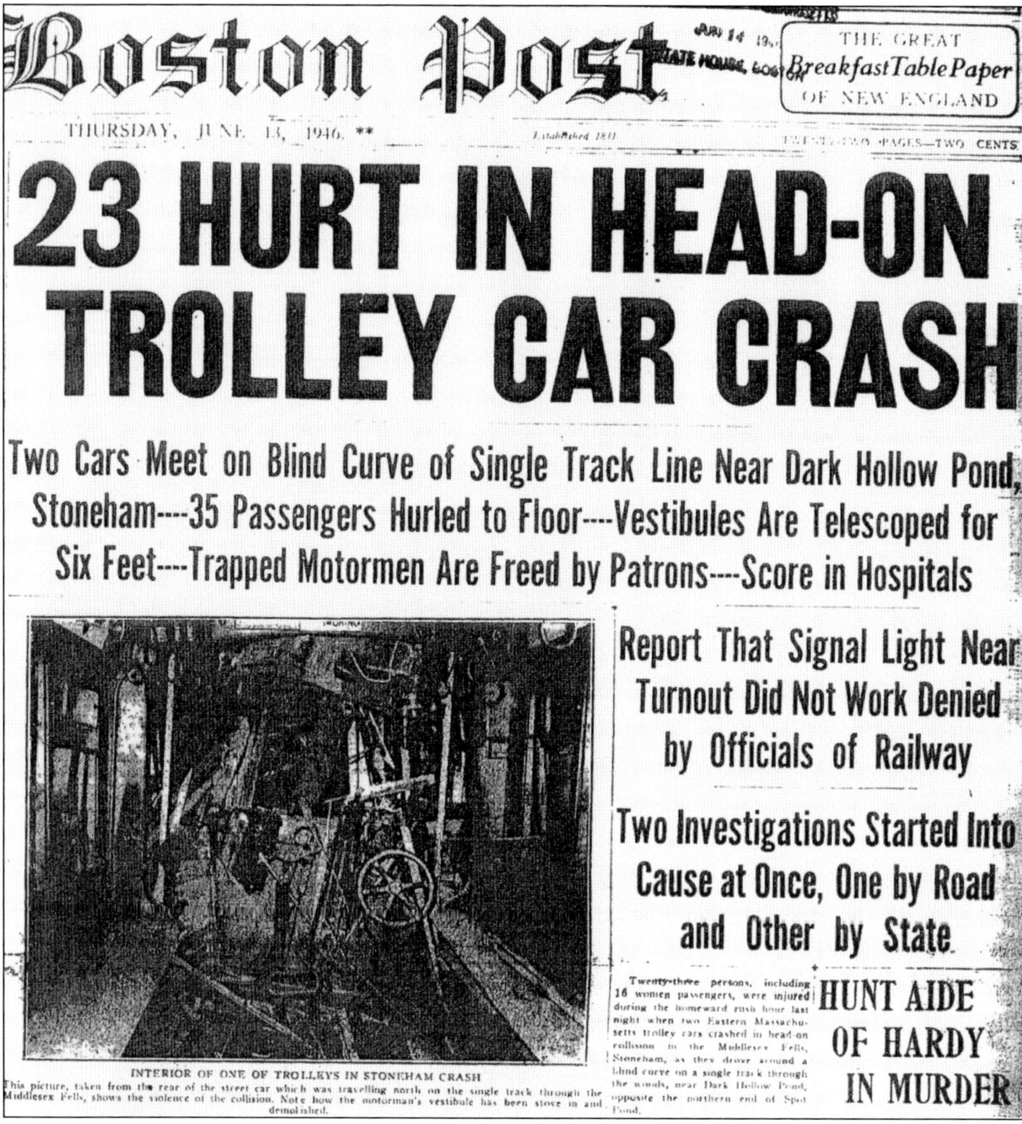

Boston Post

THE GREAT *BreakfastTablePaper* OF NEW ENGLAND

THURSDAY, JUNE 13, 1946. ** Established 1831 PAGES—TWO CENTS

23 HURT IN HEAD-ON TROLLEY CAR CRASH

Two Cars Meet on Blind Curve of Single Track Line Near Dark Hollow Pond, Stoneham---35 Passengers Hurled to Floor---Vestibules Are Telescoped for Six Feet---Trapped Motormen Are Freed by Patrons---Score in Hospitals

INTERIOR OF ONE OF TROLLEYS IN STONEHAM CRASH

This picture, taken from the rear of the street car which was travelling north on the single track through the Middlesex Fells, shows the violence of the collision. Note how the motorman's vestibule has been stove in and demolished.

Report That Signal Light Near Turnout Did Not Work Denied by Officials of Railway

Two Investigations Started Into Cause at Once, One by Road and Other by State

Twenty-three persons, including 16 women passengers, were injured during the homeward rush hour last night when two Eastern Massachusetts trolley cars crashed in head-on collision in the Middlesex Fells, Stoneham, as they drove around a blind curve on a single track through the woods, near Dark Hollow Pond, opposite the northern end of Spot Pond.

HUNT AIDE OF HARDY IN MURDER

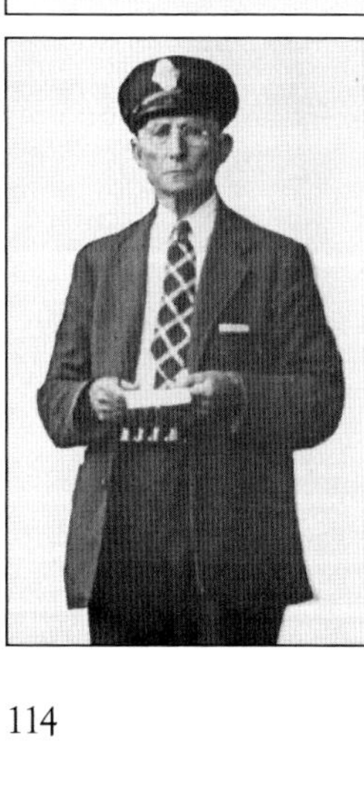

On the afternoon of June 12, 1946, two trolleys (Nos. 4382 and 4396) collided on the Bear Hill Road trestle north of the Sheepfold. The *Boston Globe* reported "the passengers in the crowded Stoneham-bound car screamed and leaped from their seats as they saw the other car bearing down on them." On impact, the trolleys telescoped six feet into each other. Panes of glass shattered, cutting passengers. Within minutes, four ambulances arrived and took 21 people to the New England Sanitarium in Stoneham and the Lawrence Memorial Hospital in Medford. The most seriously injured were motormen James A. Purtle and Herbert Fitzpatrick, both of Melrose. The image at right shows James Purtle, a native of New Brunswick, who operated trolleys for over 45 years. On July 1, he died of his injuries in the New England Sanitarium. (Above, courtesy of Boston Public Library; left, courtesy of Lester H. Stephenson Jr.)

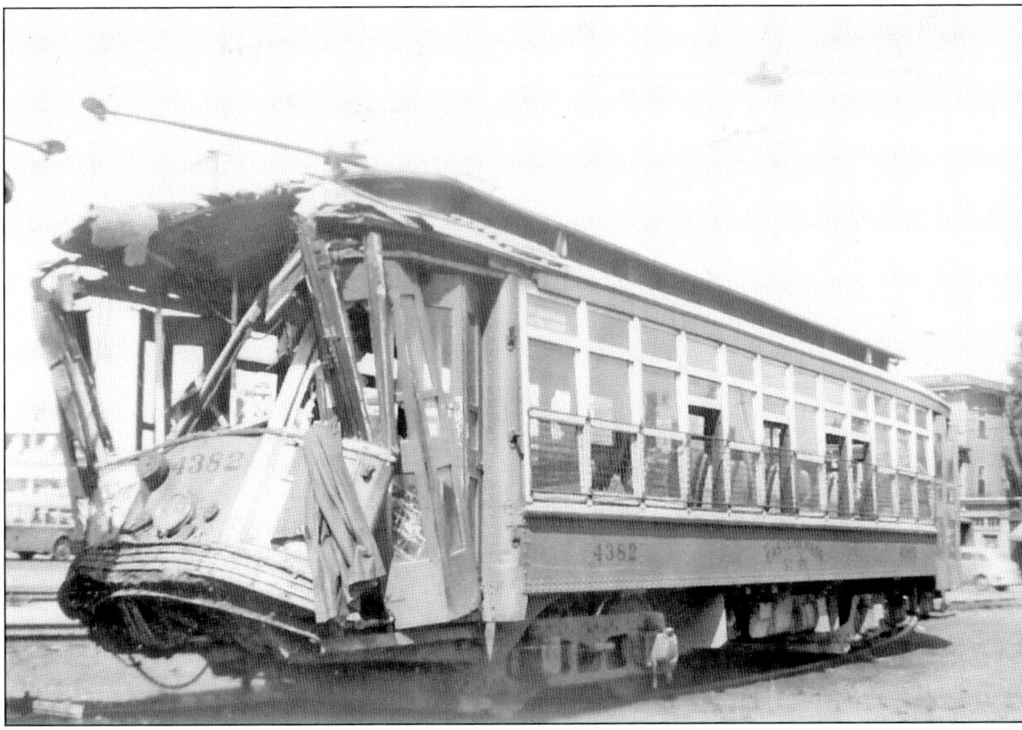

The day after the collision, motorman Lester Stephenson took these photographs of trolley No. 4382 beside the carbarn on Salem Street in Medford. The damage to trolley No. 4396 was comparable. Within a month of the accident, trolley service between Medford Square and Stoneham Square ended. All trolleys, except trolley No. 4387, which is now in a museum in Kennebunkport, were scrapped, and the route was picked up by bus services. (Both, courtesy of Lester H. Stephenson Jr.)

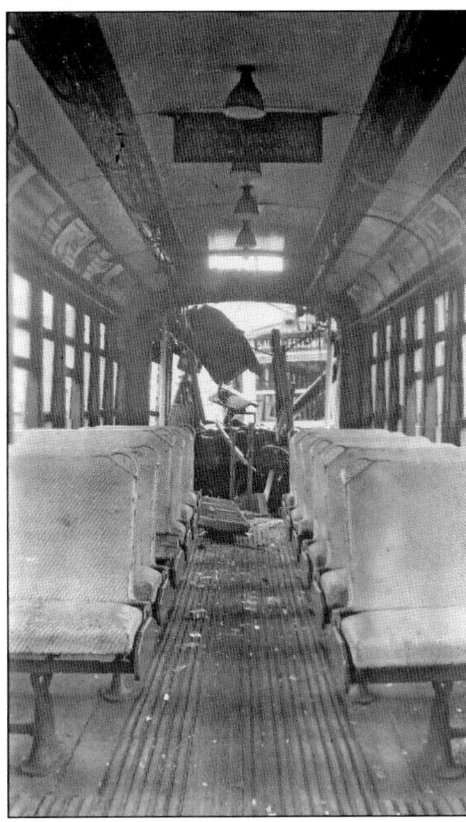

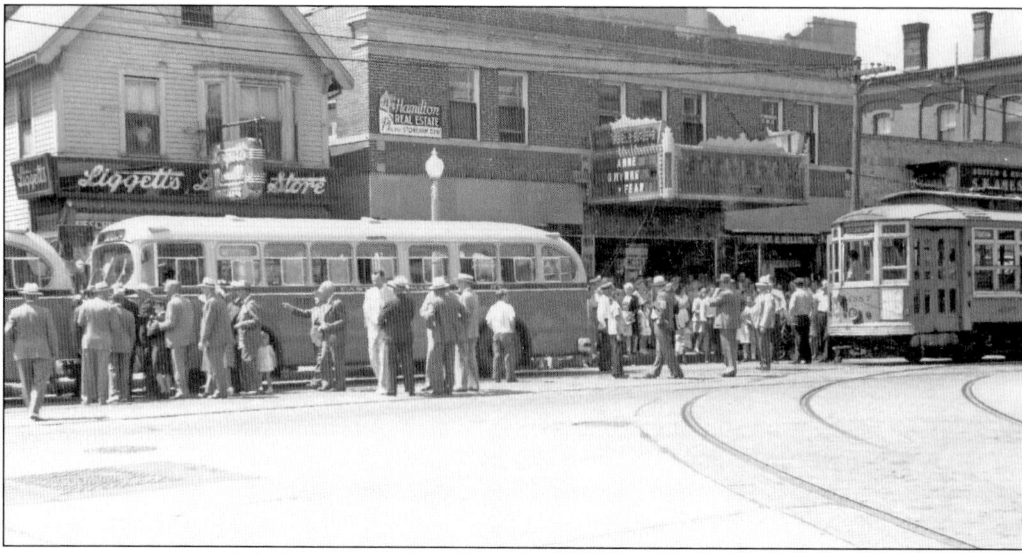

At a staged event on July 28, 1946, selected guests and employees of the Eastern Massachusetts Street Railway Company step off of trolley No. 4387 and enter buses, marking the transition from trolley to bus service. On this day, motorman Lester Stephenson drove this trolley, ending 36 years of trolley service through the Fells. The following year, Stephenson arranged for his trolley, No. 4387, to be sold for $400 to the Seashore Trolley Museum in Kennebunkport, Maine. This is the only Fells trolley saved from demolition. Below, Stephenson's son Lester Jr. stands in the doorway of this trolley at the museum. Following family tradition, Lester Jr. worked for the Boston & Maine Railroad for 40 years. He is now a volunteer motorman at the Seashore Trolley Museum. (Above, photograph by Warren Reed, courtesy of Lester H. Stephenson Jr.; below, authors' collection.)

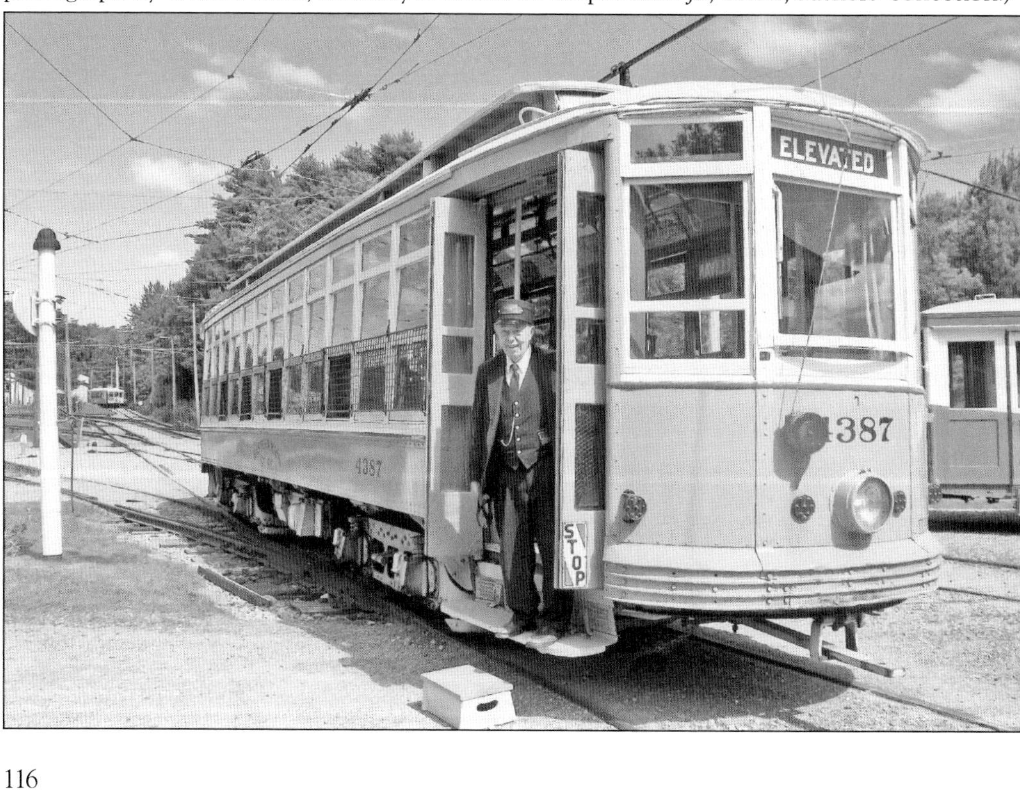

Eight

Modern Age

The life history of humanity has proved nothing more clearly than that crowded populations, if they would live in health and happiness, must have space for air, for light, for exercise, for rest, and for the enjoyment of that peaceful beauty of nature which, because it is the opposite of the noisy ugliness of towns, is so wonderfully refreshing to the tired souls of townspeople.

—Charles Eliot, 1893

At the end of World War II, the GI Bill provided returning veterans with money for college, businesses, and home mortgages. Millions of servicemen suddenly could afford to buy their own homes. Construction in the suburbs soared, along with the demand for superhighways. In the 1950s, Route 128 (called the Circumferential Highway and, later, the Yankee Division Highway) was built around Boston, and, from 1959 to 1961, Interstate 93 was built through the Fells. Whereas earlier parkways were built as scenic routes to reach recreational areas, superhighways were intended to be efficient travel corridors—a trend that continued into the 1990s. Only recently has the idea of designing highways to minimize damage to natural and cultural features become standard practice.

Today, the Fells is one of the largest forests in the country within a few miles of a major city. The variety of its features, including rocky outcrops, mixed woodland, open meadows, ponds, streams, wetlands, and vernal pools, has given it a variety of habitats. Among other findings, recent surveys have documented 129 vernal pools, 10 state-listed rare species, 5 types of priority natural communities, 183 bird species, 21 mammals, 10 amphibians, and at least 70 butterfly species. Located on the Atlantic Flyway, Middlesex Fells is also a stopover for birds during migratory flights.

Much of the Fells is now listed in both the State and National Registers of Historic Places—the Middlesex Fells Reservoirs Historic District, the Spot Pond Archeological District, the Middlesex Fells Reservation Parkways and Connector Parkways—helping ensure that future generations can enjoy this scenic woodland. The reservation offers tranquil beauty and recreation envisioned by its 19th-century founders, but protecting its natural and cultural resources remains a complex task.

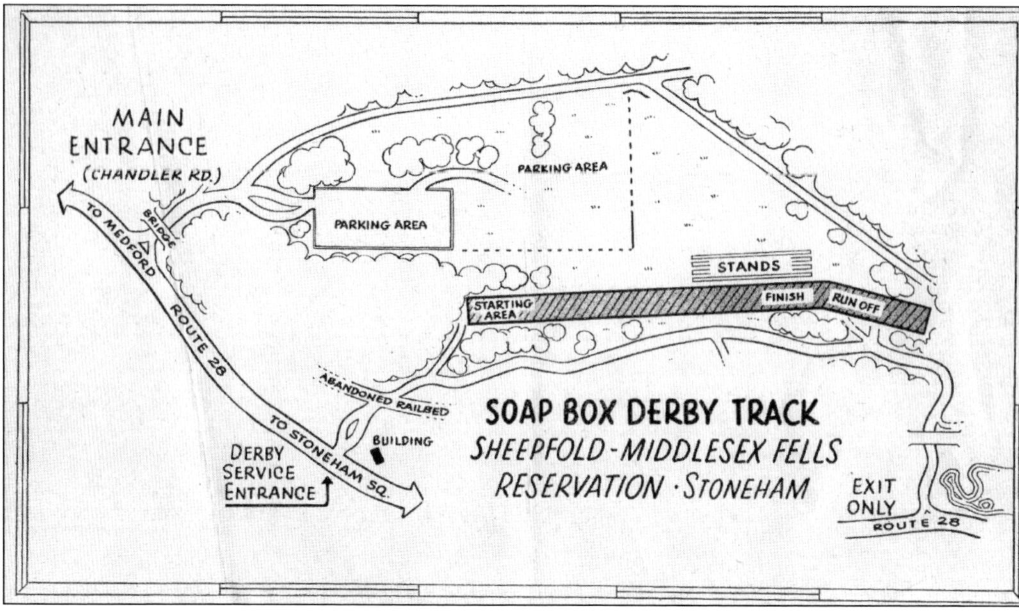

In 1953, the MDC built an 884-foot soapbox derby track in the Sheepfold and named it the Frank Taylor Memorial Track. Taylor, a native of Cochituate, was a former soapbox derby champion killed in action during World War II. The paved track was wide enough for three race cars. The map above shows three entrances to the track off of Route 28 in Medford and Stoneham. Below, hundreds of spectators crowd along the track in the early 1950s to watch a race. The track is still occasionally used for training runs before derby races in nearby towns. (Both, courtesy of DCR Archives.)

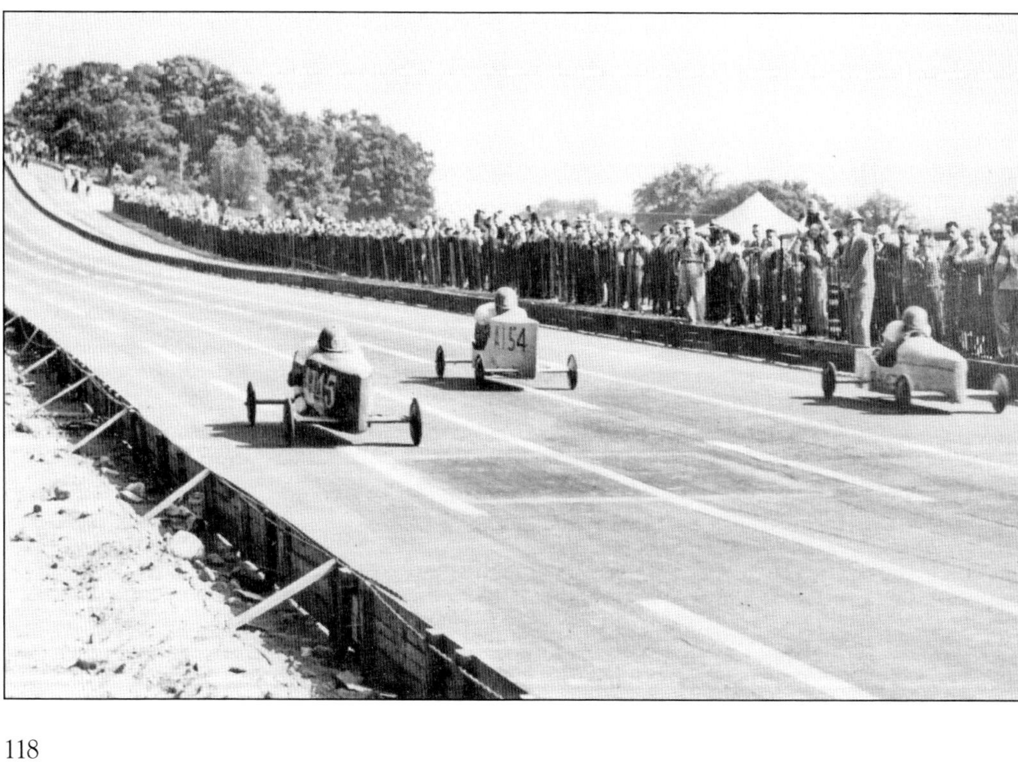

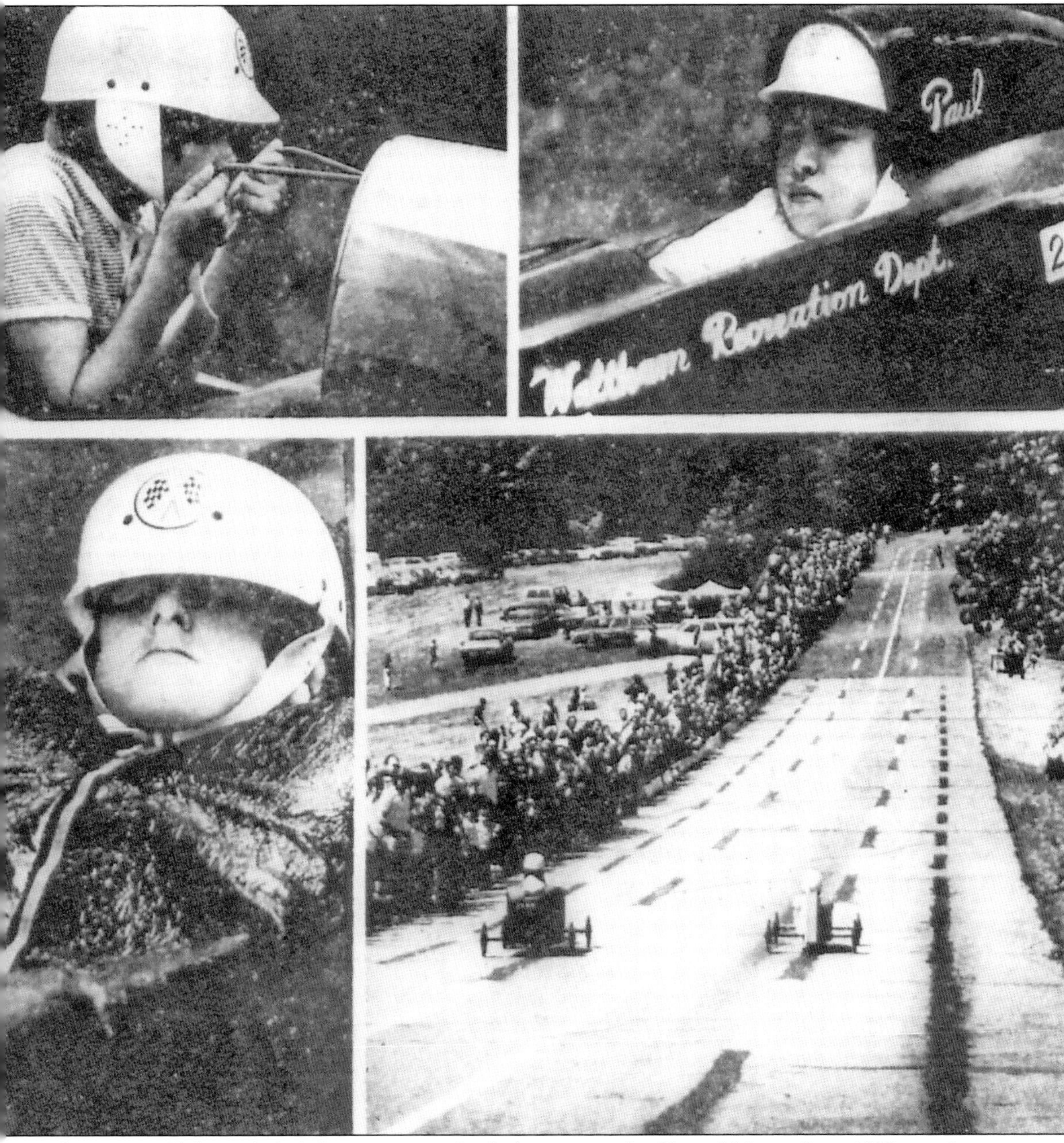

The Boston Globe included these images of a derby race in the Sheepfold in a June 1973 article, "A Fast Track and Hot Cars in the Middlesex Fells." The race, held on June 17, 1973, was part of an Eastern Massachusetts Regional Soap Box Derby competition. Clockwise from upper left are Brian Windsor of Melrose, Paul Leblanc of Waltham, and Joe Holland of Hingham. Paul's brother Ken topped a field of 31 boys and eight girls. (All, photograph by John Blanding, courtesy of Boston Public Library.)

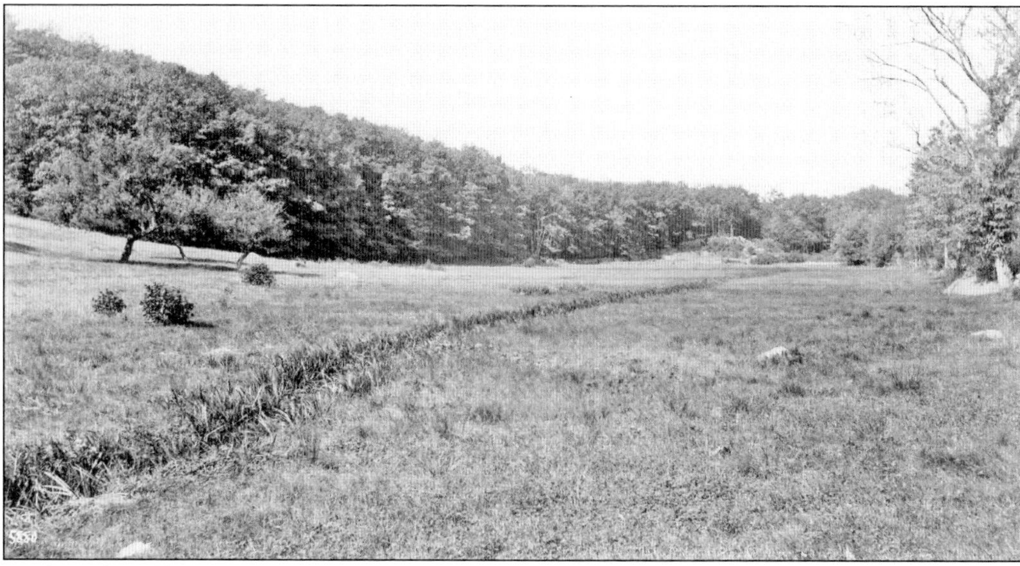

Nathaniel Stebbins took this view (above) of Gravelly Brook east of Pine Hill in October 1895. This brook, also called Intervale Brook on some maps, flows south from Wright's Pond into the Mystic River in Medford. Below, the Berke Moore Company of Providence built a culvert in 1959 to channel flow from Gravelly Brook under Roosevelt Circle as part of construction of Interstate 93. Nearby Route 28 (Forest Street) was relocated for this massive project. (Above, courtesy of DCR Archives; below, photograph by John W. Harper, courtesy of Massachusetts State Archives.)

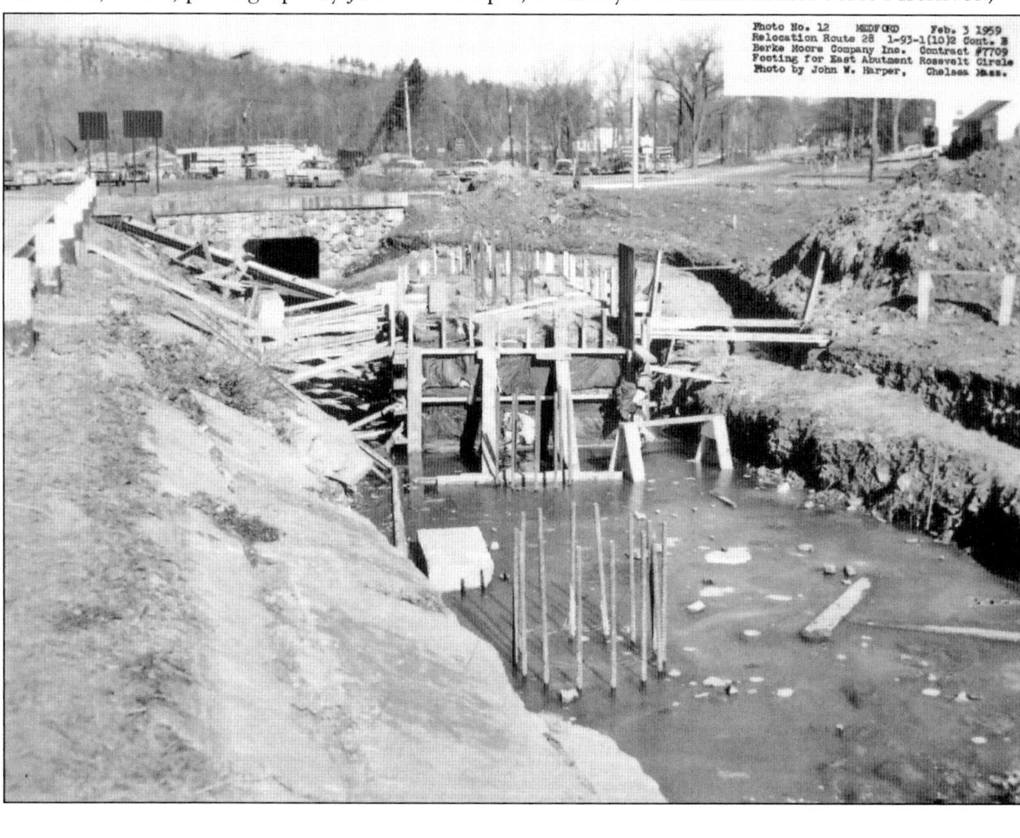

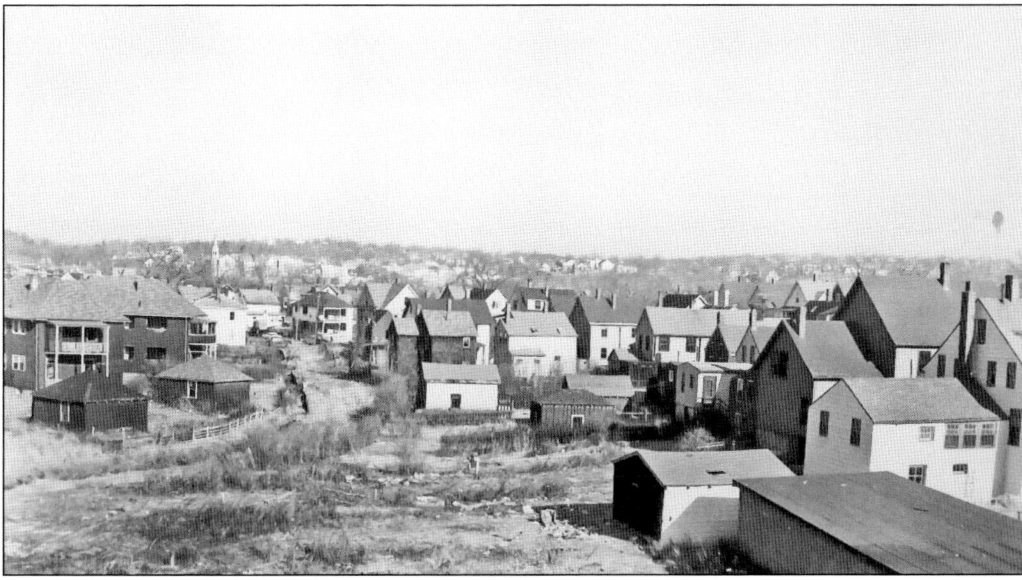

In 1959, contractors razed many buildings to make way for Interstate 93. These photographs by John Harper show Medford's Water Street neighborhood in views looking north from Salem Street (Route 60) before and after demolition. Wright's Tower is visible at far left in the image below. According to a January 18, 1959, article in the *Boston Sunday Globe*, "In the new highway's path, teams of men carrying chain saws cut down trees. Over 400 bodies from Medford's old Cross Street Burying Ground were moved to Oak Grove Cemetery. Power shovels with huge clam-shell buckets quickly reduced houses to kindling, and trucks hauled away the wood debris to a nearby dump in Wellington to be burned." (Both, courtesy of Massachusetts State Archives.)

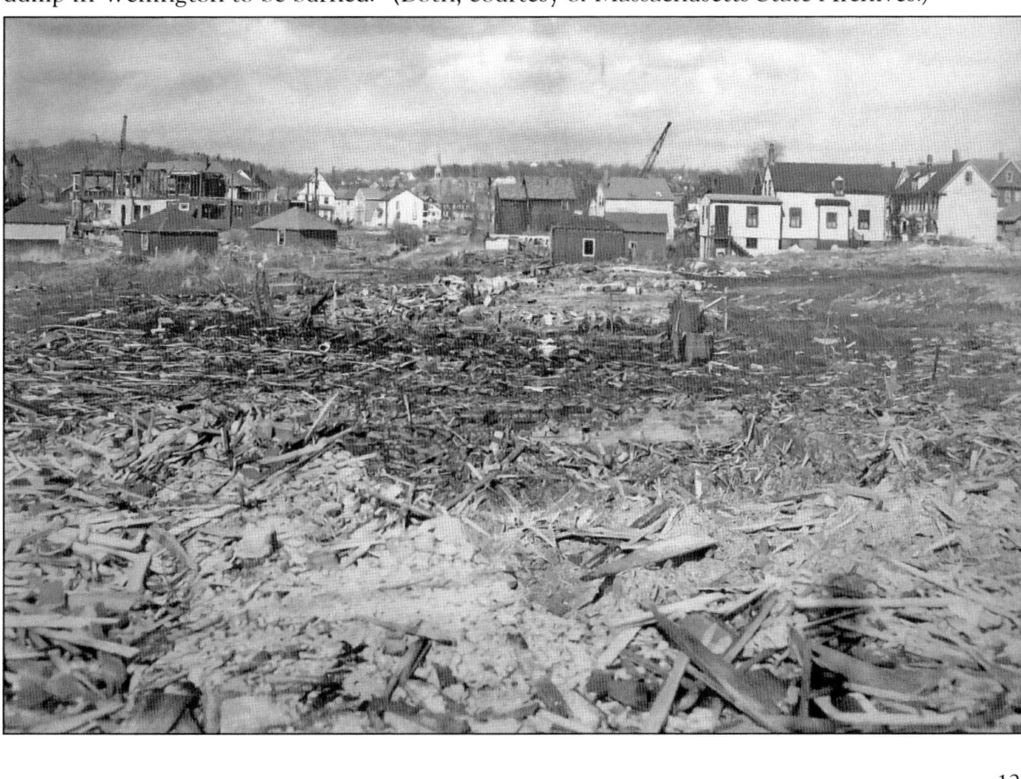

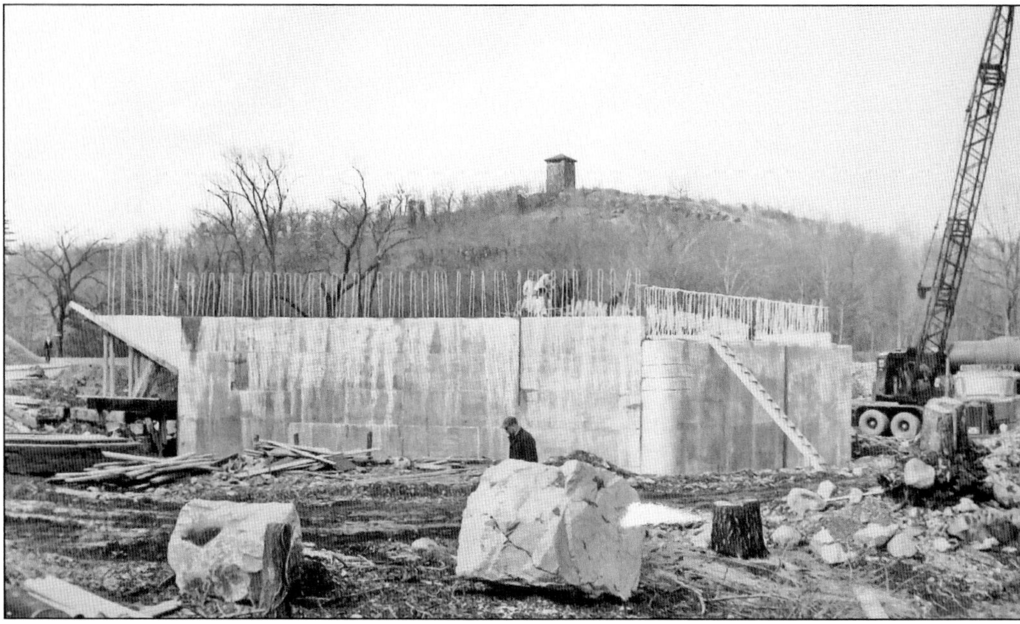

This image shows concrete and steel abutments during the reconstruction of Roosevelt Circle in early March 1959. The rotary at Interstate 93's Exit 33 provided connections with Forest Street, Fellsway West, South Border Road, and Route 28. (Photograph by John Harper, courtesy of Massachusetts State Archives.)

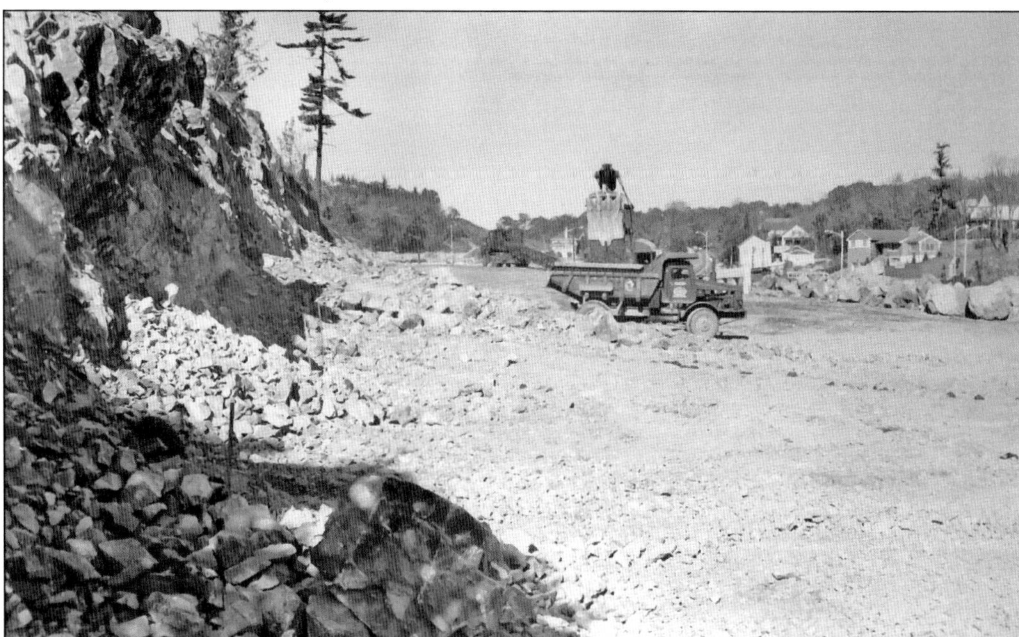

In 1959, the Berke Moore Company removed several hundred feet of the eastern slope of Pine Hill to make way for Interstate 93. This photograph, taken in October 1959 looking north from Roosevelt Circle, shows a truck removing rubble after blasting. Elizur Wright's house and orchard (see page 58) were located in the path of the highway's northbound lanes. (Photograph by John Harper, courtesy of Massachusetts State Archives.)

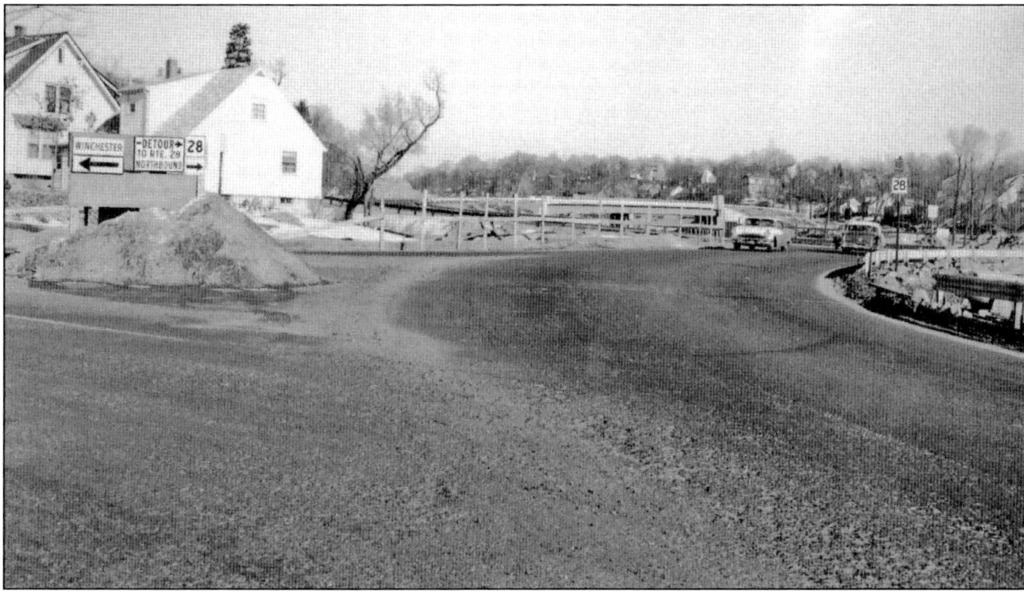

The original Roosevelt Circle linking Forest Street, Fellsway West, and South Border Road was built in 1932 by the C.J. Maney Company for about $15,000. This photograph, taken by John Harper in December 1960, shows the circle during reconstruction to connect it with Interstate 93. The entry to South Border Road leading to Winchester is at left. (Courtesy of Massachusetts State Archives.)

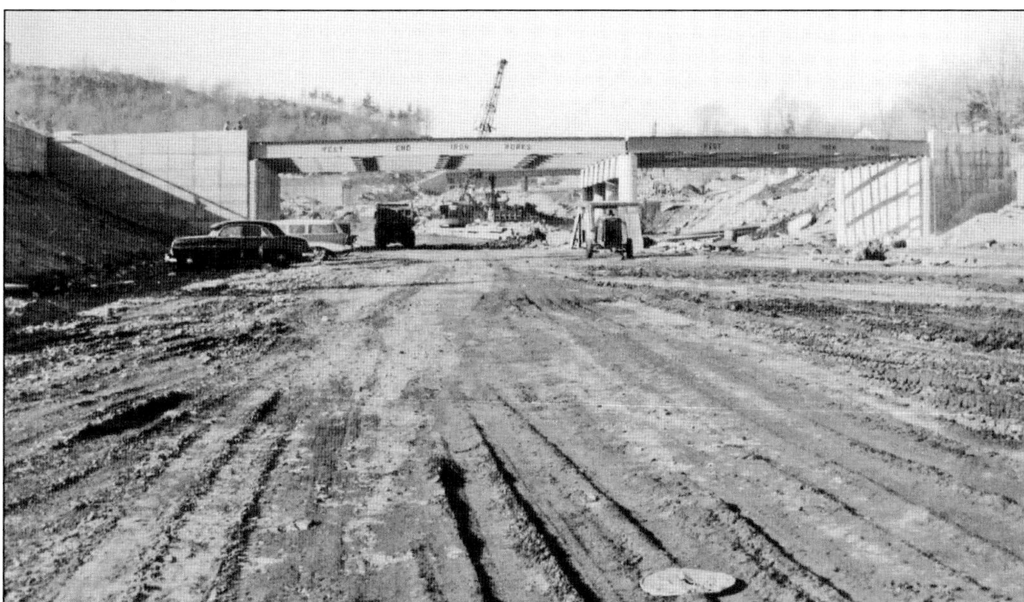

John Harper took this image of Roosevelt Circle in April 1961, looking north from an unpaved Interstate 93. The long, steel I beams for the enlarged Roosevelt Circle have been installed over the highway. Wrights Tower is partly visible at upper left. The section of Interstate 93 that runs through the Fells from Roosevelt Circle to North Border Road in Stoneham opened on June 30, 1961. Today, over 180,000 vehicles use the eight-lane highway daily. (Courtesy of Massachusetts State Archives.)

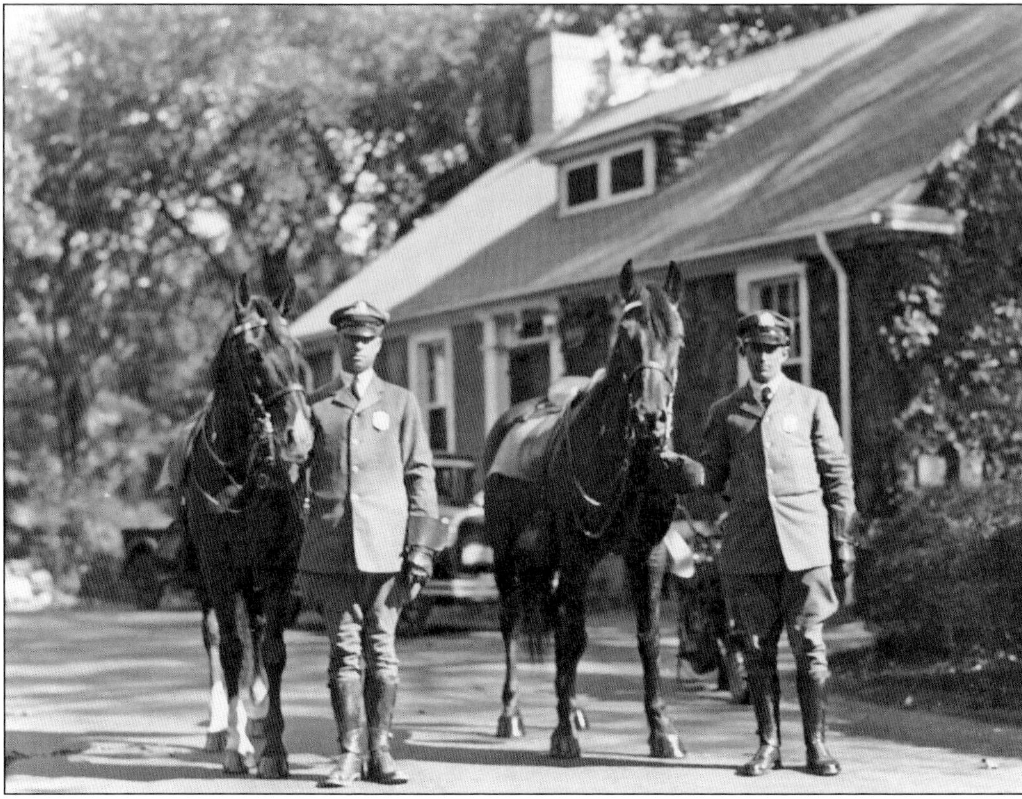

After the Metropolitan Park Commission was established in 1893, it hired police to patrol the new reservations of the Metropolitan Park System. The photograph above shows mounted police in the 1920s in front of the park superintendent's building at the Middlesex Fells Zoo (now offices for the Stone Zoo). Horses were ideal for patrolling the reservation's large, rugged territory and were kept in stables in the Fells maintenance yard across from the zoo. Police officer Bob Robinson was stable foreman for many years. The photograph below shows Middlesex Fells police in the 1940s inside the Fells' Police Headquarters in Medford. Officer Jack Danphy is at center. The building was constructed in 1908 and razed in 1959. (Above, courtesy of DCR Archives; below, courtesy of Massachusetts State Archives.)

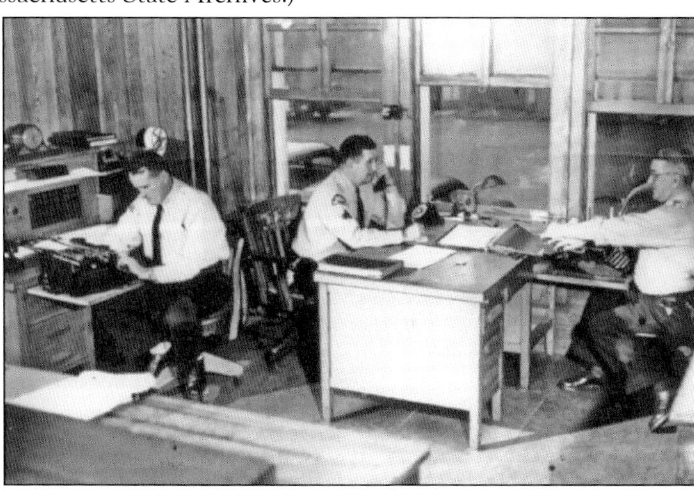

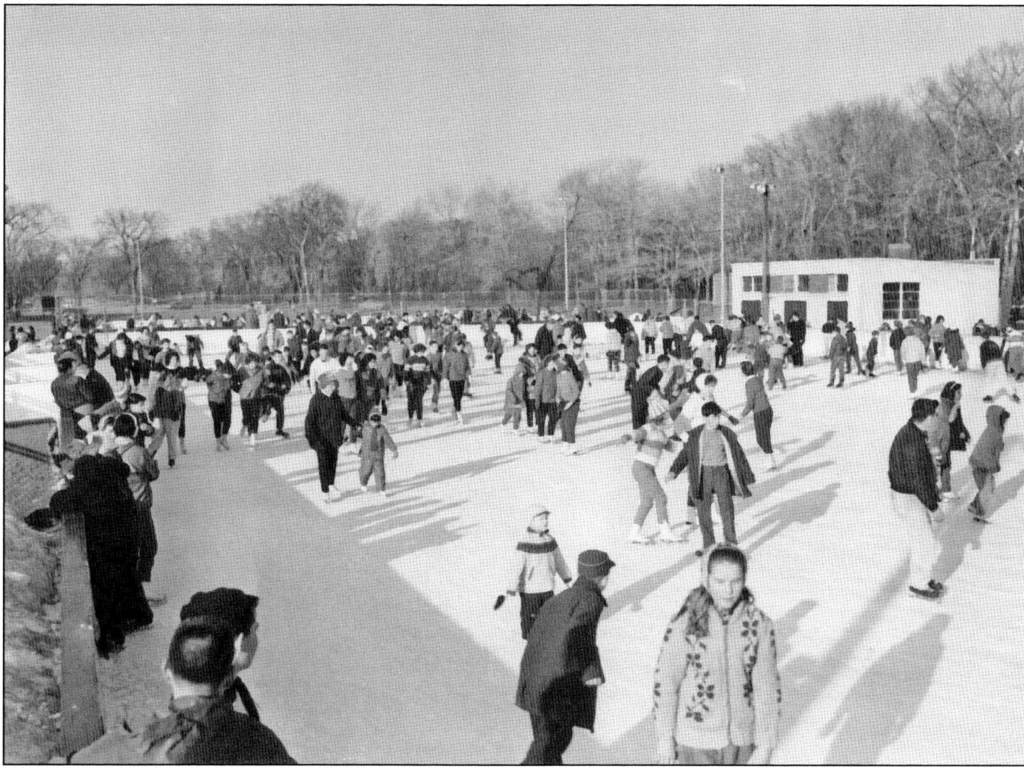

A MDC policeman lends a hand to a young skater at the John W. Flynn Memorial Rink in Medford in February 1966. Built in 1958, the rink was named four years later for a soldier killed in action during World War II. The current covered facility was built in 1995 and operates all year. (Both, courtesy of DCR Archives.)

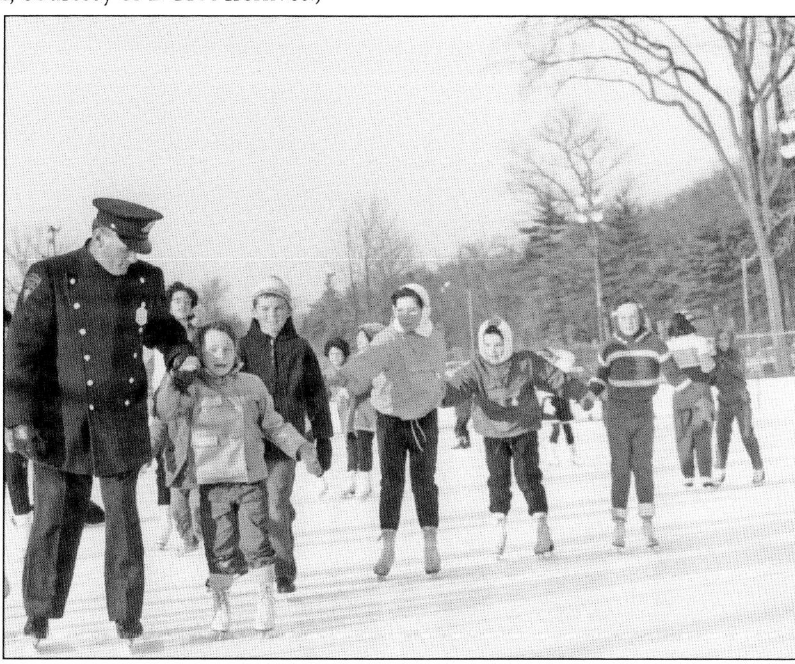

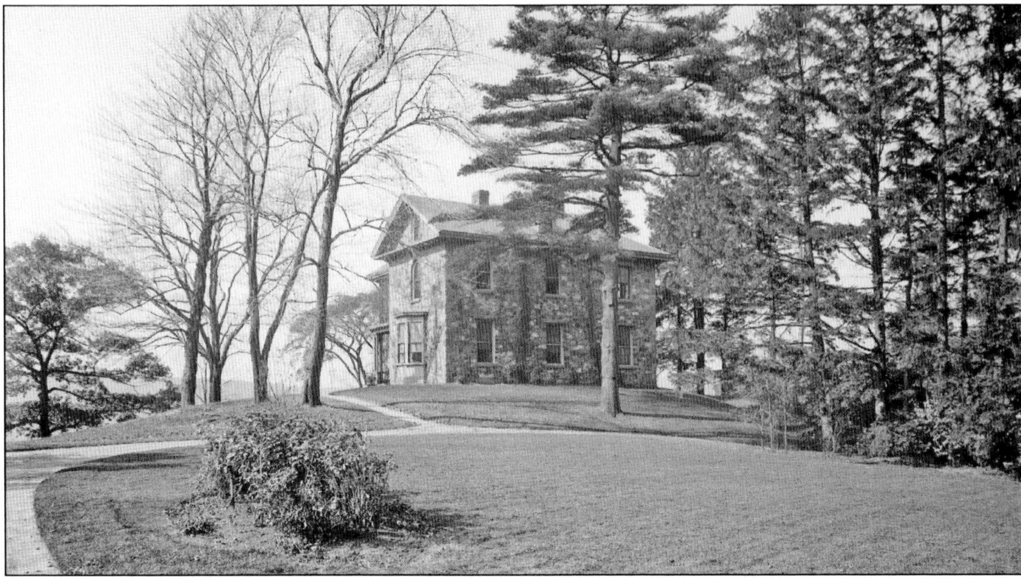

The Botume House, shown here in 1908, is now the Middlesex Fells Headquarters and Visitors Center. John Botume Jr. bought this Italianate mansion in 1855 from Charles Haynes, who bought it from its original owner, William Foster. The house is the only one still standing of four 1840s stone mansions designed by William Bailey Lang (see chapter 2). (Courtesy of Massachusetts State Archives.)

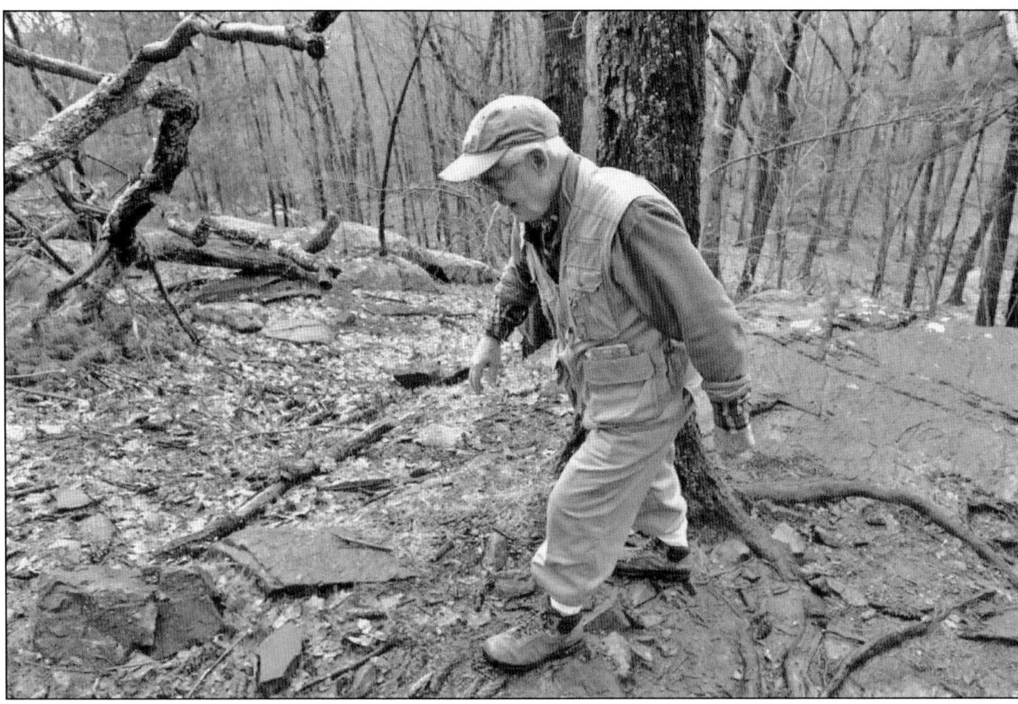

Bryan Hamlin, chair of the board of directors for Friends of the Middlesex Fells, searches for native plant species that an earlier study had considered lost. Over nine years, he and fellow botanists found 105 of the 155 lost species. Hamlin's contributions have been central to efforts to protect the Fells. (Photograph by Josh Reynolds, courtesy of the *Boston Globe*.)

Bibliography

Davenport, George B. *A Lecture on the Middlesex Fells*. Medford, MA: Press of the Medford City News, 1893.

de las Casas, William B. "The Middlesex Fells." *New England Magazine* 24, no. 6 (August 1898).

Connor, Sheila. *New England Natives*. Cambridge, MA: Harvard University Press, 1994.

Deane, W., ed. *Flora of the Blue Hills, Middlesex Fells, Stony Brook and Beaver Brook Reservations of the Metropolitan Parks Commission, Massachusetts*. Boston: C.M. Barrows & Co., 1896.

Eliot, Charles W. *Charles Eliot, Landscape Architect*. Boston: Houghton Mifflin, 1902. Reprinted in 1999 by University of Massachusetts Press.

Flagg, Wilson. *The Woods and By-Ways of New England*. Boston: James R. Osgood and Company, 1872.

Hamlin, Bryan T., Walter T. Kittredge, Donald P. Lubin, and Elizabeth Barton Wright. "Changes in the Vascular Flora of the Middlesex Fells Reservation, Middlesex County, Massachusetts, from 1895 to 2011." *Rhodora (Journal of the New England Botanical Club)* 114, issue 959: 229–308, 2012.

Hildebrand, Daniel. *An Historical Survey of the Mill Lots in Virginia Wood*. Boston: Metropolitan District Commission, 1988.

Lawrence, Rosewell B. "Middlesex Fells with a Map." Extracted from *Appalachia* 4, no. 3.

Levin, Ellen and Thomas Mahlstedt. *Middlesex Fells Reservation Historic Land-Use Study*. Boston: Metropolitan District Commission, 1990.

Lovering, Frank W. *Medford Yesterdays*. Medford, MA: Bicentennial Committee, 1962.

Massachusetts. *Annual Reports of the Metropolitan Park Commissioners*. Boston: Wright and Potter Printing Co., 1893–1920.

Massachusetts Department of Conservation and Recreation. *Resource Management Plan: Middlesex Fells Planning Unit*. Boston: DCR, 2012.

Medford Historical Society. *Medford Historical Society Register*. Medford, MA: Medford Historical Society, 1898–1935.

Rawson, Michael. *Eden on the Charles: The Making of Boston*. Cambridge, MA: Harvard University Press, 2010.

Spear, Robert J. *The Great Gypsy Moth War: the History of the First Campaign in Massachusetts to Eradicate the Gypsy Moth, 1890–1901*. Amherst: University of Massachusetts Press, 2005.

Wright, Ellen M., ed. *Elizur Wright's Appeals for the Middlesex Fells and the Forests*. Medford, MA: Medford Public Domain Club, 1893.

Zaitzevsky, Cynthia. *Frederick Law Olmsted and the Boston Park System*. Cambridge, MA: The Belknap Press of Harvard University Press, 1992.

Zellie, Carole, ed. *Stoneham, Massachusetts: A Shoe Town*. Cambridge, MA: Landscape Research and the Stoneham Historical Commission, 1981.

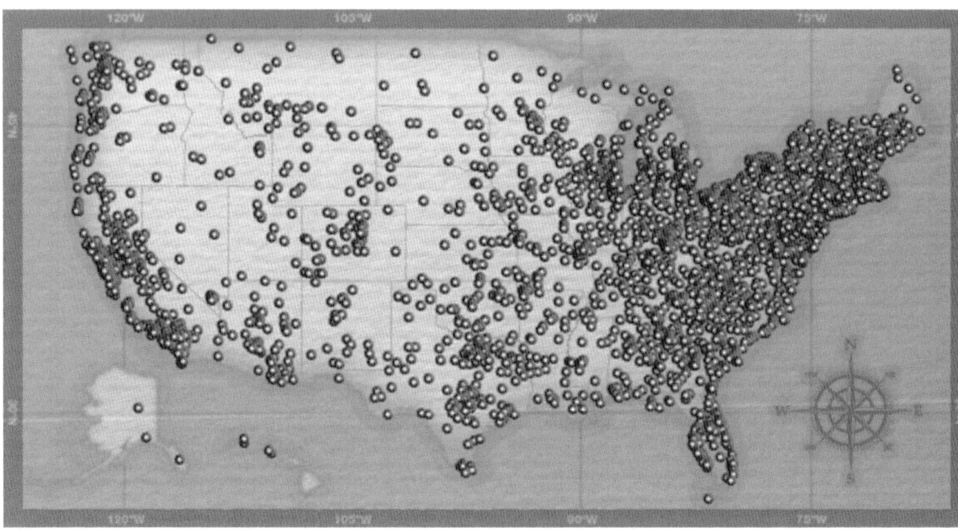